Islands' Spirit Rising

Supreme Court of Canada. *See* Haida litigation and *specific cases*

Taan Forest, 197-200
Teal-Jones Group, 138, 147, 173-74, 183
tenure system: development of, 50, 52-53; and First Nations, 70; and ICSI Consensus, 68; and private lands, 154
TFL 39: removal of private lands, 154; restructuring under Brascan, 172-73; sale from Brascan to Western Forest Products, 174-75; sale from Western Forest Products to Haida Nation, 183, 197; sale from Weyerhaeuser to Brascan, 158. *See also* Haida litigation; MacMillan Bloedel; Weyerhaeuser
TFL 60: 197
timber resources (Haida Gwaii): analysis of availability, 131-33; draft recommendations for, 146, 149(t); and ecosystem-based management, 180, legal objectives for, 194; and local manufacturing, 134; second-growth timber, 132-33, 134, 138; and strategic land use agreement, 182; timber supply review, 66, 68. *See also* forest industry (Haida Gwaii)
tourism, Haida Gwaii: draft recommendations for, 146, 149(t); and ecosystem-based management, 180; Heritage Tourism Strategy, 110, 136-37, 146; percentage of income from all sectors, 130; potential growth sector, 137; Skidegate Band Council strategy, 106-7; small business interests, 109; sports fishing industry, 110, 198
treaties: British Columbia Treaty Commission, 70; conflicting interpretations of, 33; Haida statement of intent, 71; offer to Haida Nation by BC, 99-100; and potential for resolving land conflicts, 75

Tsihlqot'in: battle, 34; title case, 207
Turning Point Initiative. *See* Coastal First Nations

UN Declaration on the Granting of Independence to Colonial Countries and Peoples, 37-38

watersheds (Haida Gwaii): analysis of on Haida Gwaii, 120-21; and ecosystem-based management, 89-90; environmental conditions report, 120-21; forest retention and strategic land use agreement, 186; legal objective for, 193; recommendations for, 143, 148(t), 149(t)
Western Forest Products: and government shareholders, 62; and Lyell Island blockade, 59, 60; TFL 24 (Gwaii Haanas), 54; purchase of TFL 39, 174-75; sale of TFL 39 to Haida Nation, 183, 197
Wet'suwet'en. and Delgamuukw case, 71
Weyerhaeuser: ecosystem-based management approach, 138-39; employee alliance with Haida Nation, 96-98; and Haida lawsuits, 72, 94; and Islands Spirit Rising blockade, 160, 162, 164, 168, 172; and removal of private lands from coast tree farm licences, 154; representatives on Process Technical Team, 139; six-point agreement with Haida and workers, 98, 160; timber projections, 138
wildlife, rare and threatened: draft recommendations, 144, 148(t)
Williams, Percy, 52, 56, 204
Williams Davidson, Terri-Lynn, 72, 95(t)
Wilson, Allan (Sgann 7iw7waans): 105-6, 150, 171, 188(f)

Yew, 105, 145, 148(t), 184, 193
Young, Nathan, 53, 54

Gwaii, 128-29, 184; and strategic land
use agreement, 182, 184. *See also* Gwaii
Haanas (South Moresby); Haida
Protected Areas
Protocol Agreement, Community, 155-56,
175, 201

Queen Charlotte Islands: name change to
Haida Gwaii, 187-88; origins of name,
6; and testimony at Royal Commission
on Indian Affairs, 36. *See also* Haida
Gwaii

Rainforest Action Network, 75, 179
Rayonier, 52, 53, 54
reconciliation table, 194-95
reserve system: inadequacy of, 34-37;
reserves on Haida Gwaii, 6; Royal Commission on Indian Affairs, 35-37; and
surveillance, 33-34
residential schools, 34
resource extraction: early history on Haida
Gwaii, 5-7; standard economic model
of, 7-8; staples development, 40-45.
See also ecologically unequal exchange;
forest industry (Haida Gwaii); forestry
sector (BC)
*Revitalizing British Columbia's coastal
economy,* 180
Richardson, Miles: and Council of the
Haida Nation, 56; and Lyell Island
blockade, 59, 204-5
riparian forests: and high-value fish habitat, 182; legal objectives for, 193; recommendations for, 143; and salmonids, 125;
and strategic land use agreement, 186;
and watershed conditions, 120-21
Royal Proclamation of 1763: and Aboriginal title, 32, 34-35, 37, 38; and government of BC, 33
Russ, Amos, 36, 206
Russ, Reynold (Iljuuwaas): 69, 69(f),
188(f)

salmon: distribution and threats to, 125;
economic contribution from, 130; and
environmental conditions, 117, 124, 125;

and Haida culture, 106; and *Haida
Land Use Vision,* 86;
Saw-whet owl: and environmental conditions report, 128; legal objective for,
194; recommendations for, 144, 148(t)
seabirds: draft recommendations for,
144-45, 148(t); threats to, 123
SGang Gwaay: and Haida Watchmen
Program, 54, 63; and UNESCO
designation, 57-58, 57(f)
share groups: and Clayoquot Sound, 73;
and forest industry, 64-65; on Haida
Gwaii, 65, 66, 68
Sierra Club, 45, 75, 179
Skidegate: after epidemic, 6; village ca.
1890-99, 31(f)
Skidegate Band Council: and Gwaii Haanas,
52, 58; interest statement at Community
Planning Forum, 106-7; pole peeling
plant, 199; submission to Pearse Com-
mission, 52-53
Smith, R.L., 61
social movement theory, 22. *See also*
power
Socio-Economic and Environmental
Assessment of Haida Gwaii/Queen
Charlotte Islands Land Use Viewpoints,
176-78, 177(t)
solutions table, 195-96
South Moresby. *See* Gwaii Haanas (South
Moresby)
Sproat, Gilbert Malcolm, 32
Staples development, 40-45
Sterling, James, 36
Sterritt, Art, 77
strategic land use agreement (Haida Gwaii):
Aboriginal tenure, 184; and annual
allowable cut, 182-83, 184, 202-3; draft
initialled, 182; ecosystem based management objectives, 184-86, 185(f), 193-
94; and *Haida Land Use Vision,* 184;
impacts to forest industry, 183; implementation of, 192-96; opposition to, 183;
protected areas, 184; support by elected
Islands' leaders, 182; timber resources,
182. *See also* land use planning (Haida
Gwaii)

timber supply review and community concerns, 66-68

Morgan, Dale, 138, 147, 167-68

Munt, Leonard, 195-96

Musqueam Nation: Sparrow case, 70

Naikoon Provincial Park, 77

Native Brotherhood of British Columbia, 37

Naylor, Glen, 53

New Democratic Party (BC): 80, 93

Ninstints: totem poles, 57(f); UNESCO designation, 57-58

Nisga'a Nation, 35, 37, 70

non-timber forest products: draft recommendations for, 146, 149(t); interest statement at Community Planning Forum, Haida Gwaii, 104-5; mushroom harvesting, 105, 130; as potential growth sector, 137

North American Indian Brotherhood, 37

Northern Gateway Project, 207

Northern Goshawk: draft recommendations for, 144, 148(f); and old forests, 122; population trends for Haida Gwaii, 122-23; and strategic land use agreement, 186

Nuu-chah-nulth: and Meares Island, 70, 73, 74

oil, 131, 207

old growth forests. See forests, old growth (Haida Gwaii)

Old Massett: after epidemic, 6; boat-building industry, 38; and saw mill partnership, 198

Pages, Barry, 106, 155

Parnell, Gilbert: and Community Planning Forum, 113; and Islands Spirit Rising blockade, 164, 170

Paul, Andrew, 37

Pearse Commission, 52-53

Perez, Juan, 5

Pinchot, Gifford, 45

planning. See land use planning (Haida Gwaii); specific resource management plans

Plant, Geoff: as chief negotiator, 176, 179; treaty offer to Haida Nation, 99-100

Plants (Haida Gwaii): and Community Planning Forum, 104; culturally important plants, 122, 145, 148(t); endemic species, 121-22; environmental conditions report, 121-22; and Haida Land Use Vision, 86; rare or endangered species, 121; and strategic land use plan, 186

political ecology: methodology, 10-11; and research implications, 14

Port Clements: blockade impacts, 172; election, 175; intervernor statement on behalf of the Haida, 156-57; local government interests, 106; and petition regarding Dale Lore, 172; Protocol Agreement with the Haida Nation, 155-56, 175; public meetings regarding blockade, 162, 166; response to 1994 Timber Supply Review, 56

post-normal science, 47-48

power: agency power, 22, 191; agenda setting, 19; analytical framework, 11, 22-28; communicative rationality, 16, 23; conceptions of, 18-22; consciousness raising, 26; consensus versus conflict, 10, 189-90; disciplinary power, 21, 25; discursive framework, 159; false consciousness, 19, 20, 25; genealogical studies, 21, 26; institutional power, 23, 191; and land use planning process, 9, 79, 93, 188-92; mobilization of bias, 19; organizational outflanking, 25; and physical force, 26; and social change, 24, 159, 190-91, 206; social movement theory, 22; socialization, 25, 26; structural constraint, 20, 25, 191; structural power, 23-24, 191; structuration theory, 20; structure and agency, 20. See also individual theorists of power

protected areas: and Clayoquot Sound, 73, 75; and co-management of on Haida Gwaii, 195, 196; conservancies, 193; and ecosystem-based management, 89-90; forest licensee perspective on, 167; marine conservation area, 193; provincial protected areas strategy for Haida

Land and Resource Management Plans: Central Coast, 75, 76, 78, 113; failed attempt on Haida Gwaii, 81

land use agreement. *See* strategic land use agreement (Haida Gwaii)

land use planning (Haida Gwaii): and blockade, 164; co-managed process, 83, 151; and Coast Information Team, 88; concerns by resident loggers, 174; consensus decision making, 79; and cut block approvals in contentious areas, 153, 158; *Ecosystem-Based Management Framework,* 88-91; environmental conditions report, 116-28; forestry projections under viewpoints, 176-78, 177(t); funding, 9, 83; government to government decision making, 83, 153; *Haida Land Use Vision,* 84-87; interests represented, 101-14; interim measures agreement, 84, 153; land use plan recommendations report, 176, 180; land use recommendations (draft), 141-53, 148-49(t); legal and regulatory constraints, 135-36, 151, 153; negotiation setbacks, 176, 179; and power dynamics, 9, 79, 93, 158, 188-92; process framework, 91-93; Process Management Team, 92, 104; Process Technical Team, 92, 102; protected areas, 177; Protocol on Interim Measures and Land use Planning (Haida Protocol), 78, 83-84; riparian forest retention, 182; and social change, 191-92; socio-economic conditions, 129-31, 177-78; standard planning model, 135; and tenure arrangements. *See also* Coast Information Team; Community Planning Forum (on Haida Gwaii); *Ecosystem-Based Management Framework; Haida Land Use Vision;* Islands Spirit Rising blockade; strategic land use agreement (Haida Gwaii)

Lantin, Peter, 207

Legacy Pole, 204-5, 205(f)

legal action. *See* Aboriginal rights and title (BC); Haida litigation

Lightbrown, Levina, 59

logging: on Haida Gwaii 1900 to 2004, 2(f); history on Haida Gwaii, 6-7. *See*

also forest industry (Haida Gwaii); forestry sector (BC)

Lore, Dale: 2005 election, 175; and blockade, 164, 166(f), 170, 172; and community petition, 172; and forest workers rally, 97-98; intervenor status on behalf of the Haida, 155; local government interest statement at Community Planning Forum, 106; perspective on environmental conditions, 138; and Share the Rock, 66; signing of *Protocol Agreement* with the Haida, 155-56, 175; on single islands forest tenure, 201

Lukes, Steven, 19-20, 25, 26

Lyell Island: blockade, 59-60; logging of, 52, 57, 58, 59, 62. *See also* Gwaii Haanas (South Moresby)

MacMillan Bloedel: and Clayoquot Sound, 74, 75; and TFL 39 (Haida Gwaii), 72, 174

Mandell, Louise, 95

marbled murrelet: analysis of population viability on Haida Gwaii, 123; draft recommendations, 143, 148(t); legal objectives for, 194; and strategic land use agreement, 186

Masset: local government interests, 106; *Protocol Agreement* with the Haida Nation, 155-56

McDonald, Jessica, 170, 179

McLachlin, Chief Justice Beverley, 156, 158

Meares Island, 70, 73

mining: draft recommendations for, 146-47, 149(t); interest statement at Community Planning Forum (Haida Gwaii), 109; mineral deposits on Haida Gwaii, 131

Ministry of Forests: approvals in contentious areas, 153; blockade negotiations, 162, 170; deregulation and new legislation, 93, 154; integrated resource management, 51; response to lack of consultation with Haida, 161; and risk management, 181; and solutions table, 195; TFL 24 licence renewal, 53-54;

litigation; land use planning (Haida Gwaii); Islands Spirit Rising blockade

Haida Protected Areas: and blockade memorandum of understanding, 170; culturally modified trees, 82; and draft land use recommendations, 142-43, 148(f); Duu Guusd, 58; and *Haida Land Use Vision,* 87; industry viewpoint, 177; mapping of, 82; and Unity Rally, 68

Haida Reconciliation Protocol. *See* Kunst'aa Guu – Kunst'aayah Reconciliation Protocol

Haida Stewardship Law, 193, 194

Haida Watchmen Program, 54-55, 57

Hammond, Herb, 137

Henley, Thom, 52

Heron, Great Blue: legal objectives for, 194

Husby Forest Products: and Bob Brash, 68, 200, 209(t); concerns regarding land use negotiations, 173-74, 183; and logging approvals in contentious areas, 158

hydroriparian ecosystems: draft recommendations for, 143, 148(t); planning guide for, 88; and watershed conditions, 120. *See also* riparian forests

imperialism: and capitalism, 32; culture of empire, 39; definition of, 28; land ownership, 30; and progress (assumptions of), 32; and social Darwinism, 31

inclusive decision making. *See* collaborative planning

Indian Act: and ban on pursuing land claims, 37, 38; and potlatch ban, 34; and residential school system, 34. *See also* reserve system

Indian Rights Association, 34, 35

indigenous rights movements: Allied Tribes of British Columbia, 37; Coastal First Nations, 75-76, 77; and Fourth World, 38-39; George Manuel, 38-40; Indian Rights Association, 34, 35; Interior Tribes of British Columbia, 32, 34-35, 37; indigenism (definition), 28;

Native American Indian Brotherhood, 37; Native Brotherhood of British Columbia, 37; and sovereignty, 38; Title and Rights Alliance, 154

industrialism: early history of, 29-32; staples development, 40-45

Innis, Harold: on culture, 30; theory of staples development, 40-45

Interior Tribes of British Columbia, 32, 34-35, 37

introduced species: draft recommendations for, 145, 148(t); impacts of on Haida Gwaii, 125

Islands Community Stability Initiative (ICSI): formation, 67; ICSI Consensus, 68, 70; Memorandum of Understanding with Province, 68

Islands Declaration, Draft, 133-34, 151-52

Islands Governance (Haida Gwaii), 135-37, 146, 175, 201, 203. *See also* co-management; Haida Nation; *Protocol Agreement,* Community

Islands Protection Committee/Society, 52, 53. *See also* Gwaii Haanas (South Moresby)

Islands Spirit Rising blockade: Aboriginal tenure, 171; backlash, 171-75; and BC government, 160, 168, 170; checkpoints, 162-65, 163(f), 167(f), 172; discursive frameworks, 13, 159, 167; and Haida culture, 165-66; and Haida title, 167-68; initiation of, 160; justification for, 162; memorandum of understanding, 170-71; negotiations to end blockade, 170-71; and resident loggers, 166; response by major forest tenure holders, 167; risk of an injunction, 160, 168; seizure of logs, 164; support for, 169, timing of, 161; and Weyerhaeuser, 160-61, 162, 168

Islands Timberlands, 173

Joint Solutions Project, 75

Kelly, Godfrey, 55-56

Kelly, Peter, 37, 206

Kunst'aa Guu – Kunst'aayah Reconciliation Protocol, 194-97, 206

Haanas National Park Reserve and Haida Heritage Site, 63; and Haida culture, 52; Haida testimony at injunction hearings, 59-60; Islands Protection Committee/Society, 52, 54, 58; and logging, 51-53, 62; Lyell Island, 52, 57, 58, 59, 62; public advisory committee, 53; Save Moresby Caravan, 60, 61(f); South Moresby Regional Planning Team, 57, 58; TFL 24 litigation, 52, 53-54; wilderness proposal, 52, 58, 60, 62

Gwaii Haanas National Marine Conservation Area Reserve and Haida Heritage Site, 193

Gwaii Trust, 62, 135, 183, 201

Habermas, Jürgen, 16, 23

Haida cultural values: culturally important plants, 145, 148(t); culturally modified trees, 5; draft recommendations for, 145, 148(t); and *Haida Land Use Vision*, 85; interest statement at Community Planning Forum, 105-6; legal objectives for, 193. *See also* strategic land use agreement (Haida Gwaii)

Haida Enterprise Corporation (HaiCo): 197-98

Haida Forest Guardians: and islands governance, 135; mapping capabilities, 82

Haida Gwaii: geography of, 4; Haida's historical occupation of, 5; and ICSI, 64-70; logging history, 2 (f), 6-7; maritime fur trade, 5; name change ceremony, 187-88; quality of life, 111, 133; reserve villages, 6; unique plants and animals, 4. *See also* forest industry (Haida Gwaii); Haida Nation; land use planning (Haida Gwaii); and *names of villages*

Haida Gwaii/Queen Charlotte Islands Forest Workers, Association of: formation, 96-97; rally and support for Haida Nation, 97-98; six-point agreement with Weyerhaeuser, 98, 160

Haida Gwaii Black Bear. *See* black bears

Haida Gwaii Management Council, 194-95, 202-3

Haida Gwaii Reconciliation Act, 194-97

Haida Gwaii Working Forest Action Group, 174

Haida heritage sites, 58, 62

Haida Land Use Vision: central aspects, 86; and community support for, 140; and Constitution of the Haida Nation, 84; and draft recommendations, 147; as guiding document for land use planning, 83; and Haida Protected Areas, 87; on logging impacts, 87; maps, 87; overview of, 84-87; presentation to Community Planning Forum, 102; and strategic land use agreement, 184

Haida litigation: statement of claim (title), 94-95; statement of defence to Haida title claim, (Government of BC), 99; TFL 24, 52, 53-54; TLF 39 (BC Supreme Court), 72-73, 94; TFL 39 (Supreme Court of Canada), 154-58; title case, 94-96, 99, 207

Haida Nation: Aboriginal tenure, 171, 176, 184; Aboriginal title (early fight for), 37, 38 ; capacity building, 206-7; co-management of land, 63, 194-96; and Coastal First Nations, 75-55; connection to land, 5; epidemics and depopulation of, 6; first contact with Europeans, 5; and forest management, 53, 56, 194-96, 198-203; founding of Council of the Haida Nation, 55-56; Haida Enterprise Corporation, 197-98; Haida House of Assembly, 83; *Haida Land Use Vision* summary, 84-87; interest statement at Community Planning Forum, 102; land claim, 55, 56, 70; oral history of, 5; *Protocol Agreement* with Port Clements and Masset, 155-56; purchase of TFL 39, 197; reserve villages, 6; six point agreement with Weyerhaeuser, 98, 160; strategic land use agreement, 182-84; Taan Forest, 197-200; testimony at Royal Commission on Indian Affairs, 35-36; traditional management practices, 29-30; traditional use of plants, 5; treaty offer by the Province, 99-100. *See also* Gwaii Haanas (South Moresby); Haida

Islands' Spirit Rising

Reclaiming the Forests
of Haida Gwaii

LOUISE TAKEDA

UBC Press • Vancouver • Toronto

22 21 20 19 18 17 16 15   5 4 3 2 1

Printed in Canada on FSC-certified ancient-forest-free paper (100% post-consumer recycled) that is processed chlorine- and acid-free.

Library and Archives Canada Cataloguing in Publication

Takeda, Louise, author
   Islands' spirit rising : reclaiming the forests of Haida Gwaii / Louise Takeda.

Includes bibliographical references and index.
Issued in print and electronic formats.
ISBN 978-0-7748-2765-2 (bound). – ISBN 978-0-7748-2766-9 (pbk.). – ISBN 978-0-7748-2767-6 (pdf). – ISBN 978-0-7748-2768-3 (epub)

   1. Land use – British Columbia – Haida Gwaii – Planning – Citizen participation – History. 2. Environmentalism – British Columbia – Haida Gwaii – History. 3. Forests and forestry – British Columbia – Haida Gwaii – History. 4. Haida Indians – British Columbia – Haida Gwaii – History. 5. Rain forests – British Columbia – Haida Gwaii – History. 6. Haida Gwaii (B.C.) – Environmental conditions – History. I. Title.

HD319.B8T34 2015   333.73'130971112   C2014-904677-4
                                                     C2014-904678-2

Canada

UBC Press gratefully acknowledges the financial support for our publishing program of the Government of Canada (through the Canada Book Fund), the Canada Council for the Arts, and the British Columbia Arts Council.

This book has been published with the help of a grant from the Canadian Federation for the Humanities and Social Sciences, through the Awards to Scholarly Publications Program, using funds provided by the Social Sciences and Humanities Research Council of Canada.

Printed and bound in Canada by Friesens
Set in Garamond by Artegraphica Design Co. Ltd.
Copy editor: Deborah Kerr
Proofreader: Dianne Tiefensee
Cartographer: Eric Leinberger

UBC Press
The University of British Columbia
2029 West Mall
Vancouver, BC V6T 1Z2
www.ubcpress.ca

To
Solvai and Nicholas
and the people of their generation,
who will become the next stewards
of the earth

We decide the fate of our lands,

    or someone else will decide that for us.

We determine how we will live our lives

    or someone else will determine that for us.

We plan for our future,

    or someone else will plan for us.

– Guujaaw

Contents

List of Illustrations / xl

Acknowledgments / xiii

1 Navigating Change on Haida Gwaii / 3

2 The Nature of Power / 15

3 Clash of Nature, Culture, and Economics / 28

4 War in the Woods: 1974-2001 / 49

5 Collaborative Planning in the Face of Conflict / 79

6 Actors and Interests / 101

7 State of the Land and Community / 115

8 Land Use Recommendations and the Widening Gap / 141

9 Uprising / 159

10 New Political Landscape / 187

Appendix / 208

Notes / 210

References / 224

Index / 238

Illustrations

TABLES

1 Harvest forecasts based on different management assumptions / 132

2 Summary of recommendations and viewpoints / 148

3 Forestry projections under viewpoints 1 and 2 / 177

FIGURES

1 Logging Haida Gwaii 1990-2004 (map) / 2

2 Skidegate Village, ca. 1890-99 / 31

3 Logging in Naikoon Park / 43

4 Totem poles at Ninstints, SGang Gwaay / 57

5 "Save Moresby Caravan" final destination, Vancouver / 61

6 Unity rally / 69

7 Cedar bark robe / 69

8 Culturally modified trees at Spirit Lake, Skidegate / 82

9 Delivering the writ for the Haida's title case / 95

10 Rally at Ferguson Bay by wives and friends of loggers / 97

11 Steaming a cedar canoe / 105

12 Logging truck near Juskatla / 108

13 Old forest ecosystem in Windy Bay / 119

14 Black bear near Sandspit / 124

15 Grizzly bear figure from the Bill Reid Pole in Skidegate / 127

16 "Stop the bear hunt" signage / 144

17 Blocking the road to Weyerhaeuser's log sort / 163

18 Checkpoint on Highway 16 in Queen Charlotte / 163

19 Seizure notice on logs cut by Weyerhaeuser / 165

20 Discussing around the fire / 166

21 Robert Davidson addressing the crowd at the Queen Charlotte checkpoint / 167

22 Witnessing Islands Spirit Rising / 169

23 Haida Gwaii Land Use Plan (map) / 185

24 "Giving the Name Back with Respect" ceremony / 188

25 Legacy pole raising at Windy Bay / 205

Acknowledgments

It is an honour to share this story of the people of Haida Gwaii as told through the extraordinary events of the recent land use planning process and the broader Haida and community efforts to build sustainability. As I remember those who helped me along the journey, I am reminded of my very first encounter on Haida Gwaii. Awaiting my luggage at the Sandspit Airport, I found myself conversing with a fellow traveller. After following events unfolding on Haida Gwaii for years, I was excited to finally be on Haida soil. The first goal of this visit was to secure approval from the Council of the Haida Nation to conduct research in Haida territory. When I revealed my intentions to my conversational partner, she immediately introduced herself as April Churchill-Davis, the council's executive assistant (later vice-president). Surprised, I explained that I had been advised to contact her as soon as I arrived in Haida Gwaii. "What a coincidence," I exclaimed, delighted at our chance meeting. Her expression became momentarily serious as she looked me straight in the eye and said: "*Nothing* happens by coincidence." Looking back on that first encounter as I put the final touches to this manuscript, April's words take on an extra layer of significance.

This book has been made possible by the contributions and assistance of many people. I would like to begin by recognizing the Council of the Haida Nation, particularly Guujaaw, Arnie Bellis, and April Churchill-Davis, for their support and assistance. A special thank you to Guujaaw for his thoughtful reflections and extensive feedback on the manuscript.

Guujaaw was president of the Haida Nation from 2000 to 2012, a period encompassing many transformative changes on Haida Gwaii. A gifted carver, singer, and astute political leader, Guujaaw has dedicated much of his life to protecting the land and culture of Haida Gwaii.

I am also indebted to the many participants of the Community Planning Forum and the people of Haida Gwaii who shared their experiences, insights, and reflections with me. Many thanks to Betsy Cardell, Nika Collison, Vince Collison, Margaret Edgars, Travis Glasman, Mike Hennigan, Dale Lore, Dale Morgan, Jacques Morin, Delina Adea Petit Pas, Barb Rowsell, Gary Russ, Leandre Vigneault, Allan Wilson, and several anonymous interviewees. An extra thank you to Nika Collison and Dale Lore for their valuable comments on the manuscript. A special thank you to John Broadhead, Simon Davies, and Leslie Johnson, co-directors of the Gowgaia Institute, for sharing their knowledge and insights, and for providing valuable feedback on the manuscript. In addition, many thanks to John Broadhead for providing the Haida Gwaii Logging History map, and a big thank you to Simon Davies for assisting with the selection of photos. Thank you also to Len Munt, district manager for the Ministry of Forests, Lands and Natural Resource Operations in Haida Gwaii, for sharing his knowledge and insights. Finally, a big thank you to Lenore Lawrence and Peter Cook of Premier Creek Lodging for their generous hospitality, and to Tassilo Goetz Hanisch for two unforgettable trips (by Zodiac and '76 Volkswagen van) from Victoria to Haida Gwaii.

A special thank you to the people and organizations that generously provided photographs for the book. Many thanks to Roberta Aiken, the Council of the Haida Nation, Simon Davies, Gowgaia Institute, and Richard Krieger, Mare Levesque, Joanne Mills, and Robert Mills for their great photos. An extra thank you to Richard Krieger for the cover photo, which beautifully captures the Haida's historic occupation of the land and continued strong connection to it, both physically and spiritually.

I am also very grateful to Michael M'Gonigle at the POLIS Project on Ecological Governance at the University of Victoria for his tremendous support and encouragement throughout the research process. Thank you also to Kelly Bannister, Oliver Brandes, and Ann Zurbrigg from the POLIS Project for their ongoing support.

This research was originally made possible with the generous support of the Research Center on Development and International Relations at Aalborg University in Denmark. I am particularly grateful to Johannes Dragsbæk Schmidt and Inge Røpke, whose guidance and enthusiasm were invaluable. Many thanks also to Pernille Gooch, Jacques Hersh, and Joan

Martinez-Alier for their valuable comments and insights. A special thank you to Joel Ornoy and Faith Takeda for their editorial assistance.

Finally, my heartfelt gratitude goes to my family, who have been unwavering in their support and encouragement. Deep appreciation goes to my parents, Kinji and Fudge Takeda; my sisters, Gay, Valerie, and Faith; my brother, Blaine; and my dear friend Wendy – pillars I have relied on through the years. A special thank you to Bedstemor, Kirsten Kjærulff, for always being there for us, and to Jens Kjærulff for making the big leap across the Atlantic many times. Last but not least, thank you to my children, Solvai and Nicholas, for all the love and laughter they have brought to my world.

Islands' Spirit Rising

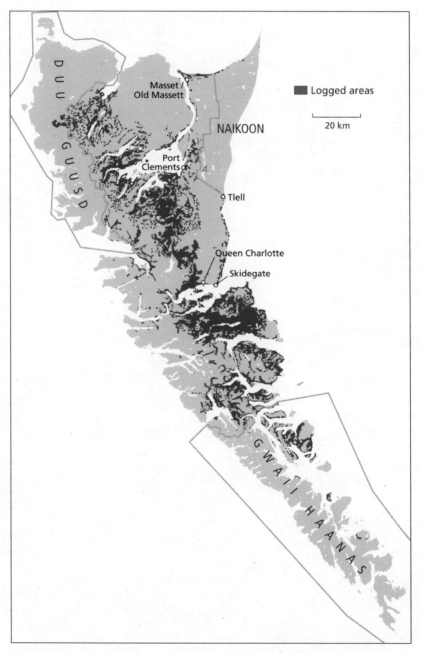

1 Logging Haida Gwaii 1990-2004. *Source:* Gowgaia Institute (John Broadhead).
Adapted by Eric Leinberger

I

Navigating Change on Haida Gwaii

We have an insatiable appetite for trees, an age-old pattern that stretches back to the dawn of time. Wood and the numberless things we make of it are so much a part of us that it is impossible to imagine a life without it. Perhaps the only thing equal to the extent of our interdependence with trees is the extent to which we take them for granted.

> *— John Broadhead, "Islands at the Edge"*

The land and waters of Haida Gwaii can and must be made well again. Our economic needs can and must be brought into balance with the capacity of the land to function and provide. We have the political will and we accept the responsibility to see that this is done.

> *— Council of the Haida Nation, Haida Land Use Vision*

The enchanted islands of Haida Gwaii contain some of the richest natural, cultural, and political landscapes in the world. Known for a time as the Queen Charlotte Islands, Haida Gwaii is the homeland of the Haida Nation, an indigenous people whose way of life has been intertwined with the land and waters of the islands for millennia. Located at the edge of Western Canada, this isolated archipelago is also home to some of the world's last remaining tracts of intact coastal temperate rainforest and is a globally significant repository for biological diversity.

Over the past century, however, the forests have been logged at an ever-accelerating rate. This has threatened not only the irreplaceable biodiversity and habitat values, but also the cultural and social values of the forests that the Haida have relied on for centuries. In response, the Haida, together with their local environmental and community allies, have launched political campaigns, blockades, and lawsuits to demand logging reductions. At the same time, they have pressed for greater local control through community-based forest tenures and legal recognition of Haida title to the land. Since the 1980s, this grassroots indigenous-environmental-community movement has evolved into a powerful force with the capacity to take on the multinational forest industry and the political structures that enable it.

This book traces the evolution of this dynamic force, from the early days of Haida resistance to the modern context of alliances, movement building, and evolving forms of governance. Within this broader context, the study focuses on the latest stages of the conflict and the provincial government's efforts to ameliorate it through collaborative ecosystem-based planning.

ISLANDS AT THE EDGE OF THE WORLD

The natural wonders of Haida Gwaii were first brought to the attention of a wider public in the 1980s, when the Haida and their allies launched a successful campaign to protect the old-growth forests of Gwaii Haanas. Since then, Haida Gwaii's reputation as an environmental jewel has spread.

Haida Gwaii is geographically positioned on the edge of the continental shelf, nestled under the Alaska Panhandle to the north and separated from the mainland of British Columbia by the treacherous Hecate Strait. It consists of two main islands, Graham and Moresby, which are surrounded by hundreds of smaller islands and islets. Its isolated geography and role as a glacial refugium during the last ice age led to the evolution of at least thirty-nine plant and animal species and subspecies found nowhere else on earth (Holt 2005). These include the Haida Gwaii black bear, ermine, pine marten, dusky shrew, and a number of plants and mosses. Because of this ecological distinctiveness, environmentalists in the 1970s strategically dubbed the islands the "Galapagos of the North."

Whereas the unique ecological features of Haida Gwaii have only recently become well known, the Haida's relationship to the land stretches back more than 10,000 years. Haida oral history traces their roots on Haida Gwaii to before the last ice age, recalling, among other things, two great floods, rising and falling sea levels, and the coming of the first tree (Council of the Haida Nation 2004, 3). This oral history is supported by recent archaeological evidence, showing that people hunted bears on Haida Gwaii as far back as 13,000 years ago and have deepwater fished since 10,700 years ago (Fedje et al. 2005).

Over the centuries, the Haida have relied on the ocean and forests for their material, cultural, and spiritual well-being. Culturally modified trees can be found throughout the forests of Haida Gwaii, providing evidence of occupancy and forest use going back centuries. The Haida have used a variety of trees for food, teas, medicine, fuel, and building materials. The red cedar has been, and continues to be, of particular cultural significance. Its durable wood has been used for longhouses, canoes, totem poles, rope, mats, and storage boxes. The bark of the red and yellow cedar has been used for clothing, hats, and baskets. The Haida have also used over sixty species of plants for sustenance, health, and medicinal purposes (Nancy Turner 2004, 57-61).

The historical profusion of seafood allowed a relatively dense and sedentary population to flourish on Haida Gwaii. Combined with the Haida's sophisticated boat-building and fishing technologies, this natural marine abundance allowed leisure time for the Haida to develop their world-renowned art forms. Despite recent declines in fish stocks and aggressive logging of the forests, the Haida's intimate connection to the land and waters of Haida Gwaii continues to this day. As ethnobotanist Nancy Turner (ibid., 23) writes: "The mountains, the waters, the plants and the animals of Haida Gwaii are all part of a magnificent system, supporting and nourishing the Haida, and in turn, respected and embraced by them as an integral part of their culture and identity."

Nevertheless, the delicate balance that existed between the Haida and their natural surroundings during the long pre-colonial period was radically affected by the arrival of Europeans.

LEGACY OF COLONIZATION AND RESOURCE EXTRACTION

With the arrival of the maritime fur trade in the eighteenth century, Haida Gwaii became known to the outside world for its superior and profitable raw materials. First contact – with the Spanish explorer Juan Peréz – was recorded in 1774. Thirteen years later, Captain George Dixon arrived in

Haida Gwaii as part of a sea otter trade mission and gave the islands their colonial name, "Queen Charlotte," after his ship and the queen consort of England. By the 1780s, the maritime fur trade had established itself, and within a few decades, increasing European presence and trade generated an intensifying clash of economics, nature, and culture. An 1852 gold rush created a new frontier economy and the establishment of the islands as a Crown colony.

More devastating than the political, economic, and cultural upheavals that followed from colonization were the successive waves of epidemics introduced by the newcomers. The worst smallpox epidemic hit Haida Gwaii in the 1860s, eventually reducing the Haida from their pre-contact numbers of 10,000 to 15,000 to an estimated mere 588 by 1915 (Van den Brink 1974, 77; Fedje et al. 2005, 119).[1] The survivors of about twenty permanent villages regrouped into two villages: Old Massett at the north end of Graham Island and Skidegate at the south end. Both remain to this day as the two Native reserves in which most of the islands' Haida people reside. The abrupt and tragic depopulation, which occurred among so many First Nations in British Columbia, facilitated the imposition of new forms of governance.[2] The colonial government designated small reserves, and though BC First Nations never ceded their rights and title to the land, the remaining land was claimed by the Crown.

With European settlement and control over resources, Haida economies were soon replaced by colonial economies. Historian Richard Rajala (2006, 15) notes: "A society based upon Euro-American settlement and capitalist enterprise dictated that from the outset land and resources would be allocated to those deemed able to extract the highest value from their market potential." In British Columbia, the clearest example of this was the forest industry. Government policies transformed the land into a form of private property that could be leased cheaply to timber corporations for development and short-term profit extraction. First Nations people were sometimes employed as loggers, but they were systematically excluded from entrepreneurial and personal access to timber (Marchak 1995; Harris 2002; Rajala 2006). Meanwhile, they would bear the brunt of the ecological and social impacts. Despite First Nations' consistent defence of their land title, the BC government ignored their concerns in favour of resource extraction and profit for multinational corporations.

Logging on Haida Gwaii increased exponentially through the twentieth century. Corporate domination of the forests was well established by the onset of the First World War and the drive for high-quality Sitka spruce to build fighter planes. Although most logs were processed elsewhere, several sawmills were built on the islands at that time. However, when the brief war-inspired boom ended, most of Haida Gwaii's industrial infrastructure disappeared (Rajala 2006, 2-40). The islands subsequently reverted to their role as supplier of raw materials to processing facilities in Victoria and the southern mainland, with little or no manufacturing occurring locally. In an extensive historical study of the forest industry on the BC north coast, Rajala (ibid., 7) concluded that Haida Gwaii "represented the clearest example of hinterland resources being drawn off without appreciable local benefit."

An estimated 105 million cubic metres of raw logs, valued at over $12 billion, left the islands during the twentieth century (Gowgaia Institute 2007, 9).[3] Rather than supporting the long-term social and ecological interests of the region, resource extraction on Haida Gwaii (as in many other resource-rich regions of the world) has enabled the development of distant political and financial centres. Modern technology has simply exacerbated the impact of logging and increased the speed at which the most accessible and valuable resources are depleted. The associated threats to local livelihoods, culture, habitat, and biodiversity has never been figured into the prices paid for the resources.

This problem of the unequal distribution of costs and benefits between primarily extractive and manufacturing regions has been extensively discussed by such well-known social theorists as Andre Gunder Frank (1969, 1975) and Harold Innis (1936, 1956). More recently, the field of ecological economics has extended these insights by examining energy and material flows to reveal the ecologically unequal exchange associated with resource extraction (see Bunker 1985; Martinez-Alier 1987; Giljum and Hubacek 2001). Ecologically unequal exchange highlights the fact that local resources are sold at prices that do not take into account the local environmental and social impacts or the exhaustion of natural resources caused by overextraction.

Nevertheless, the prevailing economic model relies on high levels of material extraction and cheap resources for continued industrialization and economic growth. The ideology of developmentalism, with its uncritical emphasis on the benefits of resource development, job creation, and capital accumulation, is largely shared by resource managers, industry proponents, and state officials alike. Monetary value is the assumed operational definition and neutral standard of value, whereas the interests and concerns of host communities are often discounted as parochial or vested (Howitt 2001). Moreover, the priorities of corporate actors are reflected in state policies and legislation that ensure continued access to

resources by the powerful of the world. This overarching institutional and
ideological framework has made it exceedingly difficult for resource-rich
regions like Haida Gwaii to avert the destructive social, cultural, and
ecological consequences of resource development.

In response to this concern, political ecologist Stephen Bunker (1985)
suggested, in his extensive study of resource extraction in the Brazilian
Amazon, that either central political and institutional structures must
work to protect the long-term interests of local communities, or the communities themselves must develop their own politically effective social
organization and self-sustaining economies in order to resist exploitative
extractive enterprises. The former proposition includes such things as
government-backed collaboration and resolution of conflicts in a way that
respects the long-term interests of place-based actors. The latter proposition
suggests the need to build a cohesive collective movement to challenge
structures of domination and to implement alternative community-
based strategies. The case of collaborative planning on Haida Gwaii con-
tains elements of both these propositions, offering an interesting entry
point to examine state and grassroots responses to resource conflicts.

POWER AND COLLABORATIVE PLANNING

The 1980s saw opposition to industrial logging rise dramatically in British
Columbia, with conflicts erupting in one valley after another. The need
to restore social order and end the escalating "war in the woods" compelled
the BC government to make a conceptual shift from top-down technical
approaches toward more democratic and inclusive approaches to resource
management. In 1992, the government introduced an inclusive decision-
making approach for the province that incorporated comprehensive
community-based participation into resource management planning. Its
stated intent was to empower "those with authority to make a decision
and those who will be affected by the decision ... to jointly seek an outcome
that accommodates rather than compromises the interests of all concerned" (CORE 1992, 25).

Yet, past inclusive decision-making forums in British Columbia and
elsewhere have often fallen short of expectations (see Wilson 1998; Brosius
1999a; Burrows 2000; Mascarenhas and Scarce 2004; Whelan and Lyons
2005). Although incorporation into decision-making institutions may
appear to offer indigenous and other marginalized groups a chance to be

heard and to achieve their goals, such processes have often served to limit debate on substantive issues and to exclude the moral and political imperatives of grassroots groups. The experience of indigenous peoples, moreover, has often been that state planning processes are unable or unwilling to understand and respect their distinct needs in the use and management of land (Gedicks 1994; Howitt 2001; Lane 2006). At the same time, inclusive processes have provided a degree of political legitimacy to dominant actors and decision-makers, which they might not otherwise have had.

Despite these caveats, the collaborative land use planning process on Haida Gwaii had several promising aspects. First, from a process angle, it had progressed farther than most planning efforts in terms of levelling power imbalances. The process was co-managed by the provincial government and the Council of the Haida Nation, a unified political body of the Haida people. Co-management not only gave the Haida greater control over the direction and design of the planning process, it also acknowledged the authority of the Council of the Haida Nation in land use decisions.

Recommendations for land use were to be made by an inclusive Community Planning Forum consisting of representatives from the Haida Nation, provincial government, forestry and mining industries, local environmentalists, local government, businesses, and community members. In addition to co-hosting the process, the Haida ensured that their values and concerns would play a central role by requiring that the process be guided by the *Haida Land Use Vision* (Council of the Haida Nation 2004), a planning document developed by the Council of the Haida Nation. In addition, land use recommendations were to incorporate the principles of ecosystem-based management as laid out in a framework developed specifically for the three coastal planning tables (north coast, central coast, and Haida Gwaii). A technical team of experts from the Haida Nation, the Province, industry, and the community was also put in place to provide key pieces of information and analyses, and to ensure that all parties had equal access to relevant data.

The Haida Nation had previously acquired substantial philanthropic resources for mapping and planning purposes. In addition, a mitigation fund was set up for the three coastal planning tables to compensate industry and workers for losses that they might incur as a result of planning outcomes. An alliance known as the Coastal First Nations also created the Coast Opportunity Funds, a substantial trust fund, to assist communities with the transition to more sustainable forms of economic development.

Due to these promising institutional, procedural, and monetary factors, the collaborative planning process on Haida Gwaii appeared to present a real possibility for resolving conflict in a way that might respect ecological and cultural values. Perhaps most importantly, Haida Gwaii is a place rife with agency – individual, organizational, and cultural. With a history of strong leadership, grassroots institution building, broad community alliances, and multiple victories on the ground and in the courts, the Haida have become a formidable force. If collaborative planning were ever to result in outcomes that not only reflected the priorities of the indigenous community but also transformed an unsustainable and inequitable model of development, Haida Gwaii was the kind of place where it would happen.

A Political Ecology Approach

Several studies have examined collaborative planning in British Columbia (see Salazar and Alper 1996; Duffy et al. 1998; Owen 1998; Burrows 2000; Gunton, Day, and Williams 2003; Mascarenhas and Scarce 2004; Frame, Gunton, and Day 2004; Jackson and Curry 2004a). Some of these studies have taken a primarily consensus approach to power, focusing on the components for successful collaboration, often in reference to the objectives set out by government policy. Such studies pay little attention to broader power relations and the problems that they present for traditionally marginalized groups. Other studies have taken a conflict approach to power, often concluding that collaborative planning processes constrain grassroots actors from challenging the status quo and fail to address their concerns. Whereas such studies suggest the need for greater power symmetry so that marginalized voices may be heard, they barely explore how this might be achieved. This book aims to broaden the discussion by exploring both the relations of power and domination at work in the collaborative planning process, as well as the ways grassroots actors might use such processes to enhance their collective power in order to counter domination. The emphasis is on understanding how relations of domination and oppression can be changed.

The approach adopted for this research is that of political ecology. At a general level, political ecology examines the way in which environmental change and ecological conditions connect to political processes and power relations (Robbins 2004, 5-7). The analytical focus is "on factors that shape power relations among human groups, and that influence relations between these groups and diverse aspects of their environment" (Paulson, Gezon, and Watts 2003, 205; see also M'Gonigle 1999). A common feature in political ecology research is an interest in furthering political and social justice. Thus, it often strives to expose, from a bottom-up perspective, the problems with the dominant approaches to resource management that are generally favoured by corporate and state actors. Individual cases are contextualized within a broader understanding of economic, political, and cultural forces. At the same time, political ecology inquires into the alternative development strategies and innovative actions taken by those who face environmental change resulting from mismanagement and exploitation.

The field research for this book was conducted concurrent to events unfolding inside and outside the land use planning process. The author made four research trips to Haida Gwaii to attend Community Planning Forum meetings and to speak with participants. Twenty-three forum participants were interviewed at three different points: March 2005 immediately following the final Community Planning Forum meeting, July 2005 shortly after a blockade action, and six years later, when the outcome of the process was becoming clearer.[4] A range of documentation was reviewed, including policy papers, the local newspaper, meeting minutes, agreements, academic literature, and a wide range of research and reports prepared specifically for the planning process. The POLIS Project on Ecological Governance at the University of Victoria provided the institutional home base from which to follow events.

The conflict on Haida Gwaii, like environmental conflicts more generally, can be understood as fundamentally about clashes between different systems of thought or languages of valuation. These include monetary values, indigenous rights and title, biodiversity conservation, wilderness, environmental justice, and others. However, as ecological economist Joan Martinez-Alier (2002) points out, the critical difference between them is not in their epistemological understandings, but, rather, in their power to influence land use outcomes.

To help unravel the complexities of power, Chapter 2 introduces various theoretical perspectives on power, including the insights of Habermas (1987), Lukes (1974), Foucault (1977, 1988), and Giddens (1984). A three-layered analytical framework is presented that offers both a methodological and theoretical framework for examining power and reflecting on outcomes. Although a theoretical understanding of power is useful, the events on Haida Gwaii can be appreciated without it. For this reason, some readers may wish to skip Chapter 2 and go directly into the story. However, the intent of providing this theoretical toolbox is to invite readers to generate their own analyses and conclusions on the situation in Haida Gwaii, and, indeed, many others.

To better understand how certain forms of valuation have become dominant in land and resource management, Chapter 3 turns to four central forces that have shaped resource conflicts in British Columbia during the twentieth century. These include imperialism, indigenism, industrialism, and environmentalism. The histories, ideologies, and practices associated with each of these are reviewed and their implications analyzed within the context of British Columbia.

Although certain land management practices have dominated on Haida Gwaii, they have not gone uncontested. A great deal of action has occurred in the courts and on the ground, particularly since the 1970s, which has influenced the direction and possibilities for alternative visions and strategic actions. Chapter 4 examines the recent resistance and opposition on Haida Gwaii, focusing on events that unfolded between 1974 and 2001. It explores the evolving relationship between the Haida, environmentalists, and local communities, and the emergence of a powerful movement poised to challenge the status quo.

In response to escalating conflict, the BC government introduced collaborative planning processes grounded in consensus decision making and the principles of ecosystem-based management. The secret to successful planning, as suggested by past studies of ecosystem-based management, lies in ensuring that all affected parties are equally and adequately represented and that power imbalances are addressed upfront (Grumbine 1994; Hartje, Klaphake, and Schliep 2003; Mabee, Fraser, and Slaymaker 2003). To understand how the planning process on Haida Gwaii attempted to address traditional power imbalances, Chapter 5 turns to its formative stages, examining the central agreements, foundational documents, and procedural framework. The planning process, however, was only one part of the Haida's larger strategy to take back control of the land and to secure their place in a changing order. The second half of the chapter turns to the wider politics, shifting alliances, and legal strategies that occurred outside the planning process.

Chapter 6 introduces the actors of the Community Planning Forum who were tasked with reaching consensus on land use recommendations. Their interest statements reveal a mosaic of concerns and seemingly discordant goals that were to be reconciled through the process. Although the institutional set-up for the planning process addressed various power differentials, early debate revealed some of the the ways that bias could be organized into and out of the process, and the opportunities and constraints this presented for the actors.

An important focal point is the role of ecosystem-based management and its potential impact on planning outcomes. With its emphasis on an ecological bottom line, ecosystem-based management appears to present a promising counterbalance to dominant forms of monetary valuation. Nevertheless, it remains a socially constructed concept, with many areas open for negotiation. Chapter 7 takes a closer look at the concept and methodology of ecosystem-based management and the challenge of balancing socio-economic and ecological concerns.

The goal of the collaborative process was to develop a strategic land use plan that would guide subsequent resource development and more detailed planning. Chapter 8 discusses the draft land use recommendations presented during the final month of Community Planning Forum meetings. It exposes the extent to which the process addressed certain power imbalances while naturalizing others. Outside the planning process, strategic alliances continued to grow as the Haida took on the government and industry at the Supreme Court of Canada.

When the Province ignored community recommendations and court decisions, a major collective action was launched. Chapter 9 highlights the discursive frameworks that each side employed in the battle and the strategic manoeuvring and incremental ratcheting that took place in public and in private. With one side pushing to expand the current social order and the other side fighting to maintain it, years of protracted negotiations ensued before an unprecedented land use agreement was finally signed.

The final chapter examines the outcomes of the planning process and the factors contributing to its success. It considers the strengths and limitations of collaborative planning as a tool for assisting progressive environmental and social causes, while highlighting the importance of power in understanding its transformative potential. It reflects on how collaborative planning might advance community capacity and collective power to challenge the status quo, while emphasizing the importance of engaging with the wider social, cultural, and political contexts in order for this potential to be understood and realized. The chapter concludes with an overview of the new ecological, economic, and governance arrangements emerging five years after the land use agreement was signed and what they might mean for the future of Haida Gwaii.

This book has many academic aims and interests, while its creation was motivated, above all, by a sense that the story deserves to be told for its

own sake. As political ecologist Paul Robbins (2004, 190) notes: "By building a political ecological record of such movements and claims, research
does some work towards both validating local accounts and challenging
dominant ways of seeing economic and ecological change." Expanding
on the implications of such research, anthropologist Peter Brosius (1999b,
180-81) comments: "We are now participants – mostly uninvited – in
the production of identities or in the legitimation of identities being
produced by others. To the degree that these movements represent an attempt to create new meanings and identities – which in turn have the
potential to produce new configurations of power – such a role cannot
remain unacknowledged."

The story of Haida Gwaii is rich and complex, and deserves to be told
from many different angles. While much remains unsaid, my hope is that
this book provides a useful account of recent events to give back to the
people of Haida Gwaii, while inspiring the emancipatory imagination of
people elsewhere.

2

The Nature of Power

The concept of power is one of the most central yet contentious in the
social and human sciences. A fundamental element of all social organization, it is "at work in all political, organisational and institutional
life and, in some views, in every social relationship" (John Turner 2005, 1).
Although the field of natural resource management has tended to ignore
power, it increasingly acknowledges the need to engage with the concept. Practitioners and theorists alike are recognizing the important role
that power plays in achieving desired outcomes. As social scientist Bent
Flyvbjerg (2001, 7) notes: "Understanding how power works is a first
prerequisite for action, because action is the exercise of power."

Despite academic advances on the subject, inadequate accounts of power
continue to prevail in much resource management literature. Yet, if planning efforts are to respond to the problems of dominance and inequality,
the realities of power must be exposed and engaged with. Failing this,
planning is unlikely to "disrupt the practices of the already powerful" and
can be expected to reinforce existing relations of dominance (McGuirk
2001, 213). To better understand the subject, this chapter breaks down the
concept of power into its main dimensions before outlining a multi-layered
framework that can assist in both understanding and analyzing it.

CONSENSUS VERSUS CONFLICT

The contrasting perspectives of consensus and conflict provide a useful
starting point for understanding the concept of power. Flyvbjerg (2001,

88) describes the difference between them as "the tension between the normative and the real, between what should be done and what is actually done." These two facets of power can be clearly seen to play out in this study.

The two approaches can be represented by the discourse ethics of Jürgen Habermas and the power analytics of Michel Foucault. Habermas, who has been described as "the philosopher of morality," studied processes for establishing consensus as a way of dealing with power (Flyvbjerg 2001, 88). Central to his approach is the concept of *communicative rationality* – "a noncoercively unifying, consensus-building force of a discourse in which the participants overcome their at first subjectively biased views in favour of a rationally motivated agreement" (Habermas 1987, 315). In contrast to instrumental rationality, where knowledge is constructed primarily through techno-scientific analysis, communicative rationality recognizes that meaning, value, understanding, and knowledge are all socially produced. As a result, it calls for "collaborative and reflexive processes of building consensus around shared meanings and understandings which are grounded in dialogue" (McGuirk 2001, 196).

Drawing on this approach, communicative planning theory emerged in an effort to transform the power context of planning (see Innes 1995; Healey 1997; Forester 1999a, 1999b). Communicative planning attempts to create power-neutral forums by minimizing systematic distortions of communication. These distortions, produced by such things as restricting argumentation, excluding participants, obscuring issues, or limiting knowledge, are seen as leading to domination by powerful groups (Forester 1989). A power-neutral forum, on the other hand, is sought by approximating Habermas's (1984) ideal speech situation. This has five key procedural requirements: generality, such that no party affected by the discussion is excluded; autonomy, requiring that all parties have an equal opportunity to present and criticize validity claims; ideal role taking, in which participants must be willing and able to empathize with the validity claims of others; power neutrality, in which existing power differences are neutralized so as not to affect the creation of consensus; and transparency, an open explanation by participants of their goals and intentions to prevent strategic action (Flyvbjerg 2001, 91).

Where conditions for the ideal speech situation are met, Habermas contends that the sole remaining form of power is the force of the better and more rational argument. The objective is to empower a variety of forms of knowledge, rationality, and value, such that all participants can deliberate on an equal footing and eventually establish new consensual ways of thinking, valuing, and acting (Healey 1997, 29). From this, a new and mutually agreed-on policy discourse can arise, providing a framework for specific planning actions, strategies, and regulatory decisions (McGuirk 2001, 197).

Communicative planning practices have made a positive contribution to democratic planning by allowing previously excluded groups and individuals to challenge the objectivity of so-called expert knowledge. Likewise, they have provided space for alternative interpretations based on practical experience, traditional knowledge, or emancipatory views. Indeed, much of this is evident in the collaborative planning approach taken on Haida Gwaii. This does not mean, however, that power-holders are effectively controlled by such processes, or that resultant decision making reflects the views and interests of the majority. The basic weakness of such an approach, as Flyvbjerg (2001, 93) points out, is "the lack of agreement between ideal and reality, between intentions and their implementation." In part, these inconsistencies can be traced to an inadequate conception of power.[1]

Whereas Habermas perceives consensus seeking and freedom from domination as inherent parts of communication, Foucault and others emphasize that communication is at all times penetrated by power. In this latter perspective, rhetoric, eloquence, charisma, and dependency relations between participants play a larger role in communication than rational argumentation (Flyvbjerg 2001, 93-94). In addition, disagreements between actors may be more than a matter of moral or personal preference. Attitudes may be deeply rooted in differing systems of thought and conflicting worldviews. Since worldviews are not generally open to reason and negotiation, differences in meaning that derive from them will not be resolvable through the "force of the better argument." Thus, even if two sides agree on procedural requirements, conflict will remain irresolvable if a fundamental incompatibility of meanings exists at a structural level (Haugaard 1997, 160-61).

In contrast to Habermas, Foucault emphasized resistance, struggle, and conflict as the means for achieving greater democracy and freedom from domination. The focus shifts from an attempt to neutralize power by fulfilling key procedural requirements to understanding the realities of power by concentrating on actual political practices (Flyvbjerg 2001, 102). The analysis is grounded in an understanding of history and sociality as the foundation for understanding the conditions that create power relations. Efforts are directed toward an analysis of strategies and tactics, and an attempt to determine how oppressive relations might be changed. In Foucault's words, the "political task" is "to criticize the working of institutions which appear to be both neutral and independent; to criticize them in such a manner that the political violence which has always exercised itself obscurely through them will be unmasked, so that one can fight them" (Chomsky and Foucault 1974, 171). Foucault's understanding draws attention to the way in which processes at the micro level are embedded in historically and socially created structures at other levels. Regardless of whether or not these structures are acknowledged, their effect is that the interests of some actors are favoured over those of others.

This points to the need for combining a micro-analysis of strategies and tactics with a macro-analysis of institutions and structures. For this purpose, a multi-layered conceptual framework can be useful. To aid in understanding, a brief overview of a few contributions in the power debate is presented below.

CONCEPTIONS OF POWER

Although studies related to power span many centuries, Robert Dahl is sometimes credited as the first theorist to examine the subject with an emphasis on methodology and precision. In *Who Governs?* (Dahl 1961), he focused on how community leaders in the United States influenced certain issues in local political decision making. Dahl analyzed the choices of a particular community to determine who influenced its decision making and to reveal its power relations. His rationale, simply stated, was as follows: "If it was the same groups [influencing decision making], the community could be said to be ruled by an elite; if, in contrast, a variety of different groups were able to influence decision outcomes, then the community could be termed pluralistic" (Hardy and Leiba-O'Sullivan 1998, 454).

For Dahl, power was something visible – an individual exercised it by making another person comply with preferences that he or she would not otherwise choose (Clegg 1989, 9). His major contribution was to distinguish between potential or latent power, represented by the power resources held by an agent, and the actual exercise of power where one agent compelled another to do something (Haugaard 1997, 12). Dahl concluded that the unequal distribution of potential power in a society did not necessarily manifest itself as an unequal distribution of actual power. Instead, he argued that the unintentional competition between elites with power resources resulted in a relatively equal distribution of power (ibid., 13).

Peter Bachrach and Morton Baratz (1962) formulated the "two faces of power" theory partly in response to Dahl. They challenged the assumption that "decision-making arenas were open to anyone with an interest in them and, therefore, non-participation reflected satisfaction and consensus" (Hardy and Leiba-O'Sullivan 1998, 454). Moreover, they argued that power is exercised not only through overt decision making, as in Dahl's analysis, but also through "non-decision-making." This concept, also referred to as the "mobilization of bias," would become central in the power debate. As Bachrach and Baratz (1962, 949) suggested: "All forms of political organization have a bias in favour of the exploitation of some kinds of conflict and the suppression of others because organization is the mobilization of bias. Some issues are organized into politics while others are organized out."[2]

They noted that power is exercised not only by doing things to others, but also by preventing certain things from occurring. This form of non-decision-making is commonly exhibited in agenda setting, where less powerful actors are deliberately prevented from placing issues on the political agenda. In this way, decisions can be limited to issues that do not challenge the interests of the powerful (Haugaard 1997, 14-15). As a result, though democracy may apply to certain innocuous issues, those of real consequence to a community remain firmly in control of the powerful.

Whereas Bachrach and Baratz saw conflict as a prerequisite for the mobilization of power, Steven Lukes pointed out that power may actually be used to prevent conflict from arising. In *Power: A Radical View*, Lukes (1974, 21-22) added a third dimension to the debate. He stated that bias is created not only through the decisions or non-decisions of leaders but also through the socially structured and culturally patterned behaviour of groups and institutional practices. These processes, he asserted, lead to certain interests being favoured over others, even if the dominated are for the most part unaware of this. Lukes used the Marxist concept of "false consciousness" to describe the situation where actors are made powerless with regard to certain issues because they are simply unaware of their "real interests" (ibid., 23). His underlying premise was that power distorts knowledge and obscures truth, thereby ensuring that the interests of the powerful prevail. In a much-cited remark, Lukes (ibid.) wrote that

A may exercise power over B by getting him to do what he does not want to do, but he also exercises power over him by influencing, shaping or determining his very wants. Indeed, is it not the supreme exercise of power to get another or others to have the desires you want them to have – that is, to secure their compliance by controlling their thought and desires.

Lukes's understanding extends the concept of power to include the broader context of political institutions as well as the whole process of individual socialization. One problem with this approach, however, is the question of how "true interests" are to be determined. Who identifies them? What standards do they apply? The danger of claiming someone is of "false consciousness" is the implied assumption that the one making the claim is intellectually superior (Haugaard 1997, 16-17).

Anthony Giddens is one of the most influential modern social theorists. His theory of structuration took up the long-standing question of whether social reality is formed primarily by agents or by social/structural forces. A main concern for Giddens was to overcome the problem of either overemphasizing the ability of individuals to shape the world through their actions, or focusing too much on the social structure as determining human agency. Rejecting the dualism of much social theory, Giddens (1984) posited that structure and agency are a unity rather than two distinct entities, interpenetrated to such an extent that one cannot exist without the other. He understood structure as both a motivation for action and a consequence of it. Giddens proposed that human actors produce, main-tain, and change social structures through their actions, which simultan-eously produce the conditions for the reproduction of human agency in a continuing process. Structure is thus seen as a dynamic process that is both enabling and constraining.

Stressing the potential of social actors, Giddens re-evaluated structural constraint. Rather than viewing it as a force that drives social actors into essentially becoming an effect of the social structure, he emphasized that constraint works by making certain actions more costly than others (Haugaard 1997, 110). Actors may behave in a way that seems contrary to their interests, not because they are ignorant of structural constraints, but, rather, because they have reflected on their social environment and con-cluded that the costs of acting otherwise would be too high. Hence, though they are motivated and knowledgeable about what they want, they are still a part of their social environment.

Foucault took a quite different approach to the question of agency and structure. Rather than pointing to an excluded structure or the power of agency, he focused on how the relations between structure and agency are constituted: how agency is given to some but not to others, how structure determines certain things but not others (Clegg 1989, 167). Foucault's analysis shared Lukes's concern with the relationship between power and knowledge. His emphasis, however, was on how certain representations are constituted rather than on their truth or falsity. Foucault rejected the assumption that knowledge can ever be separated from power and domination. Instead, he argued that truth is an effect of power that enforces social order by seeming normal or taken for granted. As Foucault (1988, 36-37) explained: "History serves to show how that-which-is has not always been, i.e., that the things which seem most evident to us are always formed in the confluence of encounters and changes during the course of a precarious and fragile history." The key to understanding the present is, therefore, to explore the past.

By undertaking what Foucault referred to as archaeological or genealogical studies, the hidden meanings and histories of concepts and things can be revealed to show their culturally specific nature. Foucault explored how certain taken-for-granted notions are formed through discourse – that is, the way in which language, stories, images, and so on define the limits of what is considered normal and acceptable. Moreover, he showed how certain social systems or practices convert these discourses into truths. For example, he demonstrated how medicinal science came to determine the best treatment of illness and how criminology came to determine the preferred treatment of deviant behaviour (Foucault 1973, 1977). In this way, he revealed that truths in discourses do not just happen, but are the result of struggles and tactics that disqualify certain knowledge and sanction others.

By revealing the history of certain truths, Foucault showed how they help to maintain the power of particular groups and individuals. He provided a radical critique of the present by using history to de-reify certain prevailing assumptions and truths. He did this, in part, by showing fractures and points of resistance in the constitution of things as they have come to be. In doing so, he revealed that things need not be the way they are (Haugaard 1997, 43-44).

One of Foucault's distinctive conceptions was that of disciplinary power. The goal of discipline is to shape socialization to a standardized mode in order to ensure predictable behaviour. The techniques of disciplinary power that developed in state institutions such as the prison were the focus of Foucault's *Discipline and Punish* (1977). Such disciplinary practices have also been disseminated through schools, the army, the asylum, factories, and other dominant institutions. In his historical inquiry into disciplinary power, Foucault revealed the many diverse sites and practices of power in the normal routines of everyday life. This resulted in his understanding of power not as a monolithic all-encompassing strategy, but, rather, as a complex strategic situation consisting of "a shifting network of alliances extended over a shifting terrain of practice and discursively constituted interests" (Clegg 1989, 154).

Each of the preceding theorists shines light on a particular angle of power. By combining their various insights, one can develop a multi-layered model of power that reflects the complex interplay of day-to-day agency interactions, on the one hand, and macro-processes of stability and change, on the other. The resulting framework is one in which several levels of control and resistance can be located.

A THREE-LAYERED MODEL OF POWER

Although there is no single all-embracing concept of power, the preceding overview illustrates that there are at least three broad groupings. Drawing on the multi-layered frameworks of Clegg (1989), Haugaard (1997), and Lemke (2002), power can be understood as consisting of three distinct but interconnected layers: agency power, institutional power, and structural power.

Agency power is the most visible form and what the term "power" typically refers to. It involves the use of power by agents, individually or in concert with others, to control or effect a situation to realize their goals. Related to the "first face" of power, agency power is about the capacity of agents to "name" and "frame" societal problems as political problems and to mobilize resources to formulate and realize the most desirable solutions (Arts and Van Tatenhove 2004, 350). Since power at this level often involves dominance over another agent, it often calls forth resistance.

Agency power is derived from the capacities that agents acquire as a result of resource control. Scholars of social movement theory (such as McCarthy and Zald 1977; Edwards and McCarthy 2004) suggest that resources consist of five broad types: material resources, including money and physical capital; moral support in the form of solidarity and support for movement goals; social organization, including organizational strategies, social networks, and alliances; human resources such as volunteers, staff, and leaders; and cultural resources, including prior experience, understanding of issues, and ability to initiate collective action. Success at the level of agency is based on the ability of an agent to activate these resources and target them toward their goals. In this sense, agency power is relatively coherent and important in and of itself.

However, when power stays exclusively at this level, it automatically reproduces the conditions of domination since it does not challenge existing rules or structures (Clegg 1989, 217-20). Moreover, though it tells of the power relations between two or more already constituted agents, it says nothing about how the broader institutional and structural context privileges or handicaps agents in acquiring the resources that enlarge their capacity. Questions of transformation arise only when challenges are made at the level of institutions and social structures.

The second layer of power, institutional power, addresses the systematized, regulated, and reflected modes of power that go beyond the spontaneous exercise of dominance over others (Lemke 2002, 5). It consists of institutions as sets of rules that both enable and constrain the behaviour of individual actors. The rules define such things as which norms are legitimate, how issues may be raised, and how interests are to be articulated. Institutional power relates to the setting of agendas, formulation of policies, the way in which decisions will be made, and how measures will be implemented. It also defines who should or should not be involved with decisions, how one can become involved, and the nature of the relationship between those inside and outside a particular process (Arts and Van Tatenhove 2004, 342). Agents are positioned in relation to one another on the basis of the rules and the division of decision-making power, which in turn affects what they may achieve.

This was the central point that Bachrach and Baratz made when they argued that some issues are organized into politics and some are organized out. The result is that certain agents are given more power than others, and certain goals are privileged over others. On the other hand, coalitions may challenge the rules of the game, and if they are successful, arrangements may change.

Alternatively, the intention behind Habermas's communicative rationality is to develop a set of procedures and norms at an institutional level that the parties agree do not arbitrarily privilege some goals over others. This is the idea behind deliberative planning. At the same time, conflicts may be about more than just goals – they may involve meanings and systems of thought that are created through social structures.

The third layer of power, structural power, refers to the macro-societal structures that shape the nature and conduct of agents. It encompasses forms of social order that are produced through the naturalization of societal norms, meanings, values, and standards. These forms of power are "materialized" in the institutions of the state, market, and civil society. Through these social structures, agents give meaning to the social world and evaluate the legitimacy of acts and thoughts. As a result, certain actors are enabled or constrained to mobilize resources to achieve their goals (Arts and Van Tatenhove 2004, 350-51).

The reproduction of structure involves the reproduction of meaning, where certain meanings are compatible with certain systems of thought. In this context, meaning is not something that an actor can create alone. An act is given meaning by being recognized, as the act was intended, by others (Haugaard 2003, 90-93). If a new meaning is introduced that is not compatible with the current interpretative horizon, it will be "destructured" or delegitimized, thus making it powerless with respect to the issue in question. However, if enough people endorse the new meaning, it can become a dominant interpretive scheme and may eventually even be sanctioned by state and societal institutions.[3] As Haugaard (2003, 96) notes: "What is established and taken for granted today is the result of successful, but hard fought organizational outflanking in the past."

This tension between what is considered true or legitimate and what is considered false or illegitimate lies at the core of social change (Haugaard 1997, 175-76). It is what distinguishes the difference between deviance and social innovation. In reaction to disempowerment, those who wish to raise a new issue must attempt to expand the conditions of possibility of social order. This requires building consensus around new meanings so that novel processes will be accepted as legitimate or true (Haugaard 2003, 95). New meanings, as Castells (1983, 304-5) states, may be produced by those in a dominant position who hold the power to restructure social forms according to their own interests and values. Such processes are sometimes referred to as political renewal or political restructuring. New meanings may also be developed within a particular limited space, such as intentional communities or cooperatives, which do not pose a significant threat to dominant interests. However, to impose a new meaning that contradicts the institutionalized meaning and is perceived as a threat to dominant interests almost inevitably involves a major collective action.[4] Over time, if enough people confirm the new meaning, the social order will be changed, and a capacity for action will be created relative to issues that were previously outside the conditions of possibility. This process entails empowerment – the creation of a capacity for action with respect to new issue areas. If it succeeds, systemic change will eventually be forced on those who attempt to maintain the status quo.

At the same time, the capacity of agents to engage with their surroundings to create change is always limited by structural constraint. Haugaard (2003, 94) defines structural constraint as "a process whereby actors who threaten systemic stability by new and innovative structuration practices are met by the non-collaboration of others in the reproduction of these new structures." Clearly, if certain structures are to be confirmed and maintained, others must be delegitimized or rejected. This is the irony of social order. But another significant and obvious motivation for structural constraint is to disempower others so as to maintain relations of power and powerlessness (ibid., 95).

The maintenance of structural bias and the consequent relations of power and powerlessness do not, however, necessarily entail active destructuring and rejection of new meanings. Rather, those who are dominated often seem to consent to their own domination. One explanation for this lies in the notion of "organizational outflanking," which emphasizes the lack of sufficient collective organization by those who are subordinated (Clegg 1989, 218-22). This may stem from ignorance of the ways in which power is exercised such as through rules, agenda setting, and so on, or it may result from uncoordinated action due to isolation or a lack of awareness of potential allies. On the other hand, organizational outflanking may be based on the knowledge that the cost of action outweighs the probability of success or the perceived benefits of achieving the desired outcome. Collective action must be seen as a feasible form of resistance if it is to be seriously pursued. Thomas Mann's (1986) historical account of social power stresses that if a resistance group is to overcome organizational outflanking, it must create a stable field of extensive, coherent, and solid alliances.

Another aspect of structural constraint is that of socialization. Actors who are "socially competent" know what is socially acceptable and will generally refrain from acting in ways that transgress it. This is the purpose of socialization. It ingrains in a person's social consciousness certain taken-for-granted knowledge that sustains particular structural practices while making other structures appear arbitrary or incoherent. This is the basis of Lukes's concept of false consciousness – that actors unconsciously reproduce certain structures that are incompatible with their discursive beliefs or that even contribute to their own domination.

Disciplinary power, as Foucault emphasized, is one way of enforcing desirable practical consciousness knowledge. Discipline is achieved through enforced routine and such things as surveillance and individual assessment, so that the knowledge base that informs an action is purely practical and unlikely to be evaluated. Physical coercion may also be temporarily used until the appropriate behaviour is internalized. Discipline is effective only to the extent that routines are internalized so that the use of physical power becomes unnecessary (Haugaard 2003, 103-4).

Both discipline and socialization contribute toward the reification of social structures so that they are made to appear as more than arbitrary constructs. This may occur, for example, by calling on the sacred (God's will) or the "natural" order of things (certain people are born superior/ inferior). Alternatively, Foucault emphasized the central role of modern science in producing "truth" and pointed out that this form of reification exists everywhere in the modern world. The power of reification lies in the fact that challenging a structure that is based on a foundation of "truth" implies denying truth itself, and anyone who does so appears irrational (ibid., 105).

Although no one can entirely step outside this socialized interpretative horizon, individuals can be made aware of their taken-for-granted know-ledge. At that point, they can evaluate their previously unacknowledged assumptions and reject them if they choose. This is consistent with Lukes's idea of "consciousness raising." It is also the intention behind Foucault's genealogical approach.

Only when all other methods of creating social order fail to generate the "correct" response from a person or group is physical power applied. Thus, its use is not the definitive demonstration of authority, but, rather, a sign of relative weakness or the failure of social power (Haugaard 2003, 106). As Lukes argued, the ultimate form of power is the ability to instill "correct" desires in others. This is well understood in most complex social orders, with the result that physical power or violence is used sparingly in its raw form. Most commonly, physical power appears in combination with social power in the form of threatened coercion (ibid.). Nevertheless, since physical force is not the most effective way of maintaining social control, the interests of the dominant are served by keeping its use to a minimum.[6]

To sum up, the multi-layered perspective makes clear that power is not only about tactics and strategies to secure outcomes at the level of agency and goals. It is also about securing or reproducing the conditions at the levels of institutions and social structures so that the strategies taken up at the agency level will be widely endorsed and perceived as legitimate. The level of agency power deals with the allocation of resources according to certain established meanings, whereas the institutional and structural layers create the conditions that enable this allocation. The extent to which agents manage to achieve their desired outcomes will depend, then, on their capabilities at the level of goals as well as the constraining or enabling effects of broader institutional and structural conditions. At the same time, agents who are constrained by their institutional and structural context may resist the roles and meanings assigned to them, creating outcomes that can potentially change institutions and social structures. By examining power at all three levels, a more complete understanding of power dynamics and their potential effects emerges.

3

Clash of Nature, Culture, and Economics

An important starting point for examining the conflict on Haida Gwaii is an understanding of the culturally specific assumptions underlying competing social structures. As in many colonized and resource-rich regions of the world, the contentious nature of resource extraction on Haida Gwaii can be seen in terms of four distinct but overlapping social structures: imperialism, indigenism, industrialism, and environmentalism. Imperialism refers to the processes and justifications whereby one nation imposes its power on another to expropriate land, labour, and raw materials for its own enrichment. Indigenism takes up the anti-colonial perspective of indigenous peoples and their struggle for collective rights to ancestral land and self-determination. Industrialism refers to the economic, social, and cultural system associated with the development of large-scale mechanized industries. And environmentalism is concerned with the natural environment and the question of how to achieve a balanced relationship between humans and natural systems.

Arising from divergent norms, values, and meanings, these perspectives have competed to define the best use of land, the beneficiaries, and the institutions that would prevail. An examination of their histories, ideologies, and practices reveals how established ideas became dominant as a result of struggles that sanctioned certain knowledges and disqualified others.

Occupying the Land

Canada is often described as a post-settler state. Its non-indigenous residents typically consider themselves to be native to the country, and indigenous people who once exercised authority over the land often form ethnic enclaves in sub-standard conditions (Lane and Hibbard 2005, 173). Although mainstream society often disregards the fact, it is undeniable that the post-settler state is founded on the imperial subjugation of indigenous peoples. Consequently, many conflicts between indigenous and non-indigenous groups can be traced to this fact and the differences in philosophies and cultural systems at the time of European colonization.

Before Europeans colonized Canada, indigenous people occupied the land. Organized into various nations representing at least ten distinct language groups, they had their own cultures, social organization, and governance systems (Erasmus and Sanders 2002, 3).[1] These systems were grounded in indigenous paradigms that understood all things as interrelated, and imbued with spirit (Little Bear 2005, 9). Thus,

> people, animals, plants, natural objects, and supernatural entities are not separate and distinct. Rather they are all linked to each other and to the places where they reside through cultural traditions and interactive, reciprocal relationships. Because of the integration of the secular with the spiritual, of the past with the present, and of all parts of the living universe, people have a sense of spiritual and practical respect for their lands, waters, and all the environmental components that they recognize. (Turner, Ignace, and Ignace 2000, 1279)

Arising from this understanding of spiritual interconnectedness, the notion of "respect for all life-forms and the land itself" guided indigenous peoples in the management and maintenance of their natural environment (ibid.). Practical strategies reflecting this worldview were developed through an intimate understanding of the regional ecology and generations of experimentation and observation. Management practices included plant propagation, soil fertilization, pruning, selective harvesting of fish and wildlife, assessing population health, and if necessary, harvesting moratoriums (ibid.). Certain chiefs or families often monitored and controlled specific resources within a given territory and held the rights to harvest them. In Haida Gwaii, the allotment of harvesting rights was traditionally applied to the entire coastline, various rivers and streams, hunting grounds, and patches of berries, root vegetables, and other foods (Nancy Turner 2005, 164-65, 169). Consequently, as Nancy Turner (ibid., 150) notes,

> Far from being simply opportunistic harvesters of naturally occurring wild fish and animals and random pluckers of berries and roots as the commonly used term "hunters and gatherers" would imply, First Peoples of Northwestern North America and other regions were astute and sophisticated caretakers of their plant and animal resources.

This fact, however, was neither appreciated nor understood by European colonizers, who assumed that Native land was either unused or used so ineffectively that it justified expropriation and replacement by more intensive land use. This was consistent with the official ideology that guided European claims to colonial territory and conquest over another people. It rested on the rights that followed from "discovery" and occupation, the inability of people to use land "appropriately," and the perception of weak social organization (Harris 2002). For the English colonists, landownership was secured by erecting a house, cultivating the ground, and building a fence. This understanding was derived from John Locke's "labour theory of property," which alleged that land acquired value and became property only through labour (ibid., 48). Title to the land was conferred by labour. By the same token, those who did not plant gardens or build fences could not have property rights.

Although British assumptions about property played a key role in early colonization, historian Cole Harris (ibid., 50) contends that they "were probably considerably less important in British Columbia in the latter half of the nineteenth century than the broad culture of empire." The culture of empire, explored extensively by cultural theorist Edward Said (1979), employed Western European ideology and values to distinguish between Europe and the rest of the world. The differences could be situated on a scale of sophistication ranging from savagery to civilization. The stereotypical representations and assessments of the "other" were used to justify European conquest. Canadian political economist Harold Innis (1995, 316) warned,

> We must all be aware of the extraordinary, perhaps insuperable, difficulty of assessing the quality of a culture of which we are a part of or of assessing the quality of a culture of which we are not a part of. In using other cultures as mirrors in which we may see our own cultures we are affected by the

2   Skidegate Village, ca. 1890-99. *Source:* Image B-03660 courtesy of Royal BC Museum, BC Archives

astigma of our own eyesight and the defects of the mirror, with the result that we are apt to see nothing in other cultures but the virtues of our own.

The hierarchical categorization of civilizations was legitimized by evolutionary paradigms that integrated Charles Darwin's concept of "survival of the fittest" with the social sciences. This social Darwinism likened the expansion of European power to the "realization of natural law" and provided "the key for an interpretation of history that seemed to glorify capitalism along with Europe's imperial impositions on the culture, identities, and free will of Indigenous peoples elsewhere on the planet" (Hall 2003, 226).

These notions of social evolution were grounded in ideological assumptions of what constituted progress. In the mid-nineteenth century, with industrialization and technological change rapidly transforming Western Europe, progress was increasingly perceived in material terms. As Harris (2002, 53) states: "Wherever they were in the colonized world, European officials and colonists had only to look at European technological achievements, and contrast them with those of the local indigenous society, to measure the extent of their own superiority." Progress also became associated with the ability to dominate nature. As capitalism expanded, land was increasingly seen in terms of resources, and people were perceived as an abundant and cheap labour pool to serve the needs of capital. Progress was consequently associated with an "ordered, managerial and market-oriented approach to nature" (ibid.).

According to this view, people who lived lightly on the land and in tune with natural rhythms were backward, unorganized, lazy, and unprogressive. This attitude was expressed by mid-nineteenth-century businessman and Indian land commissioner Gilbert Malcolm Sproat:

> We often talked about our right as strangers to take possession of the district ... The American woodmen ... considered that any right in the soil which these natives had as occupiers was partial and imperfect as, with the exception of hunting animals in the forests, plucking wild fruits, and cutting a few trees to make canoes and houses, the natives did not, in any civilized sense, occupy the land ... It would be unreasonable to suppose, the Americans said, that a body of civilized men, under sanction of their government, could not rightfully settle in a country needing their labours, and peopled only by a fringe of savages on the coast. (quoted in Nancy Turner 2005, 150-51)

The remaining question was how to deal with indigenous peoples who would be dispossessed of their land to make space for settlers. The British Crown laid down its policy on land acquisition and relations with Aboriginal peoples in the Royal Proclamation of 1763. In this important document, the Crown recognized Aboriginal title as continuing under British sovereignty. A main provision of the proclamation was that an indigenous population could lose its land title only through a treaty with the Crown. In this case, a First Nation would cede rights and privileges to certain lands and, in return, would obtain certain treaty rights, including fairly ample reserves and annuities.

A number of treaties were signed with First Nations, primarily between 1781 and 1867. However, European and First Nation interpretations of a treaty were often very different. As Erasmus and Sanders (2002, 5) point out,

> Ownership of land in the Anglo-Canadian "fee simple" sense of title was foreign to the thinking and systems of First Nations. Land was revered as a mother from which life came, and was to be preserved for future generations as it had been from time immemorial. Land was used for common benefit, with no individual having a right to any more of it than another. A nation's traditional hunting grounds were recognized by its neighbours as "belonging" to that nation, but that was different from the idea of private ownership ... First Nations people, then and now, believe that they live with the land, not simply on it.

The Government of British Columbia largely ignored the Royal Proclamation and established treaties for only 3 percent of the province. Its land policy was based on the assumption that indigenous people should "mingle" or assimilate with the settler population and learn the ways of industry. This was influenced by the early twentieth-century belief that First Nations would either succumb to industrialization or simply die out due to the diseases that had already drastically affected their communities. Indeed, settlement of the Haida occurred only after their numbers had diminished by more than 90 percent. Such colonial assumptions justified establishing small reserves that would both compel indigenous people into the workforce and make them more accessible to schools and missionaries. The rationale, as Cole Harris (2002, 87) explains, was that indigenous people

> should not be tucked away on reserves. Rather they should enter the workforce where, as labour was scarce and in demand, they would find employment in almost all branches of industrial and domestic life. In due course, stimulated by example and profit, they would develop their own enterprises as stock raisers, river boaters, packers, and commercial fishers and hunters. In this way, they would become participating members of civilized society. Mingling and thereby participating in the immigrant economy was the way to civilize Indians.

The reserve system imposed a strict spatial discipline on indigenous people by dictating where they could or could not hunt, fish, and gather. A variety of surveillance strategies enabled enforcement, including oversight by missionaries, who acted as "moral watchdogs" in the communities, and by Indian agents, who were charged with "protecting" Native rights and instructing indigenous people in "civilized ways" (ibid., 268-73). More pervasive were the property-owning settlers who watched for and reported Native "trespassers" on their recently acquired lands. Other control mechanisms were enshrined in the 1876 Indian Act, which gave the federal government exclusive authority to legislate on issues regarding First Nations and "reserved lands." Reflecting the values of colonial society, amendments to the Indian Act included an 1884 ban on the potlatch and the 1894 establishment of residential schools and compulsory attendance for First Nations children.[2]

The residential school system was perhaps the ultimate form of surveillance and discipline. Designed to "kill the Indian in the child," it removed children from their communities to disengage them from their indigenous identity and remould them as English-speaking members of a Christian settler society. Many students suffered not only from the social and cultural disconnection, but also from pervasive physical and sexual abuse. This would have a major impact on indigenous societies, the effects of which are still felt to this day.[3]

INDIGENOUS RESISTANCE

Despite the power of the colonizing force, First Nations people did not passively accept their oppression. They fought numerous battles, including the Chilcotin and Fraser Canyon Wars, and argued passionately for their right to title over lands they had always viewed as their own (Harris 2002, 216-64; UBCIC 2005, 14-27).[4] In 1906, a delegation of six BC chiefs travelled to London to present a petition to King Edward VII, which protested the lack of treaties and the inadequacy of reserves (UBCIC 2005, 22). In 1909, the Cowichan people presented a petition to colonial authorities in London, giving elaborate arguments for Aboriginal title based on the Royal Proclamation (ibid.). That same year, the leaders of a number of coastal First Nations formed the Indian Rights Association and raised funds to have their legal position drafted in "A Statement of Facts and Claims on Behalf of the Indians of British Columbia." This would later be submitted to the Privy Council in London as a basis for a hearing on Aboriginal title (ibid., 23). The Interior Tribes of British Columbia, also formed in 1909, prepared a "Petition of the Chiefs of Indian Bands of the Southern Interior at Spences Bridge." Calling for treaties, larger reserves, and compensation for expropriated lands, the petition was sent to the Department of Indian Affairs (ibid.). Similar petitions and declarations came from many other First Nations, including the Nisga'a, Tsimshian, Tahltan, and Lillooet (ibid., 14-27). The Province, however, refused to entertain the possibility of Aboriginal title.

Between 1913 and 1916, the "Indian land question" was addressed at hearings held by the Royal Commission on Indian Affairs (commonly known as the McKenna-McBride Commission). Its purpose was to make final adjustments to reserve acreage and to settle disputes over British Columbia's Indian reserve policy. The issue of Aboriginal title, however, was specifically excluded.

In eloquent testimonies, chiefs and others underlined the hardship and poverty caused by loss of their lands, inadequacy of the small reserves, and laws and restrictions prohibiting them from accessing off-reserve resources. On Haida Gwaii, speakers emphasized that, as citizens of Canada, the Haida should receive the right to vote and the same allotment of land as other people. However, in concert with other members of the Indian Rights Association, they resolved to settle the land title issue before discussing adjustments to reserve size (UBCIC 2005, 25).[5] At the Haida Gwaii hearings, Chief Councillor Alfred Adams of Old Massett stated,

On these Islands our forefathers lived and died, and here we also expect to make our home until called away to join them in the great Beyond ... All we have in this world, with the traditions and associations, lands and household goods are bound up on the islands that once were our own; but are now becoming the homes of others ... At the mouth of every river and stream, you will find our old camping grounds. All along the coastline are our former hunting grounds and the places where we fished, hunted and made our boats and canoes. These places are now covered by coal and timber licenses and occupied by preemptors. Year by year, the limits have been drawn, and we are now restricted to a small piece of land, here and there, the whole Band not having as much land as one prospector can cover with coal licenses. Where a foreigner can obtain 160 acres, we are allowed six ...

Without any treaty; without being conquered; we have quietly submitted to any laws made for our government, and this we intend to be our course. With other Indians, who claim to have the same grievances, we asked that our claims be taken before [the] Privy Council of the Nation; to be finally settled there, once and for all time.[6]

In a letter to the commission, Chief Councillor James Sterling of Skidegate wrote,

> We have been told that land outside of our small reserves is not for Indians. We supposed it was ours, but are surprised that we can neither pre-empt or purchase land anywhere in British Columbia. To us, this seems to be an injustice and a hardship ...
>
> Most of our young men are more or less educated yet the franchise has been denied them. It was on account of what we have already mentioned and other troubles, that we collected money [and] employed Lawyer Clarke to lay our claims before the Privy Council. We hope Gentlemen that as a result of your visit the Government shall remove what has troubled us.[7]

Highlighting the issue of land title, Chief Councillor Amos Russ of Skidegate stated,

> It came about after a little while that the Islands were the "Queen Charlotte Islands," but we don't know who gave them that name. As far back as we can remember we can claim that the Islands fairly belong to us and as far back as we can remember there was never any treaty with respect to this land, between the Government and the Indians. We have never had a fight for the Islands. No nation ever came and fought us for them and won them from us ...
>
> We know that day by day the Government is selling land far down this coast and also down the west coast of the island. We know for a fact that the government is selling the land and yet we can say the Queen Charlotte Islands are ours. You can see right around the island there are villages and villages and you can see our Totem poles which are the same to us as the white men's pre-emption stakes are to them.
>
> We cannot take a step further in the question until we hear what our lawyer Clark has to say to us. We cannot put any trouble before you people but we will hear and know later what to do.[8]

Despite overwhelming First Nations testimony regarding insufficient reserves, injustice, and hardship, the commission concluded virtually the opposite, that they "were contented and prosperous, and that there was no systematic land problem" (Harris 2002, 248). Its final report recommended reducing or cutting off valuable land from fifty-four reserves while apportioning "rocky, arid or otherwise undesirable lands" to most new or enlarged reserves (UBCIC 2005, 26; see also UBCIC n.d.).

The Allied Tribes of British Columbia was formed in 1916 in response to the royal commission process. It united the Interior Tribes of British Columbia and sixteen First Nations from all parts of the province, including the Nisga'a and some coastal nations.[9] Its objective was to provide a unified voice and a sustained and coordinated response to the encroachments of settler society and the infringement of Aboriginal political and territorial rights. Led by Reverend Peter Kelly of the Haida Nation and Andrew Paul of the Squamish Nation, the Allied Tribes took its demands to Ottawa in 1924. It challenged federal officials to respect their own laws, grounded in the Royal Proclamation of 1763, and to resolve the land question by recognizing Aboriginal title. Kelly expressed concern that adoption of the royal commission report would nullify Aboriginal title: "We shall have surrendered all our claims to the lands of the province, and the province, by granting us a few reserves here and there shall be held to have satisfied all claims of the Indians against the province" (quoted in Harris 2002, 255).

After persistent lobbying, the case for recognition of Aboriginal title was put before a Special Committee of the House of Commons and the Senate in 1927. The committee, however, not only found unanimously against the Allied Tribes, its recommendations led to an amendment of the Indian Act, making it illegal for First Nations to hire lawyers to pursue the land question. As a result, the Allied Tribes was dissolved and indigenous resistance was forced underground.

Although stifled by legal, economic, and political constraints, the fight for Aboriginal rights continued. The Haida and Tsimshian formed the Native Brotherhood of British Columbia in 1931, with the hidden mandate of seeking recognition of Aboriginal title. The North American Indian Brotherhood was subsequently formed in 1943 to organize First Nations across Canada. However, with almost no economic or political clout, First Nations' leaders depended on the power of ideas and principles to support their movement and legitimize their demands.

The post-war period saw an international shift toward greater emphasis on human rights. This led to the creation of a substantial body of legislation that oppressed people could employ to address their grievances. This included the 1960 United Nations Declaration on the Granting of Independence to Colonial Countries and Peoples, which constituted a milestone in the process of decolonization. It recognized the need to end colonialism "in all its forms and manifestations," and declared that "all people have the right to self determination" and the right to "freely determine their political status and freely pursue their economic, social and cultural development" (United Nations General Assembly 1960).[10] This shift in international discourse also affected attitudes toward indigenous people in Canada. In 1951, the law banning First Nations from pursuing land claims was repealed. In the 1960s, First Nations were given the right to Canadian citizenship, and in 1965 they were granted the federal franchise. Finally, in 1973 Ottawa recognized Aboriginal land claims.

The 1970s saw a resurgence in the fight for First Nations rights in Canada as a global indigenous movement emerged. On Haida Gwaii, this development was connected to the multinational corporate takeover of the forests. The Haida people had established fishing communities from about 1900 to the early 1960s and were engaged in boat building, fishing, and food processing. The reserve village of Old Massett had a mill and several boat-yards, and was well known along the coast for its boat-building industry. However, when large-scale forest tenures were introduced in the 1950s and 1960s, multinational tree farms displaced the smaller mills and blocked access to wood by Haida boat-builders. By the early 1970s, the Haida found themselves with little influence as the impact of accelerated forestry became increasingly evident on the mountain slopes and river bottoms. When the Crown pushed to restrict their hunting and fishing, the fight for Aboriginal rights and title re-emerged in full force on Haida Gwaii.[11]

A fundamental issue for the indigenous rights movement in British Columbia and globally is the conceptual and practical contestation of sovereignty. The indigenous movement defines sovereignty in terms of three interlocking concerns: maintaining or regaining control over land and resources; upholding "particular sets of social relations and more or less distinct cultural orders"; and having some degree of political autonomy (Lane and Hibbard 2005, 173). Indigenous claims to sovereignty not only challenge the state's allocation and management of land and resources but, more broadly, form a structure of resistance to the many cultural, social, and political processes by which indigenous peoples are subordinated by dominant society. It is toward these issues that much activism and scholarship on the "Fourth World" has focused.[12]

George Manuel, a Shuswap Nation leader, was a principal philosopher of the Fourth World and an important influence on the indigenous rights movement that developed with particular force in British Columbia. Like his predecessors, Manuel held that dispossession of indigenous lands in North America was a violation of the Royal Proclamation of 1763, an imperial law that had never been extinguished. Moreover, the centrality of the issue of Aboriginal title in British Columbia led him to promote the broader international implications of the proclamation for the Fourth World (Hall 2003, 286-87).

Manuel rejected the stereotypes of indigenous societies and argued for "a fundamental reorientation of global politics and economics to open space for Indigenous peoples to grow and develop in ways consistent with the underlying order of their own Indigenous cultures and traditions" (ibid., 237). Rejecting the modernization model of development typically applied to the Third World, Manuel emphasized the need for indigenous peoples to chart their own courses, stressing the importance of adapting to and integrating with the distinct ecologies of their homelands. In *The Fourth World: An Indian Reality* (Manuel and Posluns 1974, 4), he wrote,

> For a people who have fallen from a proud state of independence and self-sufficiency, progress – substantial change – can come about only when we again achieve that degree of security and control over our own destinies. We do not need to recreate the exact forms by which our grandfathers lived their lives – the clothes, the houses, the political systems or the means of travel. We do need to create new forms that will allow the future generations to inherit the values, the strengths, and the basic spiritual beliefs – the way of understanding the world – that is the fruit of a 1000 generations' cultivation of North American soil by Indian people.

Manuel called for the recognition and acceptance of the strong bonds between indigenous people and their ancestral lands. Indigenous spirituality, he believed, was central not as a means to oppose materialism but to provide a sustainable foundation for it. Furthermore, he argued that the ecological sensibility associated with indigenous spirituality was more a matter of pragmatism grounded in common sense than of romantic idealism. As Manuel (ibid., 256) put it,

> The traditional relationship of Indian people with the land, the water, the air and the sun has often been praised because of its spiritual nature. People seeking their own roots have praised it because it is a tradition they can grasp. But its real strength historically for our people, and its growing appeal today both for our own young people and for non-Indian people concerned for the generations still coming towards us, is not a romantic notion. Its strength lies in the accuracy of the description it offers of the proper and natural relationship of people to their environment and to the larger universe. It offers a description of the spiritual world that is parallel

to, and in fact part of, the material universe that is the basis of all our experience. The land, the water, the air, and the sun are sacred because they are
the source of all life. They are the limbs of the guardian Spirit. Their sanctity
is recognized because of their importance to our survival.

Nevertheless, despite a growing and increasingly coordinated indigenous
movement, industrial resource extraction continued to encroach on First
Nations territories.

STAPLES DEVELOPMENT AND THE FRONTIER ECONOMY

Since the early days of European colonization, resource extraction has
played a major role in the economic development of Canada and, more
particularly, British Columbia. The extraction and transportation of natural resources from hinterland regions to distant markets resulted in the
creation of the province's many resource-exporting single-industry communities (Hayter and Barnes 1997b, 8). One of the earliest systematic
analyses of Canada's frontier economy was made in the 1930s and 1940s
by the Canadian political economist Harold Innis. Prevailing justifications for staples development cited the laws of the market and commodities, but Innis pointed to culture as a key determinant in defining the
accepted norms for resource extraction. His broader point was "to show
that there is nothing natural about staples" (Barnes, Hayter, and Hay 2001,
2134). His intention in exposing the norms of staples development was
to assist peripheral areas to envision a more positive future. His staples
approach continues to provide important insights into Canada's economic
history and remains a useful framework for understanding contemporary
processes affecting British Columbia's resource economies.

Innis used the staple as a focal point to examine the interplay between
"a set of external forces of colonization and a set of internal forces of
internal institutional formation" (ibid., 2134). He rejected orthodox economic theory for being aspatial and oblivious to the role of institutions
and the unequal power relations they entailed. Instead, he emphasized
cultural institutions as central to the functioning of all markets. Innis
observed that staples production has particular space-time relations that
make these economies particularly dependent on non-market institutions
for their functioning. These space-time relations were fundamental to his
understanding of Canada's dependent status.[13] Innis understood space and
time to be made "inside larger but geographically and historically specific

social and economic systems defined by institutions, technology, and a given physical environment" (ibid., 2131). He pointed to a number of temporal or historical factors that affected staples production, including the physical geography and original size of a resource stock, unstable prices, transportation requirements over long distances, and the development of cheaper substitutes for the resource. He noted the defining effect of technology on resource accessibility, the speed of extraction, and the types of resources demanded by the core. Moreover, he pointed out that because of the large overhead costs generally associated with staples extraction, certain regulatory and institutional arrangements were necessary if extraction were to be economically feasible.

This brought to the fore the role of the state and the institutional structure of resource firms, including issues of ownership and existence of oligopolies. In British Columbia, for example, massive public investment in the form of roads, railways, and other infrastructure was made to facilitate forestry. To cover the cost of this, the Province required a continual inflow of foreign capital, which in turn created a bias in favour of large multinational corporations (Hayter and Barnes 1997a; Barnes, Hayter, and Hay 2001). Dependent on a wider international economy for capital, technology, and markets, the forest sector became tied into "a set of global relations that determine its fate" (Barnes, Hayter, and Hay 2001, 2132).

Innis also emphasized that a certain geographical or spatial relation was created between the local site of extraction and a dominant industrial metropole. This notion of a highly asymmetrical core-periphery structure was central to his staple model. The industrial metropole for Canada was initially located in Great Britain and later in the United States. In British Columbia, Vancouver served as the metropole for the rural hinterland, though its position was subject to high levels of external control. Such a structure once characterized all of British Columbia and still applies to many regions of the province.

The asymmetrical core-periphery structure can be defined by three factors. First is the "command and control" functions exercised by the dominant metropole over the periphery (Hutton 1997, 234). In general, upper management and decision-makers are situated in metropolitan regions, whereas blue-collar workers are located in the periphery. As a result, local development is largely determined by distant government officials and corporate executives.

Second, a qualitative imbalance in energy and material flows exists between core and periphery. The periphery supplies raw materials to manufacturers in the core and thus becomes a captive market for its end products. As a result, the additional value created when extracted materials are transformed by labour is generally realized in the core, not in the peripheral region where the raw material originated. In addition, an ecologically unequal exchange occurs since the resources extracted from peripheral regions may take hundreds or thousands of years to regenerate, whereas the products or services created in the core are rapidly manufactured on an ongoing basis. Thus, trade between the two areas entails an appropriation of energy and materials from periphery to core (Bunker 1985; Hornborg 1998; Martinez-Alier 2002).[14]

Finally, hinterland economies are subject to the long-term disadvantage known as the "staples trap." Because a certain set of economic and social forces characterize a staples region, including settlement patterns, labour force, methods of capital accumulation, domination by large multinational corporations, or transportation routes, moving from reliance on the primary sector to economic diversification is difficult. This fact may be reinforced by an export mindset among producers who cannot adjust to changing economics. The result is that the staple continues to be produced, even when it no longer generates an adequate income. The staples-producing peripheral regions "become part of the global economic 'margin,' their fates tied strongly to events in more powerful foreign metropoles" (Barnes, Hayter, and Hay 2001, 2130).

Nevertheless, when the different elements come together in the right institutional mix, periods of stability and prosperity do result. In this sense, the term "periphery" does not imply a lack of wealth so much as a lack of control. Indeed, the post-war forestry boom in British Columbia is a prime example of the creation of prosperity and stability based on staples production. This stability was largely the result of three sets of institutions and social relations: Fordism, the single-industry towns themselves, and managerialism (ibid., 2136-40).

Barnes, Hayter and Hay apply the term "permeable Fordism" to describe BC's post-war forestry sector and its marked dependency on the international, and particularly American, economy for capital, technology, and markets. The industry was typified by mass production of standardized products, mass markets (primarily in the United States), the use of Fordist production-line methods, a unionized workforce, collective bargaining, and corporate and frequently multinational resource firms (ibid., 2137). Under the corporatized post-war forest industry and Fordist staples regime, single-industry towns in British Columbia, once marked by insecurity, began to stabilize and grow. Their prosperity was exemplified in their stable populations, employment, social relations, and external

3 Logging in Naikoon Park. (Richard Krieger)

linkages. In addition, trade unions participated with industry and the state to ensure that everyone who was involved in the forest sector benefited (ibid., 2139). Nevertheless, the towns remained dependent on external decision making by resource firms and the provincial government. The institutions of this form of "managerialism" included the distribution of cutting rights, setting of stumpage fees, and provision of massive infrastructure development by the Province to promote forestry (ibid.). The federal government contributed by providing unemployment insurance to those who lost their jobs during temporary recessions.

Although resource extraction can and does lead to short-term gain: "even the best managed resource-based export-led communities contain within themselves the seeds of their own economic unsustainability, regardless of any associated social and environmental considerations" (Jackson and Curry 2004a, 5). In British Columbia, it became evident from the mid-1970s that the stability of the forestry sector was temporary. Changing markets, alterations in product demand, competition from low-cost producers, and a deteriorating wood-fibre base combined to destabilize the institutions and social relations of the forest sector. The new conditions required a fundamental restructuring of technology to meet the changed product demand. Lower production costs in both labour and management became central in the struggle to remain competitive. As the most accessible sites were logged and the best-quality timber taken, the industry was faced with higher extraction costs, diminishing returns, and growing scarcity of valuable old-growth stands. The financial predicament was temporarily offset by higher productivity achieved through increased mechanization and decreased employment. However, as Jackson and Curry (ibid.) note,

> Unless technological innovation can boost returns, or unanticipated boosts to market demand occur, given a fixed resource base, investment in labour saving capital will eventually reduce the productivity of capital, ensuring that returns to investments in resource based industries fall relative to those in other sectors. There is thus a limit on the extent to which capital can substitute for labour.

The only permanent solution to the problem of resource scarcity and diminishing returns on staples production is economic diversification. For rural forestry communities, which are most vulnerable to the effects of resource depletion, this means a shift toward value-added manufacturing and alternative sources of income generation. Nevertheless, despite strong indications by the mid-1970s of the need for diversification, British Columbia remained a staples economy. With the leading forestry firms under foreign or external control, the province's export structure and adaptations to fluctuating conditions were largely driven by the demands of markets elsewhere.

As the old-growth forests became progressively scarcer, the social and environmental values associated with them drew increasing attention.

Environmentalism and the Ecosystem Approach

In addition to the economic vulnerabilities associated with natural resource extraction, there are also major environmental impacts. These unaccounted-for and uncompensated environmental "externalities" include such things as the destruction of streams, watersheds, cultural sites, biodiversity, and habitat. In response to environmental damage, two broad environmental movements emerged: the conservation movement and the preservation movement. Both go back a century or more, and their legacy continues today.

The conservation movement is commonly associated with the American professional forester Gifford Pinchot. It is based on a utilitarian understanding of nature that rests on its usefulness to humans. The movement's original goal was to protect "national heritage," defined as the natural wealth of the country, from giant "profit-taking" firms (Weber 2000, 242). From this perspective, conservation and efficiency are achieved by creating government agencies to control the overly expedient development of natural resources. Scientific resource management techniques are central to the approach and are seen as providing "an objective mode of decision making capable of separating politics from administration" (ibid., 244). Moreover, techno-scientific methods are perceived as capable of balancing the long-term needs of nature with the short-term material needs of humanity within the context of industrial processes and economic development (ibid.). Conservation goals are pursued by allowing trained "experts" to decide how to harvest resources within the broad restrictions set by government. This approach is consistent with the integrated resource management paradigm found in British Columbia.

The problem with the approach is that the boundary between government decision-makers and industry players is often obscure. As a consequence, government decisions tend to favour short-term gains rather than long-term sustainability. As Weber (2000, 249) explains,

> Not only do bureaucrats and industry agree that economic growth is the top national priority, but preferred institutions prove conducive to cozy public-private relationships. In fact, the conservation approach historically has been associated with private, special-interest government by the few at the expense of the many. Significantly, industry has been the main if not only private-sector interest allowed the privilege of working together with government-based resource managers.

This form of utilitarian conservationism has been challenged by broader conceptions of the environment and the value of wilderness. The preservation movement, influenced by Henry David Thoreau, Aldo Leopold, and Sierra Club founder John Muir, sees nature not as a source of material resources but as something with intrinsic value. Its primary strategy is to set aside vast tracts of wilderness to prevent human encroachment that furthers environmental decline. Many contemporary environmentalists who fight to preserve the land and to protect endangered species take this approach. It has been considerably extended in part by the active role of conservation biologists and their great influence in the environmental coalition (Krajnc 2002, 220). Ecosystem-based management, in particular, has helped the BC environmental movement expand its arguments, clarify its goals, and build support for preserving old-growth forests (Wilson 1998, 14-15).

Ecosystem-Based Management

In many areas of the world, ecosystem-based management has gained increasing support as people experience the environmental and social costs of the post-war industrial boom.[15] Unlike conventional approaches to resource management, ecosystem-based management recognizes eco-systems as whole systems. Its natural scientific roots are in conservation biology and landscape ecology. Conservation biology emphasizes the need to maintain ecological resilience, defined as an ecosystem's ability to tolerate disturbances without collapsing (Holt 2001, 4).[16] It recognizes the importance of preserving biodiversity and of avoiding the erosion or removal of an ecosystem's structures, functions, or processes. Landscape ecology stresses the way that diverse ecosystems interconnect across broad spatial and temporal dimensions to allow for such things as the movement of animals, plants, energy, and nutrients.

Although precise definitions of ecosystem-based management vary, that of Grumbine (1994, 31) is often cited: "Ecosystem management integrates scientific knowledge of ecological relationships within a complex socio-political and values framework toward the general goal of protecting native ecosystem integrity over the long term." Dominant themes identified by Grumbine (ibid.) and others (such as Franklin 1997; Yaffee 1999) include variation in spatial and temporal scales, ecological boundaries (rather than administrative/political boundaries), adaptive management, conflict resolution, power relations, and human values.

The concept of ecological integrity is central to the approach and can even be understood as providing a larger conceptual framework for the other themes (McCarthy 1999, 29). Kay (1994, 37) describes ecological integrity as "the maintenance of system components, interactions among them and the resultant behaviour of the whole system in the face of change." The purpose of the approach, however, is not to maintain static ecosystems but rather to ensure that they are able to self-regulate and perpetuate themselves, in order to avoid the ecological, social, or political catastrophes that may result from their collapse (Holt 2001, 4).

In most instances, maintaining or restoring ecosystem integrity requires the management of human activity. This implies situating economic and political activities within the limits of a functioning ecosystem to minimize environmental "externalities" in the production process (International Network of Forests and Communities 2002, M'Gonigle 2003, 130). Ultimately, the bottom line is determined by an area's ecology, not its economy. This entails a shift in perspective where, rather than acting as controllers and exploiters of nature, humans become its stewards. At the same time, since resource-dependent communities require access to healthy ecosystems for their livelihood and survival, ecosystem-based management offers a valuable strategy for meeting this need (International Network of Forests and Communities 2002).

The concept of ecological integrity is not only grounded in ecological concepts, but is also firmly rooted in human values. As Kay (1993, 208, 203) concludes, determining whether human-caused changes to an ecosystem are ecologically acceptable or not is a human value judgment. He explains: "We can measure and analyse changes in an ecosystem, but we can only make judgements about the integrity of that system." Evaluation of a system's integrity must, therefore, be contextualized on the basis of the issues that are identified as most important (ibid., 202). Thus, understanding both ecological processes and the broader social, economic, political, and cultural context is essential to the success of ecosystem-based management (Mabee, Fraser, and Slaymaker 2003, 5). An attempt to integrate these various perspectives into ecosystem-based management practices, however, quickly reveals diverse and often contradictory values and interests. Under such conditions, the key question becomes, who chooses the issues of importance, and by extension, which changes are acceptable?

When this element of human value is combined with the ecosystem qualities of uncertainty, unpredictability, and lack of control, the concept of ecological integrity enters the realm of post-normal science. In contrast to normal science, post-normal science recognizes that expert-oriented decision making and "objective" answers are no longer ethically appropriate to matters concerning complex systems, high uncertainty, and huge stakes in terms of ecological and socio-economic impacts. As Ravetz, Funtowicz, and the International Society for Ecological Economics (2007, para. 2) explain,

> The approach used by normal science to manage complex social and bio-physical systems as if they were simple scientific exercises has brought us to our present mixture of intellectual triumph and socio-ecological peril. The ideas and concepts belonging to the umbrella of PNS [post-normal science] witness the emergence of new problem-solving strategies in which the role of science is appreciated in its full context of the complexity and uncertainty of natural systems and the relevance of human commitments and values.

Although it acknowledges the importance of science in decision making, post-normal science recognizes that all decisions are ultimately "an expression of human ethics and preferences and of the socio-political context in which they were made" (Kay et al., 1999, 737). Because of this understanding, post-normal science emphasizes the importance of extended participation in decision making:

> The dynamic resolution of policy issues in post-normal science involves the inclusion of an ever-growing set of legitimate participants in the process of quality assurance of the scientific inputs ... In this way, its practice (science) is becoming more akin to the workings of a democratic society, characterized by extensive participation and toleration of diversity. (Funtowicz and Ravetz 1993, 751)

This call for extended participation has also been taken up by planners as a way to resolve resource conflicts and create or restore social order. In general, the underlying understanding is that everyone will be better off if conflicts are resolved through compromises rather than by each group attempting to impose its will on others (Lee 2002, 3). In many places, this has led to a conceptual shift from top-down technical approaches toward more collaborative processes for resource management. Grumbine (1994) stresses that the key to success lies in ensuring that all parties are equally and adequately represented, and that power imbalances are addressed upfront. However, the extent to which this occurs ultimately depends on the way in which power is understood.

4

War in the Woods: 1974-2001

Throughout the twentieth century, forestry and conservation were the focus of much debate in British Columbia. The 1970s, however, saw a dramatic rise in the level of conflict between government and industry, on the one side, and environmentalists and First Nations, on the other. Clashes spread from valley to valley as awareness grew of increasing resource scarcity, declining environmental quality, and the rights of indigenous peoples. This was accompanied by mounting public discontent with the lack of consultation on forest management in the province.

This chapter explores the political, social, and economic context of the "war in the woods" in British Columbia, paying particular attention to several events on Haida Gwaii. It contrasts state and industry representations of forests with the views of the Haida, environmentalists, and local communities. It also highlights several important shifts, including an expansion from colonial assumptions of property to recognition of continuing Aboriginal title, and a move from utilitarian perceptions of nature to greater acknowledgment of nature's intrinsic worth. Tracing the emergence of an indigenous-environmental-community alliance on Haida Gwaii, the chapter explores the strategies and tactics used to disrupt the trajectory of the forest industry.

QUESTIONING "SUSTAINED YIELD"

In British Columbia, 94 percent of forested lands are publicly owned. Prior to the 1940s, however, there was minimal state oversight of private timber companies and sawmill operators in the province. In 1943, faced with rising public concern that the forest base was being unsustainably managed, the government established the Royal Commission on Forestry to examine the state of the provincial forests and forest regulation. The resulting regulatory model introduced two important elements: perpetual forest tenures and sustained-yield policy. Although the model has been reformed over the years, in many critical respects it remains largely unchanged (Tollefson 1998, 5-7; Prudham 2007).

The royal commission (also known as the Sloan Commission) advocated for "a form of tenure permitting the operator to retain possession in perpetuity of the land now held under temporary forms of alienation upon condition that he maintain these lands continuously productive and regulate the cut therefrom on a sustained-yield basis" (Sloan 1945, 143). The rationale for offering these long-term leases over large tracts of Crown forests was to "enable leaseholders to invest with security in the forest sector, and encourage a switch from a purely extractive approach to one that sought to maintain and enhance the province's forest stock" (Jackson and Curry 2004b, 28). In the early days of the system, companies that acquired these tenures paid little or nothing for them as the state considered it a legitimate and effective means of promoting rapid development of the young forest industry.

Two primary forms of forest tenure were introduced to govern access to timber resources: area-based tree farm licences (TFLs) and volume-based forest licences. Both remain in use today.[1] Under the tenure system, companies rent long-term timber harvesting rights on Crown land for relatively little cost and, in exchange, normally agree to maintain basic processing operations that use some or all of the wood.[2] The tenure system also confers certain rights to the licence-holders, such as the ability to bar members of the public who may interfere with logging activities and to be compensated if the government removes land from the licence.

The Sloan Commission also recommended a sustained-yield policy for Crown forest lands. Sustained yield requires that the average annual cut of the forest must not exceed its average annual growth. It involves "converting" natural forests, through logging and regeneration, into "ideally" constituted commercial forests composed of "even-aged blocks of commercially significant tree species, each to be harvested at a prescribed age – the rotation age – such that the total annual harvest remains constant over time" (Prudham 2007, 264). The intention is to maintain a steady stream of harvestable timber even after the best old-growth forests are logged.

The Forest Act was amended in 1946 to incorporate this practice, and professional foresters in the government and private sector were placed in charge of devising appropriate strategies. However, in the midst of rapid post-war economic growth, successive provincial governments turned to the forestry sector to finance the modern infrastructure of the BC economy (Jackson and Curry 2004b, 28). With greatly expanding logging from the 1960s onward, British Columbia's forest policy came under increasing fire. In response, the Province introduced the policy of "integrated resource management" in 1978. This brought attention to a greater range of resource values in the forests, including fisheries, wildlife, water, and outdoor recreation. Nevertheless, it was difficult for the Ministry of Forests to reconcile "its professional duties, which required the Forest Service to maximize sustained-yield timber production, with its new responsibilities for integrated resource management" (ibid., 29). Consequently, the goal of maximum timber harvest continued to take priority over non-timber uses. This bias became more pronounced during the economic recession of the 1980s, when integrated resource management gave way to "sympathetic management," which allowed the relaxation of environmental constraints on logging (ibid.).

Meanwhile, opposition and pressure for change were mounting in British Columbia as public attention increasingly turned to forest management practices, First Nations land claims, and the connections between the two. Conflicts occurred throughout the 1970s and 1980s, involving a combination of litigation, lobbying, and direct action by environmentalists and First Nations. These included the well-known campaigns for Tsitika/Robson Bight, Meares Island, Stein Valley, and Valhalla. It was during this time that a major forestry battle broke out on Haida Gwaii.[3]

The Battle for Lyell Island

In the early 1970s, a powerful and increasingly concentrated forest industry dominated the land base of Haida Gwaii. Local people had generally kept a respectful distance from the logging companies, aware if not resentful of their power to affect their lives (Pinkerton 1983, 74). The Haida had virtually no influence over the higher-level decisions affecting the land, and their economy consisted almost solely of a handful of fishing licences and logging jobs. Elsewhere, a fledgling environmental movement was finding its feet, testing its arguments on issues of litter and pollution.

Meanwhile Premier W.A.C. Bennett's twenty-year reign, with its ambitious agenda of industrialization and prosperity, was in full swing.

It was within this context that conflict emerged in Gwaii Haanas (then referred to as South Moresby). Logging operations of the 1950s and 1960s had left much of the northern part of Moresby Island brutalized by clear-cuts. By the 1970s, logging had moved into the southern half of the island, which contained numerous significant Haida cultural and archaeological sites, and hosted immense ecological diversity. In 1974, ITT-Rayonier, the company holding the tree farm licence in the area (TFL 24), presented a five-year logging plan to the Ministry of Forests, proposing to move its contractor, Frank Beban Logging, to Burnaby Island. This island was considered to be a cherished food and cultural site by the Haida.

In response, the Islands Protection Committee was formed by Guujaaw (known then as Gary Edenshaw) and Thom Henley, a recent resident of the islands.[4] Guujaaw had often accompanied his uncle, Percy Williams, to Gwaii Haanas to trap and gather food, and Thom Henley was an avid kayaker with a deep appreciation for the area. The committee represented the first formal organization of Haida and non-Haida islanders. Percy Williams, the chief councillor of Skidegate and a trapper and fisherman who grew up in Gwaii Haanas, also expressed concern over the destructive effects that logging could have there.[5] He lodged a formal statement with the government, requesting that the area be set aside.

Working closely with the Skidegate Band Council, the Islands Protection Committee built a local consensus on the need to establish a wilderness protection area on Gwaii Haanas. It formally lobbied the Province, creating support for its wilderness proposal through various forms of monitoring, evaluation, and education (Broadhead 1984, 130).

The government eventually agreed to defer logging on Burnaby Island but granted permission to log on Lyell Island, which was also within the proposed wilderness area (ibid.). Under continuing pressure from the Islands Protection Committee, Premier Dave Barrett made a verbal promise to place a logging moratorium on regions within TFL 24 that were used for traditional food gathering. This promise was never honoured.

In 1975, as logging was getting under way on Lyell Island, public hearings regarding the tenure system, known as the Pearse Commission, were initiated. Whereas licence-holders used the process to defend their management record, the Skidegate Band Council asserted in their submission: "To suggest ... that the people of the province should safeguard the timber resource for centuries in the warm heart of the large companies is, we submit, being naïve and blind to the actual operations of the multinationals" (quoted in Rajala 2006, 188). The council argued that the Haida had used the forests for thousands of years, and despite the fact that many Haida now earned wages as loggers, they were "denied the benefits realised from the profits of their labour" (ibid., 188). Thus, the best safeguard for continued employment and "respect for the forests" was local ownership of tree farm licences (ibid., 189). Appearing before the commission, Percy Gladstone of the Skidegate Band Council proposed that the Skidegate Band would apply to take over three licences when they came up for renewal. When asked whether the band council intended to compensate the licence-holders, Gladstone replied: "The Haida people feel that they should be compensated before anyone asks us for compensation" (ibid.).[6]

From 1976, the forest management debate intensified on Haida Gwaii. Increasingly, the Islands Protection Committee dogged the activities of forest companies, criticizing the poor management of both industry and government. Responding to the pressure, the Ministry of Forests created a Public Advisory Committee in 1977. Composed of logging company officials and a wide range of local residents, the committee undertook detailed analyses and critiques of forestry practices on the islands and eventually concluded that, in contradiction to sustained-yield principles, TFL 24 was being overharvested by 30 percent (Pinkerton 1983, 79-80). Ministry officials, however, ignored the resolutions of the advisory committee and declined to consult or cooperate with its members. By 1979, the committee had unanimously agreed to disband (Wilson 1998, 191).

As Rayonier's tree farm licence approached its next five-year renewal in 1979, the public called for hearings on the renewal. The Province ignored this request, citing the new Forest Act, which granted the automatic renewal of tree farm licences. In response, three members of the Islands Protection Society – Nathan Young (Chief Gitkun), a hereditary chief and trapper; Guujaaw (Gary Edenshaw), representing hunter-gatherers; and Glenn Naylor, who had a trapline in South Moresby – filed a joint petition (Broadhead 1984, 134; May 1990, 50-72). Young and Guujaaw received legal standing. Their intent was to have the court order the Ministry of Forests to conduct a full public inquiry before renewing TFL 24. At a minimum, the petitioners hoped that the interests of trappers and food-gatherers would be fairly considered.[7] The court found that a public hearing was not required, as the licence had not yet been renewed. However, there was still time to consult, and the court strongly recommended that the petitioners be consulted before a renewal was granted (Broadhead 1984, 135). Although their petition had been denied, this was the first time that a trapper and a hunter-gatherer had achieved standing in a BC court, a development that would open the law chambers to much more in the future.[8]

The Province and the Haida subsequently held meetings where the petitioners proposed fifteen changes to TFL 24. The Ministry of Forests agreed to only six and renewed the licence. Returning to court a few days later, Chief Gitkun and Guujaaw attempted to have the renewal struck down and were denied once again, this time on the grounds that the renewal had already occurred and the government had been responsive to their submissions. Soon afterward, the Province dropped the six changes to the renewal notice previously agreed on. In an effort to have the terms of the licence renegotiated, the petitioners appealed the case to the Supreme Court of Canada. Their application was again denied, because the court saw the issue as a provincial matter (ibid., 134-36). Despite the lack of support from the courts, some indirect gains did result, including the compilation of much information on logging rates and management, as well as a high degree of public education on forestry practices, the obligations of forestry companies, and the public's right to demand sound management (Pinkerton 1983, 83). Shortly thereafter, Rayonier sold the forest licence to Western Forest Products.

Meanwhile, members of the Islands Protection Society, now including Captain Gold (Dick Wilson, known then as Wanagan), John Broadhead, and Paul George, began an intensive campaign to influence public opinion. Enlisting qualified scientists, they eventually assembled enough information "to argue the case for preservation on scientific merit alone" (John Broadhead, quoted in Wilson 1998, 90). Working with photographer Richard Krieger, and others, they produced an effective travelling slide show and a glossy coffee-table book, which contrasted the beauty of wildlife and ancient ecosystems with logging-induced landslides and debris-filled salmon streams (ibid.).

Captain Gold, the Skidegate director of the Islands Protection Society, took up residence at SGang Gwaay (also known as Anthony Island) in an important Haida cultural area. This was the beginning of what would become the Haida Watchmen Program, a cultural and political strategy that involved Haida people occupying a series of base camps in Gwaii Haanas. Just as the watchman once warned a household of apparent danger, the Watchman camps would look after the house of Gwaii Haanas.[9] Captain Gold looked after the sacred sites and educated visitors while preventing looting and damage. The Province had previously designated the island as "Anthony Island Provincial Park," and were initially so supportive of Captain Gold's efforts that they hired him. However, following a misunderstanding with his supervisor, Captain Gold was replaced by a BC Parks staffer.[10]

Meanwhile, the Islands Protection Society had secured funding for the Haida Watchmen Program, and a crew of Haida, including Captain Gold, Dempsey Collison (Chief Skidegate), and others headed to Gwaii Haanas to get the village sites ready. When they reached SGang Gwaay, Captain Gold confronted the BC Parks staffer who had been hired in his place, informing him that the Haida were starting the Watchmen Program, and that he should vacate the island – "before lunch would be best."[11] Steering clear of conflict, the Parks employee was helicoptered out immediately as requested. This was part of the Haida's strategy to connect protection of the land with use and occupation of the land.[12]

Concurrent with developments in Gwaii Haanas was the advance of the Haida's land claim. In 1974 the Haida people formed the Council of the Haida Nation to negotiate land claims on the basis of Aboriginal title. It was one of the first indigenous governance bodies to step outside the *Indian Act*, the federal legislation binding all band councils. The Council's first leader, Godfrey Kelly, foresaw a political approach that continues to this day. He asserted: "The Council's decision making ability and managerial policies are to be completely determined by them. There is no reason to follow ways of operation which are forced on Band Councils by Indian Affairs regulations" (Council of the Haida Nation 1976, 2).

In the Convention of the Founding of the Haida Nation, the Council was given "complete authority to represent and speak on behalf of all Haida people in matters dealing with Governments, corporations, or other organizations and groups, on matters effecting [sic] all Haida people; reserving the present rights of each Haida group to determine matters that presently lie within areas of their own special concern" (ibid., 3). The primary goals were to have Haida title recognized in law and to ensure the Haida's permanent participation in the social, economic, and political development of Haida Gwaii (ibid., 4). As to how they might proceed, Godfrey Kelly wrote:

> The goals which we have set for ourselves require more than the power of the Haida people. It is generally agreed that land claims questions are best settled in the political arena by negotiation rather than legally in the courts. The legal or court route is only used to strengthen the negotiating position, to get publicity and political allies or to stop harmful development. No one wants a court settlement for it would probably result in a settlement not in the best interests of the Haida, and for the government it would involve

expensive litigation without touching on the bureaucratic mandates etc. of Indian Affairs. Who are our allies? How can we develop more allies both Indian and white? Are there white allies on the Islands? Let's identify them and work with them.

... As Council we must begin to act in ways which show that we have the vision to lead and the humility to listen to the people. (ibid., 5, 6)

Internal divisions between the Council of the Haida Nation and the two village/band councils soon led to a stalling of political activities for four years. The council was reconstituted in the 1980s, and a steering committee, including Ernie Collison, Guujaaw, and Captain Gold, set out a ten-year agenda and a basis for the constitution. The focus of the first three years was to unify and build public confidence. To facilitate this, the committee convinced Percy Williams, a well-known and respected member of the community, to run for president. Williams established a high standard of diplomacy and formalized the territorial dispute with Canada at the international level. In his time, the first formal land designations were established. He also clearly established Gwaii Haanas as a top priority on the political agenda. He would be followed as president by a younger, quick, and dynamic Miles Richardson, who would be right for the launch of a political action.[13]

One of the new council's first moves was to submit a land claim to the federal government in 1981. Canada accepted the land claim for negotiations two years later. However, negotiations required the Province to also be at the table and, at the time, the Province refused to negotiate land claims that might require the surrender of "Crown" land.

Forest management and resource policy became strong components of the council's work. In 1981, the Haida issued several policy statements on forest management, including one that called for the logging rate on Haida Gwaii to be reduced by 50 percent. They also produced commentary on the management and working plan of TFL 24, and a policy paper on the management of all island resources (Pinkerton 1983, 83). The connection between the Haida's Aboriginal rights and their commitment to protecting land and marine resources was made explicit. As Percy Williams, then president of the Haida Nation, stated,

These existing aboriginal rights are limited only by the capacity of what the land and sea can produce, and defined again by the laws of nature and common sense which ensures we sustain those rights through successive

4   Totem poles at Ninstints, SGang Gwaay, UNESCO World Heritage Site.
(Richard Krieger)

generations. Degeneration of the land and sea will further reduce our rights, therefore we have a moral obligation to defend our resources and determine the fate of our tribal territories. (quoted in Pinkerton 1983, 68)

In 1979, the provincial government initiated a new advisory body, the South Moresby Resource Planning Team, which it touted as "a model of the new public involvement process" (Broadhead 1984, 135). Composed of Haida, industry, government, and community representatives, the planning team was tasked with assessing the ecological reserve proposal for Windy Bay on Lyell Island, as well as suggesting land designations and management guidelines for South Moresby. In 1981, the team completed its first report, which expressed strong support for preserving the entire watershed.

Outside the planning process, people were paying attention to the issue and increasing numbers of tourists were arriving. As the Watchmen Program took hold, Haida volunteers began to watch over the old village sites, protecting their cultural heritage while educating visitors about them. With full approval of the Haida Nation, the village of Ninstints (Nans Dins) on SGang Gwaay was declared a UNESCO World Cultural

Heritage Site and a National Historic Site of Canada in 1981. Concurrently, the Haida Nation designated all of Gwaii Haanas a Haida Heritage Site.[14]

The Haida Nation also designated its first protected area, Duu Guusd Tribal Park, encompassing most of Graham Island's west coast, and advised the Province to defer all development in the area. The designation was recognized by the two main fishing organizations on the coast and by the Graham Island Advisory Planning Commission (Council of the Haida Nation 2010a). To assert their designation, the Haida held a feast in Naden Harbour, next to a logging camp, and declared it a "day off" for the loggers. Their intention, noted Michael Nicoll Yahgulanaas, was "to feed the loggers so their ears would be open as we told them they couldn't log Duu Guusd" (quoted in Gill 2009, 103).

The South Moresby Resource Planning Team completed its second report in 1983, which presented four alternatives for land use in South Moresby. These ranged from leaving 33 percent of the land as a "natural zone" to placing 95 percent of it off-limits to development. Reactions were mixed. Western Forest Products, the licence-holder in the area, declared that none of the options was realistic. The Skidegate Band Council expressed support for preserving 95 percent but asserted that "any further moves towards a formal land designation should be properly addressed through the Council of the Haida Nation" (South Moresby Resource Planning Team, quoted in Wilson 1998, 192)).

All the while, logging continued on Lyell Island. As time passed and the provincial government made no decision, it became apparent that the government was either unable or unwilling to choose an option. Planning team member John Broadhead (1984, 139) concluded: "In the minds of its participants, 'public involvement' degenerated in concept from a meaningful democratic exercise to a clever diversion by government of conservationist energies and a measure for avoiding embarrassing legal confrontations."

Nevertheless, the wilderness reserve idea appeared to be gaining some traction. Federal park officials supported it, and by 1985, federal environment minister Charles Caccia had indicated interest as well (Wilson 1998, 192). The Province's environment minister, Austin Pelton, even promised that he would try to halt further approvals for logging permits on Lyell Island (ibid., 193). Despite these assurances, however, new logging permits were approved in 1985.

With no decision made on the planning team report, and having achieved no success through official channels, the Haida turned to other measures. They set up camp first at Sedgwick Bay and then at Windy Bay on Lyell Island. Supported and led by people including Ernie Collison, Chief Skidegate (Dempsey Collison), Miles Richardson, and Guujaaw, the Haida proceeded to blockade the road. Only Haida people were to take a stand. Up to that point, the environment had been the central rallying cry. Now, the Haida brought the land title issue to the forefront. The president of the Council of the Haida Nation at the time, Miles Richardson, recalled: "We wanted a crystal clear, unmistakable message that this was a Haida issue – it was an environmental issue, but it was a Haida responsibility" (quoted in Gill 2009, 120).

In response to the blockade, Western Forest Products and its contractor, Frank Beban, applied for an injunction. At the court hearing, the Haida represented themselves, giving heartfelt testimony as they conveyed their hopes and passion for the land. Reporting on their testimony, Glen Bohn of the *Vancouver Sun* wrote,

They spoke of their hope that Haidas could establish a unique tourism industry and show outsiders their culture and traditional lands. They hoped the preservation of South Moresby would help them retain their culture and give their children, 'and their children's children' jobs and pride ... A Haida woman sang a traditional song in the witness box saying it showed the Haidas' love and respect for the land. [Haida spokesperson Levina] Lightbrown outlined the Haida legend of creation, in which humans emerge from a clamshell carried by a raven ... [She] said the legend is symbolic, because the sea is the Haida's lifeline, and they still harvest its foods in the area around Lyell Island. She said the Haida art form tells her people that man and nature are one. She said the Haida roots with nature are deep, and her people cannot move to another land ... Lightbrown said the government has never negotiated with the Haidas, "so we still own the Queen Charlottes and their surroundings." (quoted in Wilson 1998, 194)

Testimony by one of the women on the line at Lyell Island, Diane Brown, painted an intimate picture of the connection between the Haida, the land, and the culture:

The first lesson in my life that I remember is respect. I was taught to respect the land. I was taught that everything had a meaning. Every insect had a meaning and none of those things were to be held lightly. The food was never to be taken for granted ... [T]o gather food is a spiritual experience for me. (quoted in Ruebsaat 1988, p. 84)

Addressing the judge as Kilsli, the Haida term for a respected, honoured, and important person, she continued:

> I want to share what goes on in my spiritual self, in my body come February. And I feel it is an important point. That's what makes me as a Haida different from you, Kilsli. My body feels that it's time to spawn. It gets ready in February. I get a longing to be in the sea. I constantly watch the ocean surrounding the islands where the herring spawn. My body is kind of on edge of anticipation. Finally the day comes when it spawns ... (ibid., 14, 45, 49)

Despite the passionate testimony of many Haida, the court granted Western Forest Products and Frank Beban an injunction. Undeterred, the Haida organizers prepared to resume their blockade. A helicopter landed on the logging road carrying four Haida elders, Ada Yovanovich, Ethel Jones, Watson Price, and Adolphus Marks. Expecting a battle, the elders took over, insisting that if there were to be arrests, they would be the first to go. Their presence brought an air of dignity and legitimacy to the blockade as the Haida waited for the police to enforce the injunction. When the elders, clad in ceremonial dress, were the first to be arrested, the confrontation made headlines across the country.[15] The elders were transported by helicopter to jail in Queen Charlotte City. In the following weeks, seventy-two peaceful blockaders were arrested, with eleven people charged and convicted of criminal contempt.[16] Film footage in which Mounties escorted loggers to work as Haida people were being arrested for defending the land became a daily news item. At the BC legislature in Victoria, people rallied in support of the Haida's stand, putting the provincial government under increasing pressure to negotiate a resolution.

The Haida continued to demand that logging in Gwaii Haanas be halted and that the entire proposed wilderness area be preserved. To increase national and international support for the wilderness area, the Islands Protection Society led a cross-country Save Moresby caravan, receiving support from music icons Long John Baldry, Pete Seeger, and Bruce Cockburn. David Suzuki's *The Nature of Things* broadcast three shows featuring Gwaii Haanas and Haida culture. Support for the Haida grew further when images of recent logging-induced damage were publicized.

At the same time, there were many who opposed the Haida's stand. A "counter-caravan" was organized by park opponents from Sandspit, a logging town on the northern part of Moresby Island, to contest the "Save Moresby" caravan (May 1990, 130-40). There were also abrasive rants by

5 "Save Moresby Caravan" final destination, Vancouver. Foreground front, left to right: Chief Watson Pryce (Gaahlaay) and Grace Wilson. Foreground behind, left to right: Jim Edenshaw and Forrest Dewitt. (Richard Krieger)

popular BC talk-show host Jack Webster, which brought Gwaii Haanas to the top of the news. Closer to home, Sandspit resident R.L. Smith published the notorious "Red Neck News," unleashing his wrath on "ding-a-ling hippies" and others opposed to logging on Lyell Island. His characterization of the Haida action epitomized the "logging versus the environment" argument:

> The Haidas, by preventing the crews from going to work, are robbing the loggers of wages they would otherwise have earned. Those who will suffer the most will be the hourly-paid working people who have suffered a number of layoffs due to environmentalists [sic] actions. The Haidas are grinding the little people, the working people, into poverty with their lawlessness. (Smith 1985)[17]

Under continuing public pressure, the provincial and federal governments commenced negotiations around South Moresby. The talks were accompanied by continuing protest, court hearings, and a conflict-of-interest controversy. The BC minister of forests and the minister of energy, both members of the Cabinet's Environment and Land Use Committee, which was deciding the fate of Gwaii Haanas, were found to be shareholders of Western Pulp Mills Partnership, a company linked with Western Forest Products (May 1990, 131). The minister of forests was forced to resign, and the energy minister temporarily stepped down. With the government scandal dominating the headlines, public opinion swung increasingly behind the Haida.

Nevertheless, in the summer of 1986, new logging permits were issued for Lyell Island, and logging resumed. Subsequently, a new five-year logging plan was approved for TFL 24, which included Windy Bay, an area within the proposed ecological reserve (ibid., 160). This time, the Haida countered by building a longhouse on the site of a traditional village that was slated for logging. Unmoved, the Province threatened to destroy the longhouse. As the Haida began planning for another blockade, they invited affected loggers to a feast, where they explained that the issue was not with the loggers personally, but about looking after the land.[18] In the end, the provincial government proved unwilling to risk another public confrontation and announced a moratorium on logging permits for South Moresby.

In 1987, after many months of negotiation, the Province relented and signed a memorandum of agreement with Canada, which halted issuance of new logging permits.[19] A year later, the two governments signed the South Moresby Agreement. The South Moresby National Park Reserve was created to encompass roughly the bottom third of Moresby Island (147,000 hectares, or about 15 percent of Haida Gwaii) – the same delineation as the Haida Heritage Site. Canada committed $106 million toward the park reserve, compensation to the logging companies, and community economic development. This included a $38 million Regional Economic Development Fund to be spent over eight years. This would later become the "Gwaii Trust," a locally controlled interest-bearing fund dedicated to economic diversification and sustainable development. Both the federal and the provincial governments contributed $12 million toward the South Moresby Forest Replacement Account, which was established to develop new opportunities in sustainable forest management, research, education, and training.[20]

The Haida welcomed the end of logging but insisted that their rights to Gwaii Haanas be acknowledged in a Canada-Haida agreement before any management initiatives got under way. Their position vis-à-vis Canada was straightforward: "Without an agreement you will not set up a single outhouse."[21] Up to that point, the creation of parks on Haida Gwaii had meant that lands were set aside for tourists and the Haida were excluded from hunting, fishing, trapping, or living there.[22] This time, the Haida were determined to make sure things would be different.

There were real issues on both sides of the negotiating table. Neither Canada nor the Haida were willing to compromise their legal or political positions regarding title. Canada would not agree to any language that even acknowledged the existence of a "title dispute." It also insisted that the ultimate authority belonged to the minister of the environment and that this authority could not be fettered. To this, the Haida responded: "We have kids in our villages who have more authority in Gwaii Haanas than the minister."[23] When the talks made little progress, the Haida themselves proceeded to make management decisions for Gwaii Haanas. They bolstered the Haida Watchmen Program to protect all key village sites and educate visitors about the natural and cultural heritage of Gwaii Haanas. They also began issuing permits to businesses operating tours in the area. By this time, the Haida occupied all of the main destinations in Gwaii Haanas, including Hotsprings Island, SGang Gwaay, Skedans, Tanu, and Windy Bay. An active commercial *kaaw* (roe on kelp) fishery also kept Haida people in the region. Park authorities had no solution in their handbooks for this kind of situation. Moreover, visitors to Gwaii Haanas were quite content with things as they were.[24]

Finally, in 1993, after more than five years of negotiation, the federal government and the Council of the Haida Nation signed the Gwaii Haanas Agreement. The renamed Gwaii Haanas National Park Reserve and Haida Heritage Site officially came under joint Haida and federal co-management, becoming the first co-managed protected area of its kind in Canada. The agreement protects the site until the Haida land claim is resolved, while respecting the interests of both Ottawa and the Haida Nation. With priority given to Aboriginal rights, the Haida would be able to continue their traditional activities within the park. This significant change in government policy would enable the Crown to protect much more land, particularly in northern Canada. The agreement recognizes two separate authorities for the area, the Canadian government and the Haida Nation, as well as two land designations, a national park reserve and the Haida Heritage Site. Co-management is carried out through the Archipelago Management Board, consisting of an equal number of Haida and Parks Canada representatives, with board members making recommendations to their respective governments regarding planning, management, and operation of the park.

The signing of the agreement marked a triumphant conclusion to the nearly two-decade-long battle to protect Gwaii Haanas and a major turning point for the Haida. On achieving their goals, the Haida recognized the role that environmentalists had played in rallying public support and attention, and preventing the government from crushing their resistance efforts. Environmentalists acknowledged that "only the Haidas can keep the islands from being completely transformed by the larger industrial plans for the islands" (Pinkerton 1983, 83). Local environmentalist John Broadhead would subsequently found the Gowgaia Institute, a research organization dedicated to promoting sustainability on Haida Gwaii, and would continue to work closely with the Haida.

The protection of Gwaii Haanas also laid the foundation for continuing cooperation between the Haida and the federal Crown. Indigenous people throughout North America, Australia, New Zealand, and China would travel to Gwaii Haanas to learn from its model. At the same time, the new protected areas left some deep bitterness among forest workers and others who felt excluded.

Islands Community Stability Initiative

Struggles between environmentalists and loggers are almost legendary in British Columbia, with the issue of "jobs versus the environment" being a major point of contention. Forest workers have generally been strong allies of industry and loyal supporters of sustained-yield forestry policies, due in part to the social aspects of the policies, which are intended to protect resource-dependent communities from the fluctuations of a boom-and-bust economy (Prudham 2007).[25] The official ideology of forestry suggested that everyone would benefit from large-scale resource industrialization. For some, this belief made the environmental and social costs associated with rapid development more palatable.

Nevertheless, the forest industry was keenly aware that it was losing the battle for the hearts and minds of the public. The outcome at Gwaii Haanas was clear evidence of the powerful threat posed by the environmental movement. Learning from its opponents, the forest industry started its own campaign to turn the public against environmentalists. Beginning with large-scale advocacy advertising, the industry soon followed with the promotion of worker-led Share groups in forestry-dependent communities (Wilson 1998, 36-19). Closely connected with the "wise use" movement in the United States, Share expressed its message in such slogans as "Do not let your love of wilderness blind you to the needs of your fellow man: preserve special places, protect the working forest" (ibid., 38).

Angered by the outcome in Gwaii Haanas, forestry workers on Haida Gwaii formed a local Share the Rock group, determined to stop environmentalists from prevailing throughout the islands. The industry attitude at the time was "You've got your park, but we have to keep making the cut, so we're going to hit the rest of the islands harder" (Leslie Johnson, quoted in Meadows 2000, para. 1). In 1994, Share the Rock hosted a workshop on the islands titled "Forest Management and the Public – An Evolving Process." Slick speakers from off-island focused on how to maintain or increase the annual allowable cut on Haida Gwaii. They blamed environmentalists and inaccurate forest inventory data for the current reduced rate of cut (British Columbia Ministry of Forests 1996). But, the reality of resource industrialization on Haida Gwaii told a larger story. Local people at the workshop, representing logging and processing, expressed the need for local control, access to timber for local processing, and reduced export of raw logs (ibid.).

Although forestry policies had led to enhanced prosperity in many BC towns, this persisted only for a limited time. Forestry-dependent communities on Haida Gwaii and elsewhere in the province were facing destabilization and worsening unemployment (Marchak 1995; Hayter 2003). By the 1980s, it was evident that the forests were being overcut at an alarming rate.[26] By the 1990s, the forests were in a fragile condition, with inadequate replanting in large areas and an overall decline of timber stocks (Marchak, Aycock, and Herbert 1999). The problems were exacerbated when the economic slump of the 1980s hit the logging companies. This was due, in part, to rising production costs, greater competition in markets, and the protracted soft-wood lumber dispute between Canada and the United States (Marchak 1995, 95). When the slump became a long-term reality of the 1990s, companies began to restructure their labour forces to be smaller and more flexible. Improved flexibility translated to "a greater capacity of the employer to move workers from one job to another, to have open shops, to contract out work, to hire more part-time and temporary workers, and to waive credentialism for tradework if the job could be safely performed by unlicensed workers" (ibid., 100).

Although the volume of timber cut and manufactured in the province continued to escalate throughout the 1980s, employment in the industry steadily declined. Between 1980 and 1995, logging production rose by 21 percent, whereas employment diminished by 23 percent (ibid., 104-5). People were replaced by machines such as the grapple yarder, which reduced the crews required to transport trees out of cutblocks by about half, and the feller-buncher, which could "log far more trees in a morning than the skilled faller of the past could have done in several days and the driver never leaves his cab" (ibid., 102). The increasing mechanization was imperative if companies wished to compete internationally in low-priced minimally processed commodities, the main forest exports of British Columbia. Mechanization was really the only cost advantage that BC logging companies had over their competitors in other parts of the world, where trees grow faster and labour costs are far lower (ibid., 101).

Because integrated companies controlled most of the harvesting rights, almost all the timber was committed to an affiliated mill or plant. The purpose of this was to ensure that wood was at least minimally processed in the province, but the reality for rural communities was that accessing a steady supply of timber needed to maintain a local independent manufacturing sector was virtually impossible.[27]

To get a closer look at Share the Rock, Guujaaw and Skidegate Chief Councillor Tom Green joined the group and attended its "Forest Management and the Public" workshop. During the workshop, Guujaaw challenged the glib American speaker and suggested that Share's tactics were part of the problem, not the solution. He and Tom Green then publicly quit. Shortly thereafter, Guujaaw set up a meeting with local Share organizers Dale Lore and Bill Beldessi. At the time, Dale Lore was an outspoken anti-environmentalist who saw the Haida as his adversaries. The Haida perceived Lore and Beldessi as little more than mouthpieces for big industry. On the surface, their positions were light years apart. Yet, as they delved into their concerns, they discovered that once the extraneous rhetoric was peeled aside, there was not much difference between them.[28] Over time, both Lore and Beldessi would become allies of the Haida Nation and strong advocates for community stability through sustainability.

The seriousness of forest mismanagement and declining community benefits was becoming ever more apparent on Haida Gwaii. In 1994, the provincial Ministry of Forests released its *Timber Supply Review,* which reported that the amount of wood cut in the Haida Gwaii timber supply area was 2.2 times higher than the long-term sustainable harvest rate (ICSI 1996). This admission, coming from the Province itself, alarmed all islanders – Haida, environmentalists, loggers, politicians, and community members. A socio-economic analysis, subsequently released by the ministry, revealed that 94 percent of the trees logged on Haida Gwaii were being barged south for processing (BC Wild 1996). This confirmed what many residents already knew, that the majority of social and economic benefits derived from logging on Haida Gwaii were being realized in the southern mainland and Vancouver Island.

Concerned by the data in the *Timber Supply Review*, the Village Council of Port Clements, the main logging community on the islands, wrote to the Ministry of Forests, requesting that the annual allowable cut for the timber supply area be halved in accordance with the long-term sustainable rate (Lordon 2000). This letter was also sent to elected officials of all the other island communities. A few days later, Port Clements hosted a community-wide workshop to discuss the matter. Its participants reached the same conclusion: that the cut must be reduced to its long-term sustainable level.

In a united effort unprecedented on Haida Gwaii, elected representatives from all the island communities wrote to the chief forester, asking that the cut be reduced to the long-term sustainable level. Then a letter was sent to the minister of forests, which stated,

> The current allocation of timber cutting rights in the Queen Charlotte Timber Supply Area (TSA) represents a significant threat to the future of our islands community. The Socio-Economic Analysis prepared recently for the Timber Supply Review confirms that the return to our islands community is unacceptably low. It is our belief that 100 percent of the TSA should be managed by the communities of these islands. (ICSI 1996, 1)

For the first time, an issue had become so critical to all the island communities that they set aside their differences and acted in concert to have it addressed. "We realized that the companies didn't have the interests of the employees or the community at heart," recalled community organizer (later town councillor) Leslie Johnson. "We saw the trees disappearing. We finally understood that community needs are more important than any of our special interests" (quoted in Meadows 2000, para. 1). The Province neither officially recognized the community's letter nor responded to it.

To more effectively convey their apprehensions about forestry with a unified voice, elected representatives from each community formed the Islands Community Stability Initiative (ICSI) in 1995. The Province's new district forest manager for Haida Gwaii, Bob Brash, heard their concerns and agreed that the situation could not carry on this way. They were "up against the wall," he told them and things were going to change. He challenged ICSI to generate a concrete proposal within the next few months to address its issues. ICSI members took the challenge to heart and began to work on a position paper. Soon afterward, Share the Rock disbanded, recognizing that the short-term interests of loggers were trumped by the long-term health of the forests that their communities depended on.[29]

In 1996, ICSI completed its position paper, *The ICSI Consensus* (ICSI 1996), which outlined its vision for the future of Haida Gwaii's forests. It reiterated the demand that the logging rate be consistent with the long-term sustainable level and presented a community vision that included more local manufacturing and processing, greater influence in forest management, and a long-term sustainable plan for the islands. The certain drop in future logging rates (a result of what foresters euphemistically call the "falldown effect") meant that the industry must be radically restructured on Haida Gwaii if communities were to remain viable. However, as the document noted: "The major licensees have no incentive to consider or provide for the well-being of the communities. The tenure system is recognized as a formidable obstacle to establishing a sustainable forest economy on the islands" (ibid., pt. 7).

ICSI's position paper was given to district forest manager Bob Brash. But before their concerns could be addressed, Brash switched jobs to become the vice-president (later president) of Husby Forest Products and one of the Haida's greatest adversaries.[30]

Six months later, ICSI gained a number of concessions in a memorandum of understanding signed with the Province. These included a promised community forest tenure of fifty thousand cubic metres, establishment of a locally controlled Islands Forest Council, and a pledge to begin comprehensive resource planning. The community forest prospect particularly captured the attention of ICSI directors, though little real progress was made on the promises in the agreement. As the next five-year timber supply review approached, ICSI focused on examining and critiquing the logging plans that the major operators submitted to the ministry. However, when the Province's next *Timber Supply Review* report was completed in 2000, it again ignored the communities' central demand for a reduction in the annual allowable cut.

Outraged, community members held a rally at the local Ministry of Forests office and delivered 657 "votes of non-confidence" in a giant mock ballot box. They demanded that the Province diminish the cut, stay out of the Haida Protected Areas, and ensure greater benefits to islanders. People from all island communities marched together, declaring their solidarity through a joint Unity Statement, which recognized Haida Gwaii as the hereditary homeland of the Haida and committed them to care for

6   Unity rally. Left to right: Ron Brown, Iljuuwaas (Reynold Russ), and Sgiidagids (Dempsey Collison). (Gowgaia Institute)

7   Cedar bark and raven's tail robe woven by Victoria Moody; danced at the Unity Dinner. (Simon Davies)

Haida Gwaii together (*Unity Statement* 2000). Haida elders, who ten years earlier had stood on the line at Lyell Island, now inspired demonstrators with their renewed calls for justice. At the feast that followed, Chief Iljuuwaas asserted: "Today the people of Haida Gwaii walked together" (quoted in Morigeau 2000, 1). His remark captured the spirit of unity that was demonstrated by islanders that day.

The ICSI Consensus marked the beginning of a new era of community cooperation on forestry issues. However, the most significant issue for the Haida remained the resolution of their land and ownership rights.

LEGAL BATTLE FOR ABORIGINAL RIGHTS AND TITLE

Throughout the twentieth century, the forest tenure and management system in British Columbia was based on the assumption that the Crown owned most of the forests. The Province leased the lands to third-party licensees, who were assumed to have exclusive rights over the resources, whereas First Nations, most of whom had never signed a treaty with the Province, were effectively excluded from the tenure system. By the 1990s, however, a number of significant court decisions threw such assumptions into serious doubt.

Like many BC First Nations, the Haida began organizing in the 1970s to reclaim land and ownership rights to their traditional territories. This followed the landmark 1973 *Calder* case, launched by the Nisga'a Nation, which confirmed at a conceptual level the existence of Aboriginal title. Although the judges disagreed as to whether Aboriginal title still remained, the ruling nevertheless introduced a fundamentally different legal framework for First Nations and Crown relations. *Calder* led to Ottawa's 1973 decision to establish a process for Aboriginal land claims. Existing Aboriginal and treaty rights were subsequently enshrined in section 35 of the Constitution Act, 1982, though the nature and extent of Aboriginal rights remained open to interpretation.

The Haida filed their comprehensive land claim with the federal government in 1981. However, as the Province was unwilling to discuss claims that would require the surrender of Crown land, First Nations continued to turn to the courts to defend their rights. Some cases, such as the 1985 Meares Island court injunction launched by the Nuu-chah-nulth First Nation, were successfully argued on the basis of Aboriginal land claims to halt timber harvest. The seminal *Sparrow* case, initiated by a member of the Musqueam First Nation, established that Aboriginal rights could not be infringed without justification and that they must be given priority.

A number of major land claims were going through the courts when, in 1992, the provincial government, federal government, and First Nations associations established the British Columbia Treaty Commission. Its mandate was to oversee the modern treaty-making process in hopes of foregoing expensive litigation, reducing the pressure on the judicial system, and improving the chances of reaching politically negotiated agreements. In 1993, the Haida filed their statement of intent to negotiate a treaty with the commission. However, the process soon encountered difficulties. Although the traditional territory claimed by First Nations included most of British Columbia, the Province limited the amount of transferrable land to 5 percent of the provincial land base. Nor would it negotiate with a First Nation that was undertaking legal action. Moreover, First Nations had to relinquish their Aboriginal title in exchange for a treaty. Due to these limitations, litigation remained a necessary option for some First Nations, including the Haida, who refused to exchange their title for a treaty.

Up to this point, the BC government had maintained that Aboriginal title had been extinguished by accumulated events during the past century. This assumption was laid to rest when the 1993 *Delgamuukw* decision established that Aboriginal title had not been extinguished in British Columbia by colonization or settlement. The case, launched by the Gitxsan and Wet'suwet'en First Nations in the mid-1970s, went through several appeals before reaching its final ruling in the Supreme Court of Canada in 1997. For the first time, the court provided a comprehensive statement on the meaning of Aboriginal title. According to the decision, land pursuant to Aboriginal title is communally owned and can be sold only to the federal government. Moreover, Aboriginal title includes the right to the land itself, not just the right to use it for traditional purposes such as hunting and fishing. However, lands under Aboriginal title are also subject to an "inherent limit," meaning that the "land can be used for a variety of purposes, but cannot be used for things which destroy its traditional value" (Curran and M'Gonigle 1999, 723). To prove Aboriginal title, a First Nation must provide evidence of continuous occupation after the introduction of British sovereignty in 1846.

At the same time, the court found that Crown title gives the federal and provincial governments the power to infringe on Aboriginal title if they demonstrate a compelling and substantive legislative objective. The ruling also highlighted that the Crown has a fiduciary duty to First Nations, "a trust like obligation to handle dealings with First Nations honourably" (Boyd and Williams-Davidson 2000, 136). Therefore, the Crown must justify infringement of Aboriginal title and undertake meaningful consultation with First Nations, a process that, in some cases, requires consent and compensation for infringements (Williams-Davidson and Mandell 2002, 14).

In 1995, as *Delgamuukw* was working its way through the court system, the Haida initiated litigation regarding the replacement of TFL 39, the largest tree farm licence on the islands, comprising almost a quarter of the land area. They had previously requested that the replacement and unsustainable cut levels of the licence be addressed at the treaty table, but the Province asserted that it was not obligated to consult with the Haida at the licence replacement stage and would do so at the operational stage (Williams-Davidson, Guujaaw, and Walkem 2005, 3). The Haida then turned to litigation, arguing that the minister of forests had no authority to replace the licence without consultation, because the land was encumbered by Aboriginal title. The British Columbia Supreme Court ruled in 1995 that "Aboriginal title ... is not capable of constituting an encumbrance" (*Haida Nation v. British Columbia* 1995, s. VI, para. 22). The Haida appealed and in 1997 the British Columbia Court of Appeal handed down a favourable decision that the land was indeed encumbered by Aboriginal title – but only once title was proven (*Haida Nation v. British Columbia* 1997; Williams-Davidson, Guujaaw, and Walkem 2005, 3). The court, nevertheless, strongly urged the Crown to consult with the Haida. Although the licence renewal was permitted, the ruling gave the Haida increased negotiating leverage in their dealings with the Crown.[31]

In 2000, the Province again replaced TFL 39 without consulting the Haida. Once again, the Haida Nation requested that it be consulted, both regarding this latest replacement and MacMillan Bloedel's 1999 sale of the licence to Weyerhaeuser. The government, however, refused to do so. In response, the Haida applied to the BC Supreme Court to have TFL 39 cancelled, arguing that the minister of forests had no authority to replace it without consultation and accommodation of Haida interests. This time, however, the case was reframed to assert that the minister's fiduciary duty as the Crown was engaged as soon as the government "has noticed and acknowledged Haida title and rights" (Williams-Davidson, Guujaaw, and Walkem 2005, 3). To demonstrate the depth of government knowledge on this matter, the Haida legal team led by Louise Mandell and Haida lawyer, Terri-Lynn Williams Davidson provided evidence that the Haida had asserted their title and rights to the islands throughout the past two hundred years. The team also presented evidence to show the importance of the forests to Haida culture (ibid., 4).

In 2001, the BC Supreme Court ruled that TFL 39 did indeed affect the Haida's Aboriginal rights and title. However, the court held that "the province had a moral and not a legal duty to consult and accommodate prior to proof of Aboriginal Rights" (Eagle Law 2008, 66). As the next chapters chronicle, the case would continue through several appeals before reaching its final groundbreaking decision, which would fundamentally change the legal, political, and economic landscape for First Nations.

Evolving Tactics in the Forests

Whereas the 1980s and 1990s provided new legal avenues for BC First Nations, environmentalists found litigation of limited use in achieving their goals. As a result, they continued to emphasize education and shaping public opinion in their attempt to change government policies (Hoberg 2000, 34-37). In the mid-1990s, however, environmentalists began to discover new strategies that would prove highly effective in the war in the woods.

A contentious battle over the forests of Clayoquot Sound had been waging since the early 1980s. The Clayoquot old growth comprises the largest relatively intact temperate rainforest on Vancouver Island. The conflict had involved Canada's first-ever anti-logging blockades, on Meares Island in 1984, two more in 1988 and 1992, an ongoing legal struggle by the Nuu-chah-nulth Nation, organization of pro-logging Share groups, and sustainable development planning processes by the Province and various committees.[32]

In 1993, despite strong opposition from First Nations and environmentalists, the provincial government announced that logging would be allowed in two-thirds of Clayoquot Sound's old-growth forest (Hoberg 2000, 44). Although this actually represented an increase in protected areas from 15 to 33 percent, much of it consisted of shoreline or bog forest, with significant areas of ancient forests remaining open for business (Shaw 2003, 38). Outraged by the announcement, environmentalists responded with a massive blockade action.[33] This unprecedented campaign, which involved some ten thousand people and more than eight hundred arrests, was the largest act of civil disobedience in Canadian history.

The arrests received extensive media coverage, both nationally and abroad, putting the provincial government and the forest industry in an unfavourable international spotlight. In response, the Province established the independent Scientific Panel for Sustainable Forest Practices. Consisting of both academic and First Nations experts, the panel was tasked with combining indigenous and scientific knowledge to develop new world-class standards for sustainable forest management (Dobell and Bunton 2001,

15-16). Although the issue was now receiving greater attention, logging continued.

Frustrated by the state of affairs, environmentalists re-examined their strategy. Unable to persuade government to change its policies, they decided to focus on the logging companies and what mattered most to them – their markets (Berman 2006). They began to expose how large, pulp-consuming companies were using thousand-year-old trees from Clayoquot Sound to create such mundane things as phone books. When Greenpeace and other international environmental organizations threatened a consumer boycott, two large companies, Scott Paper and Kimberly Clark, cancelled their orders. Under pressure from the campaign, MacMillan Bloedel, the main logging company in Clayoquot Sound, was forced to diminish its operations in 1993 and temporarily stopped logging in the area by 1997 (Shaw 2003, 50).

Negotiations between the Nuu-chah-nulth and MacMillan Bloedel led to the formation of a joint logging venture in 1998. The Nuu-chah-nulth obtained 51 percent ownership of the new company, which was called Iisaak, or "respect" in Nuu-chah-nulth.[34] In 1999, Iisaak signed a memorandum of understanding with environmental groups, which committed it to stay out of the intact ancient-forested valleys of Clayoquot Sound and to promote ecosystem-based forestry on the rest of the tenure. This marked a "truce" in the environmentalist campaign and paved the way for official recognition of Clayoquot Sound as a United Nations Biosphere Reserve in 2000.

While the success in Clayoquot Sound was being celebrated, logging merely shifted to more remote parts of the province. At the same time, Clayoquot Sound served as a convenient public relations tool for MacMillan Bloedel. As Shaw (2003, 50) notes,

> By making Clayoquot their "poster child," the environmentalists realized that they might only have transferred the basic problem of excessive and damaging clearcut logging to other parts of British Columbia. The problem that had brought them to the barricades had been addressed only superficially, as a conflict over the future of a particular area, rather than structurally, as a contest over the future of forestry in British Columbia.

In 1997, faced with the futility of fighting logging in one valley at a time, environmentalists turned their attention to 6.4 million hectares of temperate rainforest along the north and central coast of British Columbia. The forests were still relatively intact but were being increasingly opened to new logging. Hoping to avoid another Clayoquot Sound, the government commenced a multi-stakeholder planning process for the central coast. However, it would commit to an increase of only 2-3 percent for new protected areas in the region (Tjornbo, Westley, and Riddel 2010, 9). Environmental groups refused to accept this limitation and launched a new campaign.

The area, known to the Province as the midcoast timber supply area, was branded by environmentalists as the Great Bear Rainforest. It was many times the size of Clayoquot Sound and more remote and inaccessible, which meant that sustaining a similar direct action campaign was logistically impossible. Applying their previous experience from the marketing campaign against MacMillan Bloedel, environmentalists combined direct action aimed at big retailers in England, Germany, and later the United States with an intense global market campaign. The threat to boycott companies that purchased wood from British Columbia's central and northern coast motivated many investors, including Home Office Depot and Ikea, to cancel their orders. The Royal Bank of Canada divested shares in logging companies that operated in the area, and another twenty-seven major companies, including Xerox, FedEx, 3M, and Bristol-Meyers-Squibb committed to purchasing only sustainably harvested wood products (Shaw 2003, 52). The campaign drew so much attention that *Time Magazine* listed it as "the best environmental news of the year" in 1999 (ibid.).

Frustrated by the lack of progress in the government-led planning process and in danger of losing their markets, companies targeted by the campaign approached the four big environmental organizations, Greenpeace, Rainforest Action Network, ForestEthics, and the Sierra Club of BC. After lengthy talks, they agreed to a conflict-free negotiation period. This co-operation eventually evolved into the Joint Solutions Project, which endeavoured to find a sustainable resolution of the conflict.

Meanwhile, leaders of coastal First Nations were monitoring the conflict between loggers and environmentalists. Although treaty negotiations offered some potential for resolving land conflicts, the process was very slow, and First Nations were concerned that land and marine resources would be irreversibly destroyed while treaties and land claims were being settled. Moreover, they wanted to ensure their active and meaningful involvement in plans for the land and coastal economy. Deciding that the time had come to take charge, the Haida and other coastal First Nations joined forces.

In 2000, the Turning Point Initiative (later known as the Coastal First Nations) was formed by the leadership of eight coastal First Nations and band councils, initially with financial support from the David Suzuki Foundation. The nations included the Haida, Haisla, Heiltsuk, Kitasoo/Xaixais, Gitga'at, and Metlakatla. This alliance would play a major role in opening new possibilities and opportunities for the Haida. The First Nations laid out their concerns in the "Declaration of First Nations of the North Pacific Coast" (2006):

> The North Pacific Coast is a rich, varied and fragile part of the natural world. The connection of land and sea with people has given rise to our ancient Northwest cultures.
>
> We recognize this life source is under threat like never before and that all people must be held accountable.
>
> This united declaration is the foundation for protecting and restoring our culture and the natural world.
>
> We are the ones that will live with the consequences of any actions that take place in our territories ...
>
> Our life source is vital to the sustenance and livelihood of our culture and our very existence as a people.
>
> The First Nations of the North Pacific inherit the responsibility to protect and restore our lands, water and air for future generations.

The Coastal First Nations committed to making decisions that would ensure the well-being of the land and water, to preserving and renewing its territories and cultures, to respecting all life, and to standing together (ibid.). Each First Nation subsequently developed its own land use plan and worked out ecologically sustainable alternatives to industrial forestry and fishing.[35]

The Coastal First Nations brought together representatives from the provincial and local governments, industry, labour, and environmental NGOs. They emphasized that First Nations would not stand by as others argued over the fate of their lands. At the same time, they were willing to work with others to find solutions. Those who were involved knew that any solution must address the concerns of all parties if it were to have a chance of succeeding.[36] Members of the Coastal First Nations and the four environmental organizations were strongly in favour of ecosystem-based management, the details of which were still being developed. Although other parties expressed some reluctance, all eventually supported the approach (Tjornbo et al. 2010, 14-15).[37]

Recognizing the need for new economic opportunities if logging was to be reduced, Coastal First Nations secured commitments of $60 million in seed funding from major American and Canadian charitable foundations, including the Packard Foundation, the Hewlett Foundation, and the Nature Conservancy. This amount would later be matched by contributions of $30 million each from the provincial and federal governments. This substantial $120 million fund would become known as the Coast Opportunities Funds.

When the Province's negotiator met with the Coastal First Nations, he advised that the government was prepared to sign protocol agreements and to contribute toward planning processes, but first there was a problem that needed to be resolved. The Haida were building a "clam shack" in Naikoon Provincial Park, where clam diggers could seek shelter from the rain. Naikoon was a sore spot for the Haida, and one reason that they were opposed to parks. In their experience, the park designation simply protected the land for tourists while excluding the Haida from carrying on their traditional activities. The provincial negotiator warned that the deal would collapse if the Haida did not remove the clam shack. Guujaaw replied that the government could proceed as it wished, but the shack would stay. He was supported by Art Sterritt of the Gitga'at Nation, who stated that the Gitga'at would be out of the deal as well, since their seaweed shacks would be next. In protest, all the First Nations representatives walked out of the meeting.

The following day, the Province contacted the Coastal First Nations' policy consultant, Gary Wouters, offering to buy the shack and let the Haida use it. The Haida responded that they had all the money they needed and were not interested in using a park-owned facility. Looking for a way to make the shack fit under park parameters, the government asked if the shack could be open to the public. The Haida responded that people could use it as guests or in emergencies, but it would not be a public building. In a last attempt to justify the shack, the Province asked if they could say it was for seasonal use only. The Haida answered that there were four seasons and that they expected to use the shack during all of them. Finally, the government conceded – "There are enough points of agreement, the clam shack can stay."[38] The Haida's strategy of connecting protection of the land with use and occupancy was once again successful.

On 4 April 2001, the General Protocol on Land Use Planning and Interim Measures (British Columbia/Coastal First Nations 2001) was signed between the Province and the First Nations involved in the Turning Point Initiative. The agreement took First Nations involvement in land and resource planning to a new level. Not only did it recognize their unresolved land and title claims, it committed the Province to engaging with them on land planning issues at a government-to-government level. The Province also endorsed the recommendations of industry, labour, environmentalists, and First Nations, and announced the Interim Land Use Plan for the Central Coast. Better known as the Great Bear Rainforest Agreement, it included protection of forty-two ancient rainforest valleys of the central coast, deferred logging in seventy-seven other valleys, and made a commitment to ecosystem-based management (Shaw 2003, 52).

In connection with the General Protocol, on 17 April 2001, the Haida Nation and the Province signed the Protocol on Interim Measures and Land Use Planning (Haida Protocol). This marked the first concrete step toward establishing a collaborative land use planning process for Haida Gwaii.

5

Collaborative Planning in
the Face of Conflict

Growing dissatisfaction over forest management in British Columbia led the provincial government to introduce collaborative land planning processes as a central element in its strategy to resolve conflicts. These processes were to engage all relevant interests and groups, with the aim of developing consensus land use plans and mutual-gain solutions. The consensus plans would theoretically address the main environmental and social concerns of a community in the most fair and competent manner. They would be consistent with the beliefs and aspirations of local actors, thereby increasing the probability for successful implementation and continued community support.

If excluded forms of reasoning and value are to be empowered, consensus decision-making processes must address the unavoidably "politics-laden and power-laden" context of planning processes (McGuirk 2001, 197). This chapter examines several of the means used in the Haida Gwaii planning process to address traditional power imbalances and expand the limits of norms and values. These included a co-management framework and the foundational documents of the *Haida Land Use Vision* (Council of the Haida Nation 2004) and *Ecosystem-Based Management Framework* (Coast Information Team 2004a).

At the same time, the planning process was only one element of a larger strategy to challenge the colonial and industrial social order. The second part of the chapter turns to the Haida's continuing legal action, emerging community alliances, and shifting political terrain occurring outside of the planning process.

DEFUSING CONFLICT

In 1991, the New Democratic Party (NDP) was elected in British Columbia after sixteen years of rule by the pro-business Social Credit Party. In large part, the election was won on the promise to deliver greater public participation and to bring "peace in the woods." This mandate reflected the concerns of two main forces in the NDP constituency: labour unions (wood workers) and environmental activists. It also reflected the increasingly popular discourse of participatory planning, which called for "greater public participation in the decisions that affect the environment ... [by] decentralising [sic] the management of resources upon which local communities depend" (World Commission on Environment and Development 1987, 63). The provincial government's rationale for participatory planning has varied throughout the years, but it has consistently included "resolution of potential competing uses through land allocation," "delivery of major government protection or conservation programs," and perhaps most importantly, "resolution of resource use conflicts" (British Columbia 2006, 4).

Building on the work of the previous government, the NDP launched a number of initiatives to increase public participation in land use planning. The most comprehensive was the Commission on Resources and Environment (CORE), which was created in 1992. CORE's mandate was to develop a strategy for facilitating regional planning processes in some of the most contentious areas of the province. The planning processes were to incorporate community-based participation and a system for dispute resolution (CORE 1992, 31-32). Resulting plans were to "resolve land use disputes by defining protected areas and providing greater certainty on lands available for integrated resource management" (Premier's Office 1992).

CORE chose a consensus-based, shared-decision-making approach as a key element of its strategy. Shared decision making was understood as follows: "Those with authority to make a decision and those who will be affected by the decision are empowered to jointly seek an outcome that accommodates rather than compromises the interests of all concerned" (CORE 1992, 25). This marked an important shift from the previous techno-corporate approach toward a more democratic, inclusive approach. Incorporating principles presented in Fisher and Ury's *Getting to Yes* (1983), CORE eschewed "positional bargaining" and advocated "interest-based" negotiation. The difference between these two stances, as Fisher and Ury (ibid., 42) explain, is that "your position is something you have decided upon. Your interests are what caused you to so decide." According to their rationale, when a problem is defined in terms of interests, a solution can often be found that satisfies all parties. By contrast, when parties come in with fixed positions, there will always be a loser (ibid.). Adopting this perspective, CORE (1994, 1.3) emphasized that participants must carefully consider whether a proposed option achieved more than their best "alternative to a negotiated agreement." The aim was to improve the potential for agreement through compromise.

CORE's mandate was cut short in 1996, when it was dissolved due to critiques of its progress (Wilson 1998).[1] Nevertheless, the spirit of consensus decision making lived on in the Province's sub-regional planning processes, which were known as Land and Resource Management Plans (LRMPs). These processes were intended to develop consensus-based regional plans that would provide a "comprehensive, broadly accepted and approved management framework to guide resource development and more detailed planning" (CORE 1993, 1). The strategic or higher-level plans were to designate zones for protection, zones that were open to logging and other forms of resource extraction, and zones for special management. The plans would then be used to guide the development of more detailed operational plans pertaining to a specific site and/or resource.

Working with the new set of principles, the Province and the Haida agreed to undertake collaborative planning.

AGREEMENT FOR A CO-MANAGED PROCESS

The need to complete a strategic land use plan for Haida Gwaii had been discussed throughout the 1990s, and although initiatives were undertaken for smaller planning regions on the islands, the Province had not succeeded in launching an island-wide planning process. When it attempted to initiate an LRMP for the islands in 1997, the Haida were skeptical about a process that was designed and managed by the Province. Moreover, they were expected to participate as one of many "stakeholders" in discussions regarding land that they saw as belonging to them. The Haida offered to host the process but received no answer from Victoria.[2] At the first meeting, when it became apparent that the Haida would not be participating, other community participants withdrew as well. Some did so on principle, whereas others wished to avoid wasting time on "something that could be overturned by the Haida."[3]

8   Culturally modified trees at Spirit Lake, Skidegate. (Simon Davies)

   Meanwhile, the Haida Forest Guardians and the local Gowgaia Institute were developing their own mapping and planning capabilities. The
relationship between Gowgaia and the Haida Nation was formalized in a
protocol agreement in which Gowgaia acknowledged the hereditary title
and leadership role of the Haida Nation, and the Haida committed to
consult with and respect the institute (Council of the Haida Nation and
Gowgaia Institute 2002).[4] Gowgaia's co-director John Broadhead was at
the cutting edge of mapping technologies, and with his assistance the Haida
expanded their own technical and mapping expertise.[5] The Haida Forest
Guardians began tracking and assessing all proposed forest developments
in addition to producing their own planning maps. Part of their initiative
to create a land use vision based on Haida values and concerns entailed
mapping all the major Haida Protected Areas and the "sacred workplaces
of their ancestors," where evidence of culturally modified trees and past
projects could be found. Their technical capabilities soon surpassed those
of the Province, which progressively deferred to industry for mapping and
inventory studies through the 1980s and 1990s.[6] Ironically, after a hundred
years of colonialism, there was still no provincial plan for the land.

By 2001, when the Haida Protocol was signed by the Province and the Haida Nation, the Province's stance had changed considerably. It now agreed to a co-managed planning process with the Haida Nation, in which the Haida and the government had an equal say. The *Haida Land Use Vision* (Council of the Haida Nation 2004) was to be the guiding document of the process.[7] This gave the Haida some assurance that their priorities would not be overridden by the usual dominating economic interests. Both parties committed to "cooperatively develop a strategic land use plan, while ensuring meaningful participation for residents and stakeholders on Haida Gwaii and third parties" (British Columbia/Council of the Haida Nation 2001, 2).

The planning process was to consist of two stages. First, land use recommendations were to be developed through a consensus-seeking inclusive planning forum guided by the *Haida Land Use Vision* and the *Ecosystem-Based Management Framework.* Critical issues that fell outside the scope of the planning process, including who would do the logging, the transfer or replacement of forest licences, cooperative forest management, and potential forest business arrangements for the Haida, would be addressed through a separately negotiated interim measures agreement. The second stage would deal with any significant issues that remained outstanding at the end of the Community Planning Forum, including matters for which the forum had not reached consensus or had produced recommendations with which either the Haida Nation or the Province did not agree. These would be resolved through government-to-government negotiation. Finally, land use recommendations would be forwarded to both the Haida House of Assembly and the provincial Cabinet for approval.

To ensure adequate resources for participation, the Province agreed to seek funds to assist the Haida with negotiations and implementation related to both the interim measures agreement and the land use planning process. To reduce impediments to change, a $35 million mitigation fund was set up to compensate industry, contractors, and workers for losses that might be incurred as a result of land use planning on Haida Gwaii and the north and central coasts. In addition, the Coast Sustainability Trust was created to assist communities with the transition to sustainable forms of economic development in place of conventional timber extraction.

On contractual and legal matters, the Haida Protocol stated that on signing, "the Participants intend that they will take such actions as are necessary to ensure no further steps are taken in certain legal proceedings" – namely, those involving the Haida Nation and the Ministry of Forests.

Furthermore, the parties were to "immediately discontinue" these legal proceedings, once the interim measures agreement was completed. The protocol also reiterated that the Province must comply with existing policy and legislative frameworks, including tenures, contracts, regulations, and authorities (British Columbia/Council of the Haida Nation 2001, 1, 2, 7). Similarly, it stated that the agreement should "not be interpreted or implemented in a manner which fetters the discretion of statutory decision makers" (ibid., 7). The protocol itself was declared "a statement of political intent by the Participants," not a legally binding document, and it could be terminated by either party with sixty days' notice (ibid.). It would also not bind successor governments.

Although the documents that outlined the *Haida Land Use Vision* and the *Ecosystem-Based Management Framework* were not completed for another three years, most of the central points were well developed by 2001.

LAYING THE FOUNDATION: *HAIDA LAND USE VISION*

The *Haida Land Use Vision* employs central aspects of Haida culture, practices, knowledge, and worldview in an "attempt to balance the ecological, cultural and economic interests on Haida Gwaii" (Council of the Haida Nation 2005a, 4).[8] Completed by the Council of the Haida Nation in May 2004, it brings together thirty years of efforts to protect the land. Taking its opening lines from the Constitution of the Haida Nation, it begins,

> The Haida Nation is the rightful heir to Haida Gwaii.
> Our culture, our heritage, is the child of respect and intimacy with the land and sea.
> Like the forests, the roots of our people are intertwined such that the greatest troubles cannot overcome us.
> We owe our existence to Haida Gwaii.
> The living generation accepts the responsibility to ensure that our heritage is passed on to following generations.
> On these islands our ancestors lived and died, and here too we will make our homes until called away to join them in the great beyond. (Council of the Haida Nation 2004, 2)[9]

The *Haida Land Use Vision* revolves around the concept of *Yah'guudang*, or "respect for all living things." It implies that a successful relationship between humans and the natural world is based on respect. The centrality of Yah'guudang is relayed through countless Haida stories, songs, and dances that tell of the special relationship between humans, the supernatural, and the natural world, and how it is to be maintained. As the Foreword elaborates,

> Our physical and spiritual relationship with the lands and waters of Haida Gwaii, our history of coexistence with all living things over many thousands of years is what makes up Haida culture. Yah'guudang – our respect for all living things – celebrates the ways our lives and spirits are intertwined and honors the responsibility we hold to future generations.
>
> Haida Gwaii Yah'guudang is about respect and responsibility, about knowing our place in the web of life, and how the fate of our culture runs parallel with the fate of the ocean, sky and forest people. (ibid., 3)

As these passages convey, land is not just an important part of Haida culture – it is constitutive of who the Haida are. The centrality of land to the Haida identity and way of life stands in stark contrast to the abstracted and decontextualized representations of land that are common to corporations and the state. Unlike in these detachable representations, land for the Haida consists of concrete reference points, sensory-rich experiences, and seasonal events, as illustrated by the following:

> Know that Haida Culture is not simply song and dance, graven images, language or even blood. It is all of those things and then ... awakening on Haida Gwaii anticipating the season when the herring spawns. It is a feeling you get when you bring a feed of cockles to the old people, and when you are fixing up fish for the smokehouse, or when walking on barnacles or moss.
>
> It has something to do with bearing witness when a falcon takes a seabird, and being there when salmon are finishing their course.
>
> Along the way you eat some huckleberries, watch the kids grow up, and attend the funeral feasts.
>
> And then there is the matter of dealing with squabbles within, and the greater troubles that come to us from the outside.
>
> It is about being confronted with winter storms and trying to look after this precious place. (ibid. 3-4)[10]

The *Haida Land Use Vision* consists of three parts: "Well-Being of the Land," "Condition of the Land," and "Natural Ability of the Land to Function and Provide." It relates the Haida's knowledge of the natural world, how things function together, and how things have changed over time. It also articulates a modern vision of their lives and place within nature, and "what must be done in accordance with the principle of *Yah'guudang* to bring land and resource use into balance to ensure the continuity of Haida culture and ultimately the health of all human society" (ibid., 6). Of particular concern is the damage that has been caused by industrial activity in recent times and what must be done to ensure that future generations can live and prosper on Haida Gwaii.

"Well-Being of the Land" describes, from a collective Haida understanding, key aspects of the forests, rivers, and lakes. It focuses on the six central elements of cedar, salmon, black bears, birds, plants, and beaches, and discusses the interconnections between them as well as their significant roles in the natural world and their importance to the Haida (ibid., 9-12). The cedar tree is essential to Haida culture and is used for a variety of material and cultural items, including canoes and totem poles. It is also important as habitat for bears, birds, and other forest creatures. Salmon, the "single most important source of nourishment" in the Haida diet, are essential in the transferral of nutrients from the ocean food web, as salmon carcasses are brought on land by bears (ibid., 10). Forest plants are used for food, medicine, clothing, mats, and baskets. Birds spread seeds, consume insects, and provide fertilizer. And beaches and the ocean are associated with food, transportation, supernatural beings, weather, and adventure.

The second part, "Condition of the Land," turns to the changes that have occurred due to industrial forestry. The overall impact is summarized as follows:

> On the land, logging has greatly changed the age and character of the forest – out of balance with the ability of the land to function and replenish itself. Habitat places for cedar, salmon, bear, nesting seabirds, hawks and many other things have fallen to economic interests in timber. The measured flow of water from hillside to stream and ocean has been disrupted, and the modern community economy is at risk because of a few short decades of short-sighted policies and practices. (ibid., 13)

The *Haida Land Use Vision* (ibid., 15) notes that accessible monumental cedar trees for canoes, totem poles, and longhouses have all but disappeared, that sockeye salmon have been depleted to a fraction of their former abundance, and that bears have been affected by the loss of dens and the upsurge in commercial hunting – an "unforgivable exercise in disrespect and disregard for the lives and spirits of creatures we hold to be our relations." It explains that people must now travel farther to find food and medicinal plants; that bird numbers have declined, including those of two threatened species, the goshawk and the marbled murrelet; and that heavy logging near streams has resulted in damaging landslides and erosion.

This leads to the third part: "Natural Ability of the Land to Function and Provide," which considers "what must be done in accordance with *Yah'guudang* to bring land and resource use into balance to ensure the continuity of Haida culture and the economic well-being of the entire Island Community" (ibid., 17). A major concern is how to sustainably manage commercial activities, especially logging. Seven maps indicate how this rebalancing can be achieved: one depicts fourteen Haida Protected Areas, and six others show additional regions for protection to maintain cedar, salmon, bears, plants, birds, and beaches. The fourteen Haida Protected Areas are of particular cultural significance, and no industrial activity is to take place in them." Together, they cover approximately 250,000 hectares, of which 51,000 contain "operable timber" (Lordon 2002). These areas, which have been ratified by the Haida House of Assembly, are considered non-negotiable. The other six maps are described as preliminary and are to be considered in combination with the technical analysis of environmental conditions to be conducted as part of the land use planning process.

Although the seven maps recommend a significant amount of protected area, the *Haida Land Use Vision* is not anti-logging. Outlining the requirements for a sustainable economy, it asserts: "There is room enough for forestry and other commercial activities on Haida Gwaii, but in order to be sustainable they must be managed with more respect and greater responsibility – in other words, in accordance with yah'guudang" (ibid., 18). This leads to an expanded concept of wealth that is more compatible with a sustainable future. The *Haida Land Use Vision* (ibid.) concludes,

In Haida culture, wealth is a different thing than money, which is a currency for doing business in the modern economy. Wealth flows from the well-being of the land, and from having the opportunity, knowledge and capacity to support our families, raise healthy children and organize the individual collective efforts of our clans and society. Wealth is to be shared and distributed – prestige is gained through the ability to do so.

Overall, the *Haida Land Use Vision* presents a contemporary indigenous vision of nature-society relations as an alternative to the dominant discourses of land and forests focused almost exclusively on exchange value.

Ecosystem-Based Management

The second guiding document for the process, the *Ecosystem-Based Management Framework* (Coast Information Team 2004a), provided another counterbalance to instrumental economic rationality and corporate dominance. In accordance with the 2001 General Protocol on Land Use Planning and Interim Measures, the Coast Information Team was established to provide a common set of scientific resources for the development and implementation of ecosystem-based management in the three coastal planning processes.[12] The multidisciplinary team received 50 percent of its funding from the Province, 25 percent from environmental NGOs, and 25 percent from the forest industry. This allowed for the co-production of a scientific framework and methodology, with input and agreement by differing interests. In addition to developing the planning framework, the team produced a variety of comprehensive handbooks and analyses, including the *Ecosystem-Based Management Planning Handbook* (Coast Information Team 2004b) and the *Hydroriparian Planning Guide* (Coast Information Team 2004c).

Although conservation biology's central concern for ecological integrity and the survival of the diversity of plant and animal life remained the bottom line, these concerns were integrated with social, cultural, and economic considerations. The *Ecosystem-Based Management Framework* (Coast Information Team 2004a, 2) defined ecosystem-based management as "an adaptive approach to managing human activities that seeks to ensure the coexistence of healthy, fully functioning ecosystems and human communities. The intent is to maintain those spatial and temporal characteristics of ecosystems such that component species and ecological processes can be sustained, and human wellbeing supported and improved."

The *Framework* lists the following seven guiding principles:

- *Ecological integrity is maintained.* The *Framework* defines ecological integrity as "the abundance and diversity of organisms at all levels, and the ecological patterns, processes, and structural attributes responsible for that biological diversity and for ecosystem resilience" (ibid.).
- *Human well-being is promoted.* Healthy communities require diversified local economies and careful planning so as not to "further dislocate individuals, families and communities" (ibid., 3).
- *Cultures, communities, and economies are sustained within the context of healthy ecosystems.* This emphasizes the need to sustain both people

and ecosystems; the maintenance or improvement of one at the expense of the other is unacceptable "because either way the foundation of life is undermined" (ibid.).

- *Aboriginal rights and title are recognized and accommodated.* This principle acknowledges that "past and current government policies and consultation processes have not adequately recognized or accommodated these rights and title." By contrast, the proposed cooperative planning process should "enhance First Nations governance structures" (ibid.).
- *The precautionary principle is applied.* Underlying this principle is the fact that our knowledge of both ecosystems and our impact on them is limited. Thus, to avoid exceeding ecological risk thresholds, decisions and actions must "err on the side of caution" (ibid., 4).
- *Ecosystem-based management is collaborative.* This refers to broad participation, to "respect [for] the diverse values, traditions, and aspirations of local communities," and to the incorporation of the best available knowledge – traditional, local, and scientific (ibid.).
- *People have a fair share of the benefits from the ecosystems in which they live.* This final principle acknowledges that externally driven resource-based activities have left local communities with greater costs than benefits and asserts the need to correct this imbalance.

In addition to these guiding principles, the *Ecosystem-Based Management Framework* outlines six planning elements: multiple spatial scales; conservation planning; socio-economic planning; risk management; interactive processes of assessment, design, integration, and implementation; and adaptive co-management.

The framework recognizes five planning and management scales as follows: region (10 million hectares or more), territory or sub-region (500,000 to 5 million hectares), landscape (30,000 to 100,000 hectares), watershed (1,000 to 50,000 hectares), and site (less than 250 hectares). In practice, however, ecosystem-based planning "is ongoing at all scales and decisions at any one scale may influence, and be influenced by, decisions made at scales above and below" (Coast Information Team 2004b, 18).

The second element, conservation planning, refers to the development of a system of protected areas and reserves. These correspond to particular spatial scales and are used to sustain important ecological and/or human values. Protected areas are "relatively large undeveloped areas, identified at regional and subregional scales and designated for protection by governments (federal, provincial or First Nation) under specific legislation or authority" (Coast Information Team 2004a, 6). Reserves are areas identified at the landscape, watershed, and site scales, where "no, or very little, extractive resource use" is allowed but that are not formally protected through legislation (ibid.). To maintain ecological structures in unprotected areas, particular trees, groups of trees, plant communities, or other important features can be designated for preservation or management at the site level.

Socio-economic planning considers the implications of ecosystem-based management for the social and economic well-being of communities. The goal here is to "create and implement plans that will generate wealth, provide sustainable livelihoods, distribute benefits and burdens equitably, and enhance cultural, community, and household wellbeing" (ibid., 7). This requires developing agreed-on cultural and socio-economic objectives as well as innovative thinking about planning, economics, and institutions.

The fourth element, risk management, starts from the assumption that "risk increases in proportion to the amount that management causes patterns and processes to depart from their natural range" (ibid.).[13] For any indicator, whether old-growth forest or bird species, risk is categorized as low, moderate, or high. Low risk begins where adverse impacts are first detected, whereas high risk begins where "significant loss of ecological function is expected to occur" (ibid., 8). The range of moderate risk is more difficult to determine due to the non-linear response of ecosystems. Nevertheless, a precautionary management approach that seeks to maintain high ecological integrity requires that the overall risk at a sub-regional scale remains at or below the low threshold. However, it is not necessary to maintain high ecological integrity at all spatial planning scales, as long as low-risk management is achieved at the overall sub-regional and landscape scales. This means that there is flexibility at the smaller spatial scales to allow for more economic/extractive activity in areas that are of little ecological or cultural significance, while maintaining a high level of ecological integrity in areas with significant conservation values. In this way, extractive activities are prevented from spreading across the landscape and occur only where they are deemed least harmful.

With the fifth element, ecosystem-based management is understood as an interactive and ongoing cycle of assessment, design, integration, and implementation within and across the various spatial scales.[14] It is seen as a circular process that often requires new assessments at the design and integration stages while simultaneously considering the entire picture of planning at the various spatial scales (ibid.).

The concept of adaptive management is defined as "a formal process of 'learning by doing' where management activities are designed as experiments to test different management assumptions and hypotheses" (ibid., 10). This recognizes that, even after plans are finalized and implemented, new information will continue to be acquired through monitoring and other sources. Thus, some plans will need modification in light of the new information. Adaptive co-management, the sixth element, adds collaboration between various planning participants to the process.

Overall, the aim of the ecosystem approach is to decrease risk to significant ecosystems while allowing for extractive activity in other areas. This may be straightforward in some cases but is likely to involve difficult trade-offs in others. Unacceptable trade-offs can simply postpone human vulnerability until some point in the future, or can cause destruction of ecological integrity over large areas with no achievable plan for recovery. Acceptable trade-offs "compromise ecological integrity in the short term at smaller scales to achieve more sustainable outcomes overall than would otherwise have been the case" (ibid., 11). Despite the complexity of choices to be made, the *Framework* (ibid.) notes: "The most challenging aspect of the transition to ecosystem-based management involves the identification and reform of resource policies or governance arrangements" that impede the implementation of agreed-on plans and objectives.[15] Underlying this challenge is the assumption that high levels of resource extraction are no longer acceptable.

CENTRAL GOALS AND PROCEDURES

The Haida Protocol, signed in 2001, committed the Province and the Haida Nation to establishing an inclusive forum to develop land use planning recommendations. Representatives from government, the Haida Nation, local communities, and other stakeholders were to participate in the forum. In March 2003, the Province and the Haida released the *Planning Process Framework* (British Columbia/Council of the Haida Nation 2003b), which outlined the general procedures and structures under which participants of the planning process would be expected to engage.

The four goals articulated for the planning process were to protect and maintain ecosystem integrity, to maintain spiritual and cultural values, to enhance sustainable economic opportunity within the inherent limits of the land, and to foster social and community well-being (ibid., 5). In addition, the *Planning Process Framework* (ibid., 6) outlined several principles with which the planning process and final plan had to be consistent; these included "respect for the traditional culture, practices and knowledge of the Haida Nation" and "use of science to support decision-making" in addition to the principles of ecosystem-based management and collaborative planning. The planning area covered approximately 1.01 million hectares and consisted of terrestrial and inland freshwater acreage.[16] As with other LRMPs in the province, the resulting plan was to include a system of land use zones, identifying the primary characteristics and values of each one and giving clear management direction for their full range of values and resource uses (ibid., 5).

The planning process was to be cooperatively designed and coordinated by a Process Management Team, which consisted of two co-chairs and two process coordinators;[17] the Haida Nation and the Province were to appoint one co-chair and one process coordinator each. The Process Management Team would draft the framework and workplan for the process and would ensure their successful implementation. It would also organize and facilitate the Community Forum Planning meetings and would eventually coordinate the delivery of the final land use recommendations to both the Haida Nation and the provincial Cabinet for approval (ibid., 9).

In addition, a Process Technical Team, consisting of technical representatives from the Province, the Haida Nation, and industry, was to be put in place. Its job was to prepare or coordinate the preparation of the technical information that the planning forum would use. It would also liaise with the Coast Information Team and ensure that information put before the table was valid and acceptable to the parties. All information, including reports, maps, and analyses, was to be integrated within the ecosystem-based management planning framework for the purposes of decision making.

The procedural framework also outlined a dispute resolution process to address potential disagreement during the planning process. This consisted of four stages: independent facilitation to guide the parties in interest-based negotiations; the use of working groups to negotiate solutions where consensus could not be reached; the use of an independent mediator if agreement remained elusive; and government-to-government talks for unresolved substantive issues at the end of the process. It was expected, however, "that most disputes [would be] addressed at or before [the third] stage in the dispute resolution process" (ibid., 12).

Finally, a tentative timeline was supplied for the process. The Community Planning Forum was to begin in April 2003 and would run for fifteen months. A final set of land use recommendations would be completed by July 2004, with government-to-government negotiations and plan approval set for December 2004. Once accepted, the new land use plan would be incorporated into the Province's next timber supply review for Haida Gwaii. The government committed to making "every effort to amend legislation and policy if required to implement consensus recommendations" (ibid., 5).

Although the collaborative planning process may have been inspired less by a desire to empower marginalized voices than by the need to resolve rising conflict and falling profits in the forest industry, the *Planning Process Framework* suggested that serious efforts were being made to ensure that the process would be fair, meaningful, and capable of expressing the will of the people. At the same time, however, political developments occurring outside the planning process put this prospect in question.

POLITICS, LITIGATION, AND SHIFTING ALLIANCES

In November 2001, seven months after the Haida Protocol on Interim Measures and Land Use Planning had been signed, the ruling New Democratic Party lost the provincial election. The incoming Liberal Party had campaigned largely on a platform of more industry-friendly reforms, raising anxieties that the government would pull out of the 2001 agreements. Although the Liberals chose to endorse them, they would go on to discard one-third of all rules to protect the environment, increase the annual number of trees to be logged, approve controversial mining, logging, and road proposals, close Ministry of Forests offices in twenty communities, and lay off 35 percent of ministry staff who were associated with environmental protection (Koberstein 2003; Marchak and Allen 2003). New "Working Forest" legislation was also introduced, condemned by some environmentalists as "the most sweeping anti-environmental forestry legislation in British Columbia's history" (Ken Wu, quoted in Koberstein 2003, para. 22). The legislation proposed to take over 48 percent of the land base for industry and ensure that environmentalists could not claim it (Marchak and Allen 2003, 6). Finally, a "results-based code" would give forestry companies a high degree of responsibility for their own environmental protection activities. These changes cast serious doubt on the government's commitment to the agreed-on objectives of the collaborative planning processes.

Meanwhile, the British Columbia Court of Appeal released its decision in the Haida lawsuit against the Province and Weyerhaeuser regarding the transfer of Tree Farm Licence (TFL) 39 and its subsequent replacement. The Haida had applied to the BC Supreme Court in 2000 to have the licence declared invalid, arguing that they had not been consulted and that the licence transfer and replacement therefore unjustifiably infringed on their Aboriginal rights and title. The court ruled that the Haida were right on facts and had good prima facie evidence, but made no order to compel the province to any action. The Haida appealed the decision.

In February 2002, the Court of Appeal found that the Province indeed had a legally enforceable duty to consult with the Haida Nation. Its ruling was based on the strength of the Haida case for Aboriginal rights and title, which it held the Province should be aware of, and the strong likelihood that these rights would be affected by government decisions (Lawson Lundell 2002). This legal victory was highly significant because, prior to the ruling, the Province had maintained that it was not legally required to consult until a First Nation had *proven* its title. The ruling further stated that Weyerhaeuser, the holder of TFL 39, also had a legally enforceable duty to consult and to find a working accommodation with the Haida (ibid.). This decision could have important implications for any private company operating on lands claimed by a First Nation. Weyerhaeuser would subsequently apply to the BC Court of Appeal for a rehearing regarding the question of its legally enforceable duty to consult with First Nations.

Ultimately, the Haida wanted the tree farm licence quashed. However, the February 2002 decision implied that they must prove Aboriginal title before this could occur. So in early March 2002, days after the February ruling, the Haida launched their title case with the Supreme Court of British Columbia. Their "Statement of Claim" (Council of the Haida Nation 2002), filed the following November, detailed the particulars of their argument. First and foremost, they asserted Aboriginal rights and title to the land, inland waters, seabed, and sea of Haida Gwaii. They intended not only to meet the legal test of title but also to show that neither the Government of Canada nor the British Crown before it had any legal claim to Haida Gwaii. The statement called for compensation for damages to the land caused by "unlawful occupation" and "infringement of Aboriginal Title and Rights," an accounting from the Province of "all profits, taxes, stumpage dues, royalties and other benefits," and a quashing of all "forestry,

9   Delivering the writ for the Haida's title case. Left to right: Alfred Setso,
Terri-Lynn Williams Davidson, and Nika Collison. (Gowgaia Institute)

fisheries, mineral and other tenures, permits and licences" issued without
accommodation with the Haida Nation (ibid., para. 20).

If the Haida win their title case, companies that have failed to accommodate Haida interests on the land could pay millions of dollars in damages
and have their licences discontinued. This arises from the *Delgamuukw*
case, which stated that there is an "inherent limit" on Aboriginal use of the
land such that it must not prevent future generations from using the land.
It follows that, for a logging company not to infringe on Haida title, its
activities must also be sustainable for future Haida generations (Williams-
Davidson and Mandell 2002, 2). As to how tenure-holders might avoid
losing their licences if the Haida prove title, Louise Mandell, a lawyer for
the Haida, informed them that, "the court will be asked to deal with the

question of remedy and the extent to which there has been a few years of good honest working together with the licensee will definitely go into the answer" (quoted in Lordon 2003, 5).

Parallel to the shift in legal landscape was a change in allegiance among employees of Weyerhaeuser, the largest logging company on the islands. Local loggers, who historically stood in solidarity with the companies, were now seeing their jobs disappear along with the old-growth timber that had previously sustained their communities. In April 2002, the wives of loggers working for Weyerhaeuser organized a protest at Weyerhaeuser's sort yard to oppose the export of raw logs from Haida Gwaii to the United States. A handout laid out their grievances:

> The export of raw logs means that Weyerhaeuser is exporting jobs out of B.C. communities. Queen Charlotte employees have been told that if Weyerhaeuser cannot export logs they will not be able to operate ... if this is the choice we are facing today, maybe we should leave these trees standing or get someone else here that will be responsible and support our communities rather than threaten them.

> Weyerhaeuser is a community wrecker. Sucking the economic lifeblood out of our communities. It is time for us, the families and friends of these workers to say no to Weyerhaeuser and to Gordon Campbell for allowing this immoral export of logs and jobs from these Islands and from this Province.

The following month, a newly formed Association of Haida Gwaii/Queen Charlotte Islands Forest Workers (2002) sent a letter to all Weyerhaeuser employees and contractors. It read as follows:

> It has become increasingly clear that Weyerhaeuser has no commitment to us as employees and residents of Haida Gwaii/QCI. At the same time, it is equally obvious that this company's whole focus is to harvest the highest quality of timber at the lowest possible cost at the highest possible rate of cut ...
>   This will lead to: a continual decrease of island employment, decreased industrial and business opportunities, [and] a further degradation of the island environment. This will also lead us into direct conflict with the Council of the Haida Nation.

A year earlier, Weyerhaeuser had laid off most of its 160 resident employees. The purpose of this appeared obvious to workers: by shutting down

10   Rally at Ferguson Bay by wives and friends of loggers. (Gowgaia Institute)

operations for eighteen months, Weyerhaeuser could effectively wipe out the union crew and proceed to rehire people back as contractors.[18] Although the resident workers were eventually rehired, bitterness persisted regarding the layoffs and the increasing use of contractors, including the contracting out of thirty-five engineering and forester jobs previously filled by locals.[19] In addition, they were concerned about the company's plan to consolidate operation teams of resident loggers with transient workers living in logging camps – a move that would carve up their crews and put their jobs at risk. They wanted the opposite: to close the logging camps and have local forestry jobs filled by local people.

The letter concluded by inviting forestry workers to join the Forest Workers Association and show their support for the Haida in the upcoming rehearing of the TFL 39 case, which was scheduled for 6 June 2002. Three days before the rehearing, the association, led by Dale Lore and Bernie Lepage, held a joint rally with the Council of the Haida Nation in the Haida village of Skidegate. According to the organizers, 135 of the 155 resident loggers who worked for Weyerhaeuser had joined the association by that time.

Lore, the recently elected mayor of Port Clements and a long-time logger and road builder for Weyerhaeuser, declared at the rally: "If we have to take sides, we are weighing in on the side of the Haida Nation. The long term interests for community stability and for the well-being of the islands expressed by the Haida Nation are more in line with our interests. We will not be pitted against our neighbours to satisfy these short term interests" (quoted in "Loggers Support CHN" 2002, 13). Convinced that the Haida would win their title case, Lore stated: "Once the Haida have Aboriginal title, and don't particularly need any cooperation with us, it will be difficult to say 'Hey, help me out. I'm the guy that wasn't a good neighbour'" (quoted in Tenove 2003, 8-9). Rally co-organizer Bernie Lepage asserted: "We are backing the Haida. We would like to work with them in some form or other, with the Haida being our employers" (quoted in ibid., 9). Whether one took the moral high ground or acted purely in self-interest, supporting the Haida was, in their view, the right thing to do.

The rally proved hugely successful, attracting about 350 people, half of them Haida and the other half loggers. It drew national media attention and forced Weyerhaeuser to suspend its logging operations for the day.[20] The event signalled a significant shift toward a new assumption: that Haida title could be beneficial not only to the Haida people but to islanders more generally.

Two weeks after the rally, representatives from the Haida Nation, the Forest Workers Association, the local International Woodworkers Association, and Weyerhaeuser met to discuss the issues. After several meetings, they agreed on the following six points:

- Reduce Weyerhaeuser's annual cut from about 850,000 cubic metres to 600,000 cubic metres.
- Log the profile of the forest (rather than taking only the most valuable species).
- Develop a cedar plan to ensure long-term viability of Haida cultural needs.
- Support maximum employment of local residents within the reduced harvest levels (that is, diminish the employment of transient workers).
- Stop the introduction of additional mechanical harvesters until further notice (one feller-buncher was already in operation).
- Respect cultural, environmental, and economic values while forestry operations are being reconfigured (Six Point Agreement 2002).

Shortly thereafter, in November 2003, the BC Court of Appeal released its decision on the TFL 39 rehearing. It reaffirmed that both Weyerhaeuser and the Province had a legally enforceable duty to consult and accommodate First Nations interests in licence transfers and replacements. The decision was another victory for the Haida. Weyerhaeuser's expectation of this ruling had no doubt prompted it to sign the six-point agreement, which it could cite as proof of consultation with the Haida and use to avoid a potential lawsuit for damages.[21] The Province's reaction to the ruling was to legislate itself out of the duty to approve licence transfers as part of its larger deregulation strategy. Weyerhaeuser would go on to appeal the decision to the Supreme Court of Canada.

In the summer of 2003, the Province released its "Statement of Defence" in the Haida title case. It asserted that "British Columbia does not admit the existence of the 'Haida Nation,'" a comment that offended more than a few islanders (Statement of Defence ... 2003, para. 2). It also argued that the Haida had abandoned their traditional sites while neglecting to mention that 90 to 95 percent of the population had been wiped out by the smallpox epidemic. Haida Nation president Guujaaw responded that this tragedy was the result of "germ warfare," not intentioned abandonment (quoted in MacQueen 2003, 4).

One week before the Community Planning Forum was scheduled to begin, in September 2003, the Province made a surprise treaty offer to the Haida Nation. It entailed transferral of 200,000 hectares, or 20 percent of the land, including all of the Haida's declared protected areas (British Columbia 2003). The deal contained no monetary offer – if the Haida wanted cash, they would have to log their protected areas, which they had consistently defended from logging in the past. In exchange for the land, the Haida were to relinquish their title case and return to the treaty negotiating table. BC Attorney General Geoff Plant released the terms of the proposal simultaneously to the media.

It was clear to the Haida that the treaty offer was a ploy – if they rejected the Province's "generous" offer, the Province would portray them as unreasonable.[22] The next day, Guujaaw dismissed the offer as "mischief" on the part of the Province. As expected, Attorney General Plant put his strategy into play and threatened that the government might not be so considerate in the future: "If the Haida aren't interested in resolving issues through negotiation then it might be harder for us as a province to informally put lands to one side pending a possible treaty settlement ... If there's no hope of progress at the [treaty] table, then there's no reason to withhold granting [logging] permits to people" (quoted in *SpruceRoots Magazine* 2003, para. 26). Plant conceded that the government would continue to consult and accommodate with respect to Aboriginal rights and title as best it could – the courts left it little choice there – but added that it must ensure that land and resource decisions "also provide a benefit to the non-Haida residents of the Charlottes" (ibid.). If the declining appeal of this divide-and-conquer strategy were not already evident to the Province following the Forest Workers Association alliance with the Haida, it would be soon enough.

A legitimate treaty offer required both provincial and federal involvement, but Ottawa distanced itself from Victoria on this matter, and Plant's strategy collapsed – he could not bring the treaty offer into the courts. The Province would subsequently field some awkward questions from other First Nations who wondered why the Haida were offered (and had rejected) 20 percent of the land, whereas other First Nations at the treaty table were being offered only 5 percent.[23]

The treaty fiasco, which occurred immediately before the Community Planning Forum was about to begin, left some people wondering whether the Haida would continue to participate in the collaborative process. Many islanders doubted that the government was genuinely interested in hearing what they had to say. However, as Council of the Haida Nation member Amos Setso would tell community forum members, with no sign of a treaty settlement in sight, the land use planning process was all the more important for addressing critical issues as soon as possible (British Columbia/ Council of the Haida Nation 2003-05, Meeting 2, 3). Thus, in the midst of a major legal battle, the dismantling of forestry regulations, a failed "treaty offer," and expanding community alliances, the stage was set for the opening rounds of the Community Planning Forum.

6

Actors and Interests

The Community Planning Forum held its first meeting in September 2003, bringing together representatives from the Haida Nation, industry, the Province, and island communities for the first time ever. During the next eighteen months, participants would meet for two to three consecutive days each month to engage in comprehensive discussions. The goal of the forum was to build an understanding of the values and issues at stake, and ultimately to develop consensus recommendations regarding land use.

To make the process fair and meaningful, the main affected parties were included in discussions. To increase transparency and prevent strategic manoeuvring, each participant was asked to disclose his or her goals and intentions for the process. This chapter captures the highly diverse interests and often contradictory goals expressed by participants.

While the process had made various efforts to address power imbalances, early debates revealed the subtle ways that power could be organized into and out of the process.

Who's Who at the Community Planning Forum

In preparation for the Community Planning Forum, the Process Management Team was created. Consisting of two process coordinators, two co-chairs, and two process managers, it was responsible for co-managing everything from participant selection and workplans to meeting agendas and facilitation. By early 2003, the Province and the Haida Nation had appointed their candidates.[1]

A Process Technical Team was also established to coordinate and review the technical information that would be put before the planning table. It consisted of eleven technical experts from industry, several provincial agencies, Haida Forest Guardians, Haida Fisheries Program, the Gowgaia Institute, and a locally based consultant.[2]

By March 2003, a general call for applicants to participate in the Community Planning Forum had been publicized through newspaper ads, a planning process newsletter, public presentations, and community open houses. The forum was expected to consist of ten to fifteen members "representing a balanced cross-section of values and interests in the community" (British Columbia/Council of the Haida Nation 2003a, 3). Based on a lead/alternate structure, twenty-nine people representing fifteen interests and sectors were selected for the forum (see Appendix 1).[3] Twenty non-Haida representatives were selected by a nominating committee consisting of the two co-chairs and two process managers. Nine Haida representatives were appointed directly by the Council of the Haida Nation and Hereditary Chiefs' Council in accordance with Haida protocol. Except for four who lived off-island, all were locals. The overall composition reflected representation from a wide range of values and interests.

INTEREST STATEMENTS AND DIVERGING GOALS

Participants were asked to present statements to inform each other of the interests they planned to bring forward. Co-representatives who held common views on a subject made joint interest statements, whereas those with diverging viewpoints made individual presentations. The main elements are summarized in the following.

Council of the Haida Nation

The key interests of the Haida Nation were laid out in *Haida Land Use Vision* (Council of the Haida Nation 2004), discussed in Chapter 4. This document was presented in its entirety to the forum, with all Haida members participating. At a general level, the Haida Nation expressed three objectives: to secure greater access and control over land and resources, to protect important cultural and environmental values, and to provide sustainable economic benefits to the Haida people. A main concern was the unsustainable rate of logging.

Nika Collison and Gary Russ represented the Council of the Haida Nation at the forum. Nika spoke of the respect the Haida have for the land and the way in which people and the land are connected. She noted that some commercial logging and fishing could occur in a sustainable manner but that, ultimately, other means of revenue generation were required. She stressed the need to work together to find innovative solutions and hoped to develop a land use plan that would serve all islanders.

Provincial Government

Herb Langin expressed the Province's interest in achieving the approved goals of the process within the Province's fiscal and legal framework. He hoped that the plan would provide greater certainty for environmental, Haida, and resource industry interests; promote the social and economic well-being of all British Columbians; and resolve resource management conflicts fairly and effectively (British Columbia 2004c). He noted that the Province's input would be guided by legislation and policy, and informed by a government advisory committee staffed by members from various provincial ministries. He hoped to develop solutions that would work for everyone but acknowledged that "the provincial interests may not always align with Community Planning Forum interests" (British Columbia/Council of the Haida Nation 2003-05, Meeting 10, 18).[4]

Major Forest-Tenure-Holders

Bob Brash and Dale Morgan expressed four main interests on behalf of major forest licensees on Haida Gwaii. These were to foster an operating environment that would create long-term viability for the industry, to maintain and expand the land base available for harvesting, to secure land use certainty, and to achieve process certainty to guide strategic and operational planning (Teal-Jones Group et al. 2004, 3). They stated that though forestry was a significant source of livelihood on the islands, Haida Gwaii was the most difficult district in the province for obtaining logging permits. As a result, profits and attitudes regarding long-term investment were negatively affected, a trend that was exacerbated by increased competition from new producers, loss of traditional markets, declining log values, high stumpage rates, and heavy regulatory burdens. They added, however, that operating on Haida Gwaii did have an advantage – its trees grow very quickly, two to three times faster than previously estimated.[5] According to their projections, the volume of wood available for cutting in certain island areas would steadily rise over the next ten to sixty years as companies transitioned from logging old growth to harvesting younger, more compact second growth. They maintained that the forest sector must be globally competitive to survive but that things are "not as bad as you are being told" (ibid., 31).

Terrestrial and Aquatic Ecosystem Interests

Ecosystem interests were divided into two seats, terrestrial and aquatic. Jacques Morin and Travis Glasman represented terrestrial ecosystems, and Lynn Lee and Leandre Vigneault represented aquatic ecosystems. However, because these ecosystems are inseparable, their interest statements were jointly presented. Their intent was "to secure the well-being of all Islands ecosystems in perpetuity" and "to ensure ... that the interpretation and application of Ecosystem Based Management principles in the Haida Gwaii Land Use Plan achieve this goal and are not compromised by the ever-present economic pressures" (Ecosystem Interest Statement n.d., 22).

Calling for change, they highlighted examples of the damage caused by current management strategies in terrestrial and aquatic ecosystems. They advocated for the creation of forest use zones, where the most sensitive and vulnerable uses would be accommodated before more aggressive ones.[6] Finally, they called for the endorsement of the *Ecosystem-Based Management Planning Handbook* (Coast Information Team 2004b) as the framework and planning guide for the forum, and asked that economic discussions be left until the end to allow for wise choices that might require compromises of the economy.

Non-Timber Forest Products

Margaret Edgars, a revered Haida elder, food gatherer, and plant specialist, presented on culturally important plants. She underscored the respect that Haida people have for all food and plants, noting that certain plants are of particular importance for medicinal and cultural purposes. These had become increasingly difficult to find, due in part to excessive grazing of introduced species (deer) and the logging of accessible sites.[7] She hoped that the process would reduce the rate of commercial logging and better protect creeks and rivers, where some of the most fertile soil and abundant plants are found.[8]

11   Steaming a cedar canoe. Foreground: Guujaaw. (Simon Davies)

Dwight Welwood, a veteran mushroom picker with over twenty-five years of experience in harvesting, buying, and marketing non-timber forest products on the islands, presented a commercial perspective on the subject. Speaking on behalf of mainly part-time and seasonal workers, he hoped to develop management strategies that would help keep these workers employed. He discussed the value of wild mushrooms and the commercial potential of other forest products such as yew bark, moss, floral and decorative greenery, and berries.[9] He recommended establishing regulations to ensure that non-timber commercial forest products remained available in sustainable quantities to all local residents in the future. He suggested that, as second-growth forests are harvested, the value of the mushroom crop in these areas must be weighed against that of the trees and stumpage royalties.

Haida Cultural Values

Allan Wilson and John Williams are both hereditary chiefs.[10] Wilson noted that Haida cultural values are so strong that "you almost have to live it to grasp it" (British Columbia/Council of the Haida Nation 2003-05, Meeting 13, 4). He shared stories to highlight the Haida's respect for the land and water, and how it is reflected in their way of life. In particular, he spoke of the importance of the salmon and the cedar, and how the Haida have used them with respect and humility. He asserted that the Haida had employed a thousand-year plan for the land until it was disrupted by European contact and industry. Now, in response to the dwindling supply of monumental cedars and to other concerns, they were again offering a thousand-year plan for the land.

Local Government

Mayors Barry Pages and Dale Lore represented the interests of their communities, Masset and Port Clements, respectively.[11] Masset, with a population of approximately a thousand, relies on commercial fisheries and, to a lesser extent, forestry as its main industries. Primary activities in both these sectors had declined in recent years, though some growth had occurred in value-added processing.[12] Barry Pages discussed the problems associated with a boom-and-bust economy and emphasized the need for local economic diversification to create sustainable opportunities for islanders. He referred to the unique island way of life, characterized by such things as food gathering and accessibility to nature, and called for a flexible and adaptable land use plan that would preserve it.

Port Clements, with a population of approximately five hundred, relies heavily on the forestry sector (British Columbia/Council of the Haida Nation 2003c, 7). In addition to logging, it has a small sawmill and dry kilns, two dry-land sorts, four custom-cut micro-sawmills, and a pole-peeling plant. Dale Lore underlined the need to "enable a local voice" and to ensure local input into the plan (British Columbia/Council of the Haida Nation 2003-05, Meeting 10, 17). He stressed the importance of a local supply of timber and fish to support manufacturing and the island way of life, and he rejected the current global supply model that directs resources to the global marketplace at the expense of local needs. Advocating for greater local processing and manufacturing, he noted that sustainability requires "reversing the number of people cutting down trees with the number of people cutting them up" and "doing things that require trees, not forests."[13]

Skidegate Band Council

Fishing and forestry are main industries in the Haida community of Skidegate, though tourism greatly expanded with the completion of the

$19.2 million Kay Llnagaay Haida Heritage Centre.[14] Councillor Eddie Russ explained that the main interest of the Skidegate Band Council was economic development, with a focus on creating jobs and a sustainable economy.[15] He stated that the band council is responsible for eight hundred people, 80 percent of whom are unemployed.[16] He presented a council initiative for economic development titled "Destination Skidegate," a tourism strategy targeting eco-, adventure, and cultural tourism. He pointed out that Canada was already the fourth-most popular destination for eco- and adventure tourism, and that experiential and cultural tourism, uniquely suited to the islands, was in high demand and low supply. However, he concluded that the success of the tourism venture depended on the integrity of the cultural and ecological resources of Haida Gwaii.

Small-Business Forestry

Stan Schiller, president of Edwards and Associates, a forest contracting company working primarily for Weyerhaeuser, represented the interests of independent forest contractors and operators. His main issue was the need for certainty and stability in the volume of wood available to small-business operators. He said that though the major licensees hold the forest tenures and manage planning, engineering, and silviculture, the small-business operators do the actual logging and road building, and are responsible for creating most local jobs in the forest sector. To remain viable, they needed access to a certain amount of wood. The current climate of uncertainty around harvesting, however, was making it very difficult for them.

Mike Hennigan, owner of Slarktooth Logging, gave a different angle on small-business forestry. His main interest was in promoting an alternative logging method that selectively removes 30 to 50 percent of the trees without compromising habitat characteristics. This is achieved by maintaining the same original overall composition of the forest, with tree species remaining in their original proportion and numerous old-growth trees left untouched. Departing from current ecosystem-based management approaches, he suggested that protected areas may not even be required with this form of logging, because of the low level of disturbance at each site. Although it requires access to larger areas and entails higher training costs for operators, he contended that it could maintain both jobs and habitat.

Forest-Based Employment

Betsy Cardell, a long-time log scaler and safety representative, spoke for

12   Logging truck near Juskatla, with Simon Davies. (Gowgaia Institute)

all forestry-sector employees, both unionized and non-unionized.[17] She
pointed to the many problems that had led to declining employment and
noted the lack of effort to ameliorate the situation. Looking beyond conventional resource extraction for solutions, she advocated sustainable
forestry management and emphasized intensive restoration and silviculture
on deforested areas to increase employment and improve the environment.

Her bottom line for the land use plan was "no net job loss" in the forestry sector, a challenge that would require innovative thinking.

Subsurface Resources

Haida artist Tim Boyko represented Haida subsurface resource interests. He focused on argillite, a soft black stone that the Haida use for carving and passing down oral histories, art forms, and other ancient traditions. He noted that argillite mining is a hereditary Haida right. Haida Gwaii argillite is unique, and he hoped that the Slate Chuck argillite mine would be protected and possibly established as a Haida Heritage Site. In addition, he expressed concerns about the environmental impact of other types of mining, particularly the risks associated with acid mine drainage.

Bob Patterson spoke for the British Columbia and Yukon Chamber of Mines and the Mining Association of British Columbia. He stated that 157 minerals occur on Haida Gwaii, with good potential for gold, iron, copper, lead, and zinc. He hoped to "develop a plan that provides maximum access to the land for exploration and to ensure that land tenure is secure to accommodate the development of an infrastructure for mineral extraction" (British Columbia and Yukon Chamber of Mines and Mining Association of British Columbia n.d., 12). Although exploration requires access to a large area, he indicated that mining itself disturbs a very small area. Less than 0.03 percent of the BC land base has been disturbed by mining, and much of it has yielded high returns, on average $150,000 per hectare. However, because exploration is so expensive, companies need secure tenure and certainty regarding future mine development before they embark on it.

Tourism

Tourism is "one of the most significant growth sectors and a source of economic diversification" for Haida Gwaii (British Columbia/Council of the Haida Nation 2003b, 153).[18] Delina Adea Petit Pas, owner of a local coffee and gift shop, stressed the need to diversify and to promote small businesses on Haida Gwaii as part of the larger transition to creating vibrant sustainable communities and a healthy environment. She cited constraints on the creation of small businesses such as lack of access to start-up capital and local training, as well as potential opportunities in terms of promotion, funding, and image development. She was also apprehensive about the recent deregulation of industry and the ongoing prioritization of profits and global markets.

Urs Thomas, a local hotel owner, highlighted the economic value of guide-outfitting (big game hunting) and the sports-fishing industry. Both are controversial due to their potential cultural and ecological impacts, but Thomas asserted that they could create a sustainable tourist industry on Haida Gwaii – one capable of providing both sufficient revenue for tourism operators and high-paid jobs for workers.[19] In particular, he provided statistics from a 2002 government report (G.S. Gislason and Associates 2002), which stated that the sports-fishing lodges on Haida Gwaii had provided 115 local jobs and contributed over $6 million in local expenditures and wages.

Cultural Heritage Tourism

Vince Collison and Barb Rowsell focused on the *Heritage Tourism Strategy* (Haida Gwaii/Queen Charlotte Islands Heritage Tourism Strategy Working Group 2003), which was developed by a table of Haida and islanders in consultation with the general population. It recorded how and where people lived on the islands, and provided recommendations for protecting, celebrating, and sharing their heritage. Collison outlined five elements of the *Heritage Tourism Strategy,* which define the islands heritage as a direct relationship between healthy ecosystems and the island way of life, a deep and profound respect for Haida culture, a determination to preserve the island way of life, an inspired relationship to place, and community integrity and the importance of the local. He recommended that the forum employ these five elements in developing the land use plan.

Barb Rowsell referred to other recommendations in the *Heritage Tourism Strategy* including developing standards to prevent tourism from adversely affecting defined heritage values; undertaking local consultations to identify places of natural, cultural, and spiritual importance; and setting aside these areas for their appropriate uses. She also suggested that the forum use the definitions and objectives in the *Heritage Tourism Strategy* to evaluate current tourism activities.

Public Interest

Cathy Rigg and Carolyn Terborg represented island residents whose interests might otherwise not be included at the table, particularly those who were not directly involved in resource-based industries. They emphasized maintaining the unique quality of life on Haida Gwaii. In interviews and questionnaires that they had conducted, residents indicated that the defining characteristics of island life included self-sufficiency, proximity to wilderness and adventure, bountiful food gathering, and a slower pace. Rigg and Terborg pointed out that all these qualities were connected to the land. Local values, identified to guide decision making, included a commitment to sustain healthy ecosystems, respect for Haida culture, and the maintenance of a diverse economy that could withstand market fluctuations. The ultimate challenge, however, was to ensure that resource development did not compromise local values or the island way of life. They asserted that "Islanders believe that the people who live here must control the Islands" (Public Interest Statement 2004, 5).

Given the wide range of diverse, complex, and potentially conflicting interests at the table, a certain amount of debate and disagreement was to be expected. However, several disputes focused on the process design and who controlled it.

EARLY DEBATES

The general outlines of the process and structure for the Community Planning Forum had been established by the Province and the Council of the Haida Nation and presented in the *Planning Process Framework* (British Columbia/Council of the Haida Nation 2003b). This document was not open for negotiation. A set of operating procedures was also presented, which covered the code of conduct, the decision-making process, and the role of the management and technical teams.

As in other BC planning processes, most sectors at the Community Planning Forum were represented by two members, a "lead" and an "alternate." The lead member had primary responsibility for the seat, and the alternate was to take charge when the lead was unavailable. If both attended a meeting, the alternate was not to participate directly. Instead, he or she was to quietly convey any concern or comment to the lead, who would then relay it to the table. In this way, the number of participants directly participating in discussions was almost halved – a desirable outcome from a process management perspective, since reaching agreement on contentious issues was easier with fewer people.

Some community representatives, however, strongly disagreed with this structure.[20] They argued that the co-members had been chosen due to their collective experience and that each one was best able to convey his or her own experience to the table. Moreover, they suggested that "speaking for someone who is present at the meeting (and who is recognized as part of the decision-making process) both disempowers the silenced individual and establishes a hierarchy at a table attempting to achieve parity among participants" (British Columbia/Council of the Haida Nation 2003-05, Meeting 3, 5). They reasoned that regardless of whether one or both co-members participated directly, the power distribution among members would remain unchanged, since even under a lead-alternate structure, the alternate would have equal influence over consensus decisions provided that the lead supported only those decisions that both co-members favoured.

In response to the dissatisfaction, the Process Management Team abandoned the lead-alternate structure. By the end of the second month of meetings, all forum members were given equal footing, which increased the number of seats at the table from sixteen to twenty-eight.[21] Although a larger table meant a slower pace, the Process Management Team also recognized the advantages of a broader basis of engagement: the more people in the core decision-making group, the better the chances that the broader community would support their decisions and the more likely the plan would succeed in the long-term. Community participants saw this decision as a small victory since, from their perspective, the more community members who spoke directly at the table, the louder their message and the greater the chances of being heard.

Financial compensation was also a contentious issue. As is typical for processes of this nature, some participants, such as those from government and industry, were paid, whereas most community members were volunteers. The Province's policy on the matter was clear: it would fund the travel and food expenses of participants but nothing else. Most community members rejected the unequal financial compensation. Appealing to the principle of "equal pay for all participants," they argued that everyone dedicated the same time and attention to the meetings (British Columbia/Council of the Haida Nation 2003-05, Meeting 2, 10). When the forum was told that further funding was probably unavailable, certain prominent members threatened to withdraw unless everyone received remuneration. Under this ultimatum, the Process Management Team managed to secure funding from the South Moresby Forest Replacement Account to pay all forum participants. As a result, the planning table became the first in British Columbia in which all participants were paid.[22]

The brevity of the fifteen-month timeline was another concern for nearly everyone. No other BC planning table had completed its work in such a short time. The two processes most similar to that of Haida Gwaii, for the north and central coasts, had taken three and seven years, respectively. However, both the Province and the Haida had their reasons for agreeing to the tight timeline. The Province had experienced planning processes that had gone on for years, and was not prepared to fund another lengthy exercise. The Haida wanted to ensure that an extended "talk-and-log" situation did not develop. In addition, both governments wanted the process to conclude before the next provincial election. The Haida were willing to extend the deadline only if an interim forestry agreement were put in place to protect certain lands while the planning process was under way. However, despite several months of negotiation between the Province, industry, and the Haida, no agreement was reached. Thus, even when the Province later agreed to a short time extension, the Haida were compelled to reject it.[23]

Facilitation was another ongoing issue. The *Planning Process Framework* (British Columbia/Council of the Haida Nation 2003b) called for independent facilitation at the meetings, but opinions differed as to who the facilitator should be, or if a facilitator was even necessary. The first facilitator, brought in to introduce the subject of interest-based negotiation and consensus-based decision making, was immediately dismissed by community representatives as "out of touch" and condescending. They were unimpressed that an off-islander with limited knowledge of local culture and issues had been hired to "teach them what to do." Some of them recommended hiring Gilbert Parnell as facilitator. A former Council of the Haida Nation vice-president (and recently resigned co-chair of the planning forum), he understood local culture, history, and issues, and he was trusted. The Process Management Team, however, wanted someone with formal training in facilitation, a track record in achieving consensus, and no personal ties to the community (British Columbia/Council of the Haida Nation 2003-05, Meeting 2).

At the second month of meetings, a facilitator who had been contracted by the Province on several other occasions was introduced. He was a seasoned facilitator with previous on-island experience and a demonstrated ability to bring planning processes to consensus. However, community members soon identified his style as "clearly government biased." The table had not been consulted on his appointment, and community representatives reiterated their request to hire Gilbert Parnell. In response, the Process Management Team decided that the government facilitator would be retained as an advisor and that meetings would be facilitated by the co-chairs. After all, they reasoned, a good facilitator is often simply a good chair.

Several months later, the Process Management Team reintroduced the government facilitator, but the table responded with such strong disapproval that the facilitator himself expressed doubts about his ability to function in the face of that level of resistance. Consequently, the co-chairs resumed their role as facilitators. Gilbert Parnell, who had indicated his availability to facilitate meetings, was never hired.

Such issues raised the topic of control and the influence participants had on the process. Should table members be expected to follow along "like sheep on a tether?"[24] Or should a group of participants have the ability to influence the direction of the process? This question of control would persist throughout the forum.

7

State of the Land and Community

One of the prerequisites for meaningful participation in collaborative processes is equal access for participants to relevant and accurate information. This material must be appropriately analyzed and understood in its wider context. Ecosystem-based management, moreover, requires the integration of "scientific knowledge of ecological relationships within a complex socio-political and values framework" (Grumbine 1994, 31). To facilitate the transparent and accountable delivery of information, a Process Technical Team was created consisting of members from the Haida Nation, government, industry, and environmental organizations. This composition was intended to provide for a greater integration of science, values, and politics, as well as ensure objective results and balanced outcomes. Nevertheless, information by its very nature is shaped by unspoken and often unacknowledged social, economic, cultural, and political assumptions. These in turn produce differing degrees of advantage and disadvantage for actors and interests. Moreover, although science can predict future changes to a system based on a certain set of assumptions, the question as to whether such changes are acceptable or not is a value judgment.

This chapter examines the central information presented to the Community Planning Forum. The significance of the underlying assumptions and framings of the information becomes clearer as we turn to the table's responses to it.

ENVIRONMENTAL CONDITIONS

Assessing the state of the environment is a complex task involving considerations from genes and habitat to populations and ecosystem processes. The centrepiece of environmental information presented at the forum was the comprehensive *Environmental Conditions Report* (Holt 2005). This 180-page volume provided an overview of ecological conditions and addressed the implications of land use decisions within a broad historical context. It was initiated and guided by the Process Technical Team with input from a wide variety of experts on specific species or ecosystem elements. Community forum members also contributed on issues of particular local interest.

In general, ecological integrity entails the retention of sufficient areas of land and water to maintain viable populations across their natural range (Coast Information Team 2004a). Various approaches can be used to determine this. The *Environmental Conditions Report* (Holt 2005, 1-1) compared current conditions against a historical benchmark. The benchmark for the report was the year 1800, when ecological impacts due to European contact were still largely negligible. Thus, the full impacts, negative or positive, of ecological changes resulting from colonization, industrialization, and other influences could be taken into consideration. As the report noted, the intention of the benchmark was not "to suggest that all indicators should be 'restored' to a natural condition" but, rather, to provide an overview of "the full extent of current and future predicted change" (ibid.). In addition, modelling was used to predict changes expected to occur over the next 250 years, assuming that current management practices and policies persist. This modelling allowed significant changes to be considered, such as the maturing of previously logged forests into old growth. Together, the historical benchmark and future modelling provided a "supply curve" that spanned 450 years. Such a broad approach had never been used in a provincial planning process before, and it would prove to be very effective for providing a full understanding of current conditions within the broad context of environmental change.

The report also used species and population analysis to assess the likelihood that a species or population would survive into the future. However, because sufficiently detailed information to undertake such an analysis was unavailable for a vast number of species, the main consideration for assessing their survival was the extent to which their habitat would be maintained over time. This placed added emphasis on the need to preserve forests, particularly old growth.

A coarse filter/fine filter approach was used to select the main ecosystem elements for analyses. As described in the report,

> The coarse filter focuses on maintaining ecosystem elements that provide for the vast majority of species. This can include a) representing ecosystems across the landscape, b) using umbrella or wide-ranging species which potentially provide habitat for [a] wide array of other species, c) using keystone species (those that have a disproportionately higher ecological role than is suggested by their biomass), d) using indicator species which are sensitive and require a broad set of ecosystem elements.[1]
>
> The fine filter approach identifies special elements that are likely to not be maintained by the coarse filter. Rare species, key ecosystem processes and specialized species are good examples of candidates likely to require a fine filter approach. (ibid., 1-2)

Ten primary indicators were selected for the coarse filter approach and thirteen additional species and elements were chosen for the fine filter approach. Selection of indicators was based on four main considerations: critical environmental variables or descriptors (such as ecosystem and habitat types), keystone species (such as salmon and black bears), species and ecosystems of global significance (such as rare or endemic species), and introduced species with major ecological impacts (such as deer). Central information and "supply curves" for the indicators were presented to the Community Planning Forum.

Primary Indicators

The ten primary indicators chosen for the coarse filter approach were old forest ecosystems, watershed condition, plant species and communities, northern goshawk, marbled murrelet, seabird colonies, Haida Gwaii black bear, salmonids, non-native/introduced species, and cedar. The report provided detailed explanations of the methodology used for the various indicators and their limitations. It analyzed the conditions and trends for each indicator, outlined potential risks associated with the trends, and recommended options to lower the risks.

Old Forest Ecosystems

Maintaining old forest ecosystems in suitable abundance and distribution is crucial to preserving biodiversity and ecological processes. However, defining "suitable abundance" in relation to old forests is a highly contentious issue on Haida Gwaii and a prime example of the complexity integrating ecological relationships within a socio-political and values framework.

Generally, old-growth forests are defined as older than 250 years.[2] The analysis assumed that the closer a landscape is to the distribution and abundance of old forests in the natural (pre-1800) condition, the higher the probability of maintaining the values provided by the old forests, and the lower the risk of losing fully functioning ecosystems. More specifically, the Coast Information Team associated low-risk management at a regional scale with maintaining 70 percent of the naturally occurring levels of old forests. This was determined to be the point at which adverse ecological impacts are first detected. High-risk management was associated with maintaining less than 30 percent of the naturally occurring levels of old forests. This represented the point at which significant loss of ecological function was expected to occur.

The overall ecosystem trend for old forests was presented at three levels: for the islands as a whole, for three ecosections, and for twenty-four landscape units. Each level incorporated nine analysis units that described the leading tree species and level of productivity. The ecosystem trends were conducted over three periods: 1800, 2000, and 2250. Logging predictions for the year 2250 were based on current management practices and policies. For example, land that was currently legislated as protected or excluded from logging was assumed to remain so in the future. Likewise, unprotected land that was considered "inoperable" due to economic constraints was assumed to remain uneconomical to log in the future.

The results presented for old forests indicated that almost all logging on Haida Gwaii had occurred in good- and medium-quality forest stands, where the predominant tree species was either western hemlock, Sitka spruce, or western red cedar. Unsurprisingly, these trees hold the most commercial value. At the same time, the forests in which they grow also contain the highest habitat and Haida cultural values (Gowgaia Institute 2005, 11).

Ranking the risk to ecosystems, based on the thresholds laid out by the Coast Information Team, the analysis showed that a significant number of ecosystems did not currently meet the low-risk threshold of 70 percent retention of the natural levels of old-growth forest at the regional or ecosection scale (Holt 2005, 2.1-23, 2.1-24). At the ecosection level, eleven of twenty-four, or almost half, of the ecosystems did not meet the 70 percent threshold, and another four were predicted to exceed the threshold in the

13   Old forest ecosystem in Windy Bay, Lyell Island. (Richard Krieger)

future. Four had less than 30 percent of the natural forest level, which put them at a high risk for ecosystem failure.

As might be expected, the highest-risk ecosystems were those with the highest timber productivity and accessibility, whereas most of their low-risk counterparts were located in commercially inoperable forest areas. The data showed that 65 percent of the good and medium forest sites on Haida Gwaii had been logged. On the Skidegate Plateau, where most logging had occurred, 74 percent of the area had been cut (Gowgaia Institute 2005, 11). Given the scarcity of habitat values in second-growth forests, the Gowgaia Institute (ibid.) concluded that "65-74 percent of the best places for salmon, bear, birds, cedar, medicinal plants and people are gone."

Inoperable land status was shown to make up 38 percent of the land base (Holt 2005, 2.1-20). Although this status was assumed to persist in the future, the *Environmental Conditions Report* (ibid., 2.1-21) noted that, in fact, harvesting in such areas was precluded solely by current economic conditions. As resources become scarcer, logging in inoperable lands tends to become economically feasible. Indeed, at the time of the planning process, a considerable amount of land in the so-called inoperable areas was being cut. As a result, the report recommended: "If an area is to contribute to biodiversity values in the future *with any certainty* it must be protected" (ibid., 2.1-22, emphasis in original).

The report identified old forest areas at the landscape level where enhanced protection could immediately lower risks. In addition, it identified high-risk areas that required restoration strategies to lower risk in the future.[3] In the end, however, forum members would need to decide what level of ecological risk was socially acceptable.

Watershed Condition

Watersheds on Haida Gwaii were considered from two separate but interrelated perspectives: biological and hydrological.[4] A biological approach focuses on the biological functioning of watersheds and considers such things as habitat, rare ecosystems, and biodiversity. Of particular importance are hydroriparian zones, which include aquatic ecosystems plus the adjacent riparian forest that directly influences them. These zones are very high in nutrients, making them hotspots for biodiversity as well as habitat for numerous terrestrial and aquatic species. The hydrological approach assesses water resources in terms of volume, timing of flows, and water quality. These are influenced by a variety of factors, including vegetation, drainage efficiency, and sedimentation (Holt 2005, 2.3-1, 2.3-2).

A broad analysis of indicators was undertaken for 145 watersheds. Due to the difficulty of determining an ecological baseline for watersheds – that is, their condition in 1800 – they were ranked according to the potential risk associated with current and future levels of forest harvesting and development. The primary indicator for assessing biological functioning was the percentage of riparian areas harvested. Riparian forests were chosen as the indicator because of their important effects on aquatic ecosystems, including stabilizing stream banks, reducing erosion, and providing vital shade and organic material for fish and other species. The width of the riparian area varied from twenty to eighty metres, depending on the size of the stream and the abundance of fish. The analyses applied the Coast Information Team's breakdown of risks – high risk was associated with greater than 30 percent harvest of riparian areas, moderate risk with greater than 10 percent, and low risk with less than 10 percent.

The primary indicator for hydrological functioning was the percentage of the total watershed area harvested. This indicator was chosen because forests significantly influence the flow of water through the entire watershed. The levels of risk to aquatic resources were broken down as follows: high risk was associated with greater than 30 percent harvest of watershed areas, moderate risk with 20 to 30 percent, and low risk with less than 20 percent.[5] A secondary set of indicators for hydrological functioning includes roads in the watershed and their impact on sedimentation.

The analyses indicated that almost one-third of the watersheds on Haida Gwaii were at a high level of ecological risk. Study of the primary biological indicator (percentage of riparian forests harvested) revealed that 46 of the 145 watersheds were potentially at high risk, 25 were at moderate risk, and 74 were at low risk. Results for the hydrological indicator (total watershed area harvested) showed that 43 of the 145 watersheds were at potentially high risk, 17 were at moderate risk, and 85 were at low risk. Taken together, the findings demonstrated that regardless of which indicator was used, 40 to 45 of 145 watersheds on Haida Gwaii were at high risk.

The *Environmental Conditions Report* recommended that a more comprehensive strategy for watershed assessment and monitoring be developed as part of a larger strategy to protect, improve, or restore watershed conditions. Priority watersheds were identified as those at highest ecological risk, those with highest aquatic values (fish stocks or community watersheds), and those identified in the *Haida Land Use Vision* (Council of the Haida Nation 2004) as having cultural importance.

Plant Species and Communities

Many plants on Haida Gwaii are particularly important from a cultural and/or ecological perspective. The two main threats to plant species and communities are logging and extensive deer browse. Whereas old forest analysis is generally assumed to assess plant community representation, plant species were considered a separate indicator because of the numerous rare and/or endemic plants and ecosystems, and the local/regional scarcity of many historically common and culturally important understory herbs and shrubs (Holt 2005, 2.2-1).

Forty-six plant species are provincially listed as rare/threatened or endangered, and another seventy-six are identified as locally rare. Ten plant species and four mosses are locally endemic. Fourteen ecosystems are also rare, as defined by plant associations, and a number of other ecosystems are locally rare, uncommon, or unique. In addition, fifteen medicinal plants have been identified as reduced by deer browse.

To manage culturally important plants, the *Environmental Conditions Report* recommended the maintenance of accessible forests with a significant intact understory. To protect important plant species and communities more generally, it emphasized the need for adequate levels of old forest protection combined with strategies for managing deer browse.

Northern Goshawk

The northern goshawk, *laingi* subspecies, is a provincially red-listed (endangered) bird thought to be declining on Haida Gwaii. Its numbers are generally related to the age and amount of mature and old forest where it forages and nests.

To determine the requirement for suitable habitat, the amount of old forest present in known goshawk territory (based on nest areas) was analyzed. The results showed that the minimum amount of mature and old forest present for all nest areas (active and abandoned) was 41 percent. For active nests only, the minimum was 61 percent.

On the basis of these figures, the number of potentially suitable goshawk territories was predicted for the future. These were estimated to reach their lowest point in 2050, with eleven territories suitable for nesting based on the requirement for 61 percent old/mature forest, or thirty-two territories based on the requirement for 41 percent old/mature forest. After 2050, the goshawk population was expected to stabilize because logging of original old forests was predicted to cease after that time.[6]

A population trend was estimated from Gwaii Haanas goshawk reproductive data and from survivorship data for other goshawk populations. The results showed that the bird was declining by either 3 or 21 percent, depending on whether the data were interpreted optimistically or pessimistically. Using a population model, the study estimated the probability of goshawk survival by combining the number of potential territories with the estimated population decline. The results indicated that if the population decline were taken at 3 percent, the goshawk had a 14 to 35 percent probability of surviving (depending on whether the number of active territories was taken at eleven or thirty-two). However, if the population decline were taken at 21 percent, the bird had zero probability of persisting.

In light of this, the *Environmental Conditions Report* strongly recommended that old and mature forests suitable for goshawk habitat be maintained in adequate size and distribution to increase the chances for the bird's survival.[7]

Marbled Murrelet

The marbled murrelet is another provincially red-listed (endangered) species. This seabird also generally requires old forests for nesting. A habitat suitability model was used to estimate the amount of murrelet habitat in twenty-four landscape units. Results showed that suitable habitat had declined by 42 percent since 1800 and was predicted to diminish to 50 percent by 2050 (Holt 2005, 2.6-5, 2.6-6, 2.6-10). Thirteen of twenty-four landscape units showed a reduction of more than 30 percent in murrelet habitat, and eight landscape units showed a decline of more than 50 percent. In certain areas, significant habitat remained.

Population viability analysis estimated the current number of marbled murrelets on Haida Gwaii to be between 8,500 and 9,500 individuals. On the basis of this figure, the probability that the bird would persist on the islands was estimated at 83 to 84 percent.[8]

To maintain the marbled murrelet population, forum members were advised to focus on protecting areas where the impact on suitable habitat was greatest. However, determining the extent of protection demanded that table members decide how much risk was socially acceptable.

Seabird Colonies

Haida Gwaii is home to approximately 1.5 million seabirds, representing a diversity and abundance of global significance. Of the twelve species present, three are provincially blue-listed (threatened) and two are red-listed (endangered).[9] Information for the various species was summarized at the forum, and maps with the location and size of colonies were also presented. For many species, there were no exact estimates of population trends, but it was noted that a number of important colonies had significantly declined or perished in the recent past. The main threats included introduced predators (particularly rats and racoons), habitat loss, and degradation due largely to fishing lodge development on seabird islands and disturbance of nesting sites by tourist and recreational activities.

14   Black bear near Sandspit. (Richard Krieger)

A number of recommendations for maintaining seabird colonies were made to the table, including formally protecting nesting locations, restricting access to seabird areas during the breeding season, preventing logging and other developments near nesting sites, and managing introduced predators.[10]

Haida Gwaii Black Bear

The Haida Gwaii black bear is an endemic species found only on the islands. It is distinguished from its mainland relatives by a significantly larger body and skull. It requires a large and diverse habitat, which means that the effective management of black bear habitat also addresses the needs of many other species. In addition, the bear plays a critical role in nutrient transfer in some forest ecosystems by leaving remnants of nutrient-rich salmon carcases on the forest floor.

Black bear winter dens are usually located in old-growth structures such as large standing trees or fallen dead trees, logs, and stumps. A map of black bear residency was produced along with a preliminary map identifying relative bear habitat values based on estimated forage values, salmon biomass, and road density. However, no recommendations were made regarding the degree to which such sites should be maintained for black bear habitat.

Salmonids

Salmonids were considered important for land use planning due to the significant amount of nutrients they contribute to terrestrial areas when their carcases are left in the forests by bears. The main threats to salmon included forestry operations, mining, and associated road building in critical habitats.

Five species of Pacific salmon and three other salmonid species are found in the fresh waters of Haida Gwaii. The *Environmental Conditions Report* (Holt 2005, 2.9) described their general distribution and abundance across the islands and provided an overview of available population trends. Overall results showed a sharp decline in abundance between 1950-53 and 2000-3.[11] A number of impacts to specific fish populations were also shown, including population declines in major creeks and the apparent connection between decreasing stocks and disturbance to surrounding riparian areas.

With a mandate from the Process Technical Team, the Gowgaia Institute prepared a detailed map showing the distribution of resident and anadromous freshwater fish in relation to the adjacent riparian forests. A risk assessment of the forests was conducted for various landscape and watershed units based on how much had been logged. The locations of riparian forests that were at a high or medium ecological risk were then compared with the locations of major salmon runs.[12] The comparison showed that "in essence, every major salmon run of cultural significance to the Haida is at high or medium risk" (Gowgaia Institute 2005, 13). The map would play an interesting role in later negotiations.

Non-Native/Introduced Species

The islands are home to more than 23 non-native animals and 140 non-native plants, most of which have been introduced since the mid-eighteen hundreds. Although the effect of introduced species is an unusual concern for a land use planning process, their impact is significant enough to potentially undermine management strategies on Haida Gwaii (Holt 2005, 2.10-3). The most serious of these include excessive browsing by deer and predation of endangered birds' eggs by racoons and rats. Non-native species also compete with native species for habitat elements and food supplies.

Previous work by two groups (the Research Group on Introduced Species and the Haida Resource Restoration Project) was employed to create a list of priority species and locations. The eleven species of primary concern were the beaver, rat, raccoon, Sitka black-tailed deer, Japanese knotweed, Scotch broom, gorse, chada thistle, marsh thistle, wall lettuce, and English ivy. Holt (2005) also pointed to the complexities of managing introduced species from both an ecological and social perspective. For example, extirpation of a species, assuming it is possible, could produce complex and unexpected ecological responses. It may also be deemed socially unacceptable, as in the case of deer, which have a major ecological impact but are also an important local food source.

Cedar

The long-term supply of monumental cedar used for traditional longhouses, canoes, and totem poles is a serious Haida concern.[13] Although cedar was a primary indicator, the *Environmental Conditions Report* gave no details for it. The Process Technical Team had initiated an analysis of current and historical conditions of monumental cedar, using information from a Weyerhaeuser inventory timber cruise of TFL 39. However, before the analysis could be completed, Weyerhaeuser removed its representatives from the Process Technical Team along with the information being analyzed.[14] At that point, Weyerhaeuser was embroiled in legal proceedings with the Haida Nation. Thus, quantifying the historical trend in monumental cedars would not be to the company's advantage since such information could potentially be used to measure the losses incurred by the Haida as a result of logging.

However, two presentations to the Community Planning Forum did describe two divergent cedar inventories of TFL 39: one was conducted by the Council of the Haida Nation in 2002, and the other was performed by Weyerhaeuser in 2004. Randomly selecting fifty-six old-growth plots, the council study found that they contained only three monumental cedars. This suggested that very few monumental cedars remained on the islands. Weyerhaeuser's audit estimated that there were ten to fifteen large red cedars per hectare with a diameter of 1.0 metre at breast level (or two red cedars per hectare with a diameter of 1.6 metres at breast level). It also found one to two yellow cedars per hectare with a diameter of 1.0 metre at breast level (or 0.1 per hectare with a diameter of 1.6 metres). Although the Weyerhaeuser study rated only 10 percent of these cedars as "quality logs," their numbers were still much greater than those of the Haida inventory.

15   Grizzly bear figure from the Bill Reid Pole in Skidegate.
(Richard Krieger)

The discrepancy between the two assessments was partially explained by their differing definitions of monumental cedar. The Haida definition depended on what the log would be used for (canoe, longhouse, or totem pole), not on diameter alone. In addition, about three-quarters of the plots in Weyerhaeuser's study were taken from an operational timber cruise that was considered to be skewed toward sites of higher productivity (British Columbia/Council of the Haida Nation 2003-05, Meeting 15, 4-5).[15]

In a presentation to the forum, Captain Gold, a Haida historian and one of the first people to begin mapping culturally modified tress on Haida Gwaii, voiced an urgent need for a protective strategy to ensure the availability of monumental cedars for current and future cultural needs. He highlighted the Council of the Haida Nation resolution to develop a "thousand year cedar strategy" and noted the council's interest in designating cedar reserves. He concluded with three recommendations to the Community Planning Forum: conduct GIS modelling to address current and past conditions of cedar and to predict future growth sites, determine Haida demand trends for cedar, and protect remaining monumental cedars while the model is being developed.

Additional Species of Land Use Concern

The Process Technical Team chose thirteen additional species and elements for review. These included the northern saw-whet owl, great blue heron, bald eagle, Steller's jay, hairy woodpecker, sandhill crane, peregrine falcon, pine grosbeak, ermine, Keen's long-eared myotis, marine mammals, giant black stickleback, and Haida Gwaii jumping-slug. Many are endemic subspecies to Haida Gwaii, making their preservation of global significance. All were considered of particular importance for land use planning, but they either lacked sufficient information for detailed analyses or did not make good indicators. The *Environmental Conditions Report* briefly outlined background information on each one and mentioned the potential related land use concerns.

Although most of these species were thought to require individual management strategies, several broader land use issues were identified for them as a group. These included the need to maintain old-growth structural attributes in second-growth forests, natural undergrowth in old- and second-growth forests, key habitat areas that provide critical foraging grounds, and terrestrial riparian areas (Holt 2005, 3.10).

Provincial Protected Areas Strategy

In addition to the fourteen Haida Protected Areas designated by the Council of the Haida Nation, the Province's Protected Areas Strategy considered certain zones for protection. Initiated in 1992, its purpose was to protect 12 percent of the province in a systematic way that would conserve representative examples of ecosystems and special or unique landscape features. Areas were assessed based on their naturalness (less than 25 percent disturbance), representativeness, diversity, viability, vulnerability, and significance.

Sixteen candidate areas were identified on Haida Gwaii, ten of which overlapped with the Haida Protected Areas. A member of the Province's

Regional Protected Areas Team for Haida Gwaii noted that although conserving cultural features was one goal of the strategy, the sites proposed for protection did not have a strong cultural component. He suggested that "the Haida Nation would be in the best position to identify key areas for cultural reasons as has been done with the Haida Protected Areas" (British Columbia/Council of the Haida Nation 2003-05, Meeting 13, 8).

Overall, the environmental information presented to the Community Planning Forum highlighted the importance of old-growth forests in maintaining the well-being of the land, the water, and all the creatures that depended on them. It clearly conveyed the level of risk posed by current management practices to particular indicators and ecosystems but left table members to decide whether certain changes were acceptable or not. Is there a point, for example, at which providing jobs and revenues justifies a moderate or even a high level of ecological risk? To better understand the socio-economic context of land use decisions, a number of studies were conducted.

Socio-Economic Conditions

To assess the socio-economic implications of land use recommendations on Haida Gwaii, the *Socio-Economic Base Case* (Holman and Nicol 2004) was prepared to serve as a benchmark and general context. The report focused primarily on population, jobs, and income, and it concentrated on the sectors most strongly linked to land use. It incorporated some input from community forum members and local representatives, but relied heavily on secondary sources of information.[16]

Employing census data from Statistics Canada, it reported a 12 percent drop in Haida Gwaii's general population between 1996 and 2001. This was due largely to the closure of a Canadian Forces base and the decline of forestry and fisheries employment. The Haida population, however, had increased by about 60 percent between 1981 and 2001, rising from 16 to 34 percent of the total population (ibid., 4, 6).[17] This trend was expected to continue, with many Haida returning to the islands following Bill C-31, which restored Indian status rights to many Haida women who had lost their status on marrying non-Aboriginal men.

The report also noted that employment rates, education, and labour force participation on Haida Gwaii were lower than in the rest of the province. Statistics Canada data revealed that 72 percent of the Haida

Gwaii workforce had been employed in 2001, though only 39 percent had held full-time jobs for the entire year. The public sector, which engaged 966 people, was the top source of employment, followed by forestry at 672 jobs (direct and indirect), tourism at 292 jobs, and fishing/trapping at 191 jobs (BC Ministry of Sustainable Resource Management 2004, 4).[18] The highest employment growth was in business, personal, and miscellaneous services.

In terms of income, forestry was the largest source, accounting for 36 percent of income in 2001. This was followed closely by the public sector at 30 percent, tourism at 5 percent, and fishing and trapping at 4 percent. Transfer payments in the form of government pensions, employment insurance, and welfare cheques accounted for another 13 percent of income (ibid.). In 2001, the forest sector saw a 10 percent drop in the annual allowable cut, which decreased from about 1.9 to 1.7 million cubic metres per year. Actual logging on public lands was about 25 percent below the allowable cut. This was partially due to poor market conditions and the deferral of logging in the declared Haida Protected Areas (Holman and Nicol 2004, 5). In 2003, the harvest dropped to just over 40 percent of the annual allowable cut. This corresponded with a 40 percent decline in local forestry employment (direct and indirect) between 2001 and 2003, with a large proportion of the jobs held by non-residents (BC Ministry of Sustainable Resource Management 2004, 6). In terms of wood processing, a mere 3.5 percent of the harvest went to local mills. Ironically, despite their location in a prime timber area, no local mill had a secure supply of wood (Holman and Nicol 2004, 5).

Tourism was the second-most important private sector industry, though it contributed proportionately less in income per job due to lower average wages and its seasonal nature. The most important aspects of the tourism sector were food and accommodation as well as saltwater fishing lodges and guiding activities. All local communities saw tourism as an important growth area (ibid.).

The third-most important sector was commercial fishing and processing. During the last decade, employment in the industry had significantly decreased due to declines in salmon stocks and recent logging restrictions. It was estimated that ninety jobs had been lost since 1996 due to fleet reduction and area licensing (BC Ministry of Sustainable Resource Management 2004, 13). On the positive side, shellfish aquaculture was seen to have good growth potential.

Other economic activities linked to land use consisted of mushroom harvesting and mining. The former was reported to provide supplemental income for about a hundred residents, with some growth potential. It was also noted that, though the islands had no working mines, there were significant deposits of gold, iron-copper, and copper-lead-zinc-gold. There were also ten sand and gravel operations (ibid., 11-12). In addition, Holman and Nicol (2004, 6) mentioned "significant offshore oil/gas development potential if the federal/provincial moratorium and Haida title can be resolved."

Ultimately, although the *Socio-Economic Base Case* provided an overview of the formal economy and what might be expected according to a business-as-usual perspective, it missed much of what islanders really cared about.

Timber Supply Analysis

At the heart of the conflict over forests was the question of how much wood could be extracted if more areas were retained for ecological and cultural purposes. To better understand how differing management strategies would affect the timber supply, an analysis of four base-case scenarios was undertaken by Cortex Consultants and Gowlland Technologies (2004):

1 current management (assumptions updated to 2004)
2 current management minus the Haida Protected Areas
3 current management minus the Haida Protected Areas and an additional 20 percent retention within cutblocks
4 current management minus the Haida Protected Areas, the additional 20 percent retention, and an additional constraint on TFL 39 not to exceed 600,000 cubic metres per year.[19]

The first scenario was based on current policies and legislation, whereas scenarios 2, 3, and 4 incorporated aspects of recent practices on Haida Gwaii. The constraint on TFL 39 in scenario 4 reflected a recent agreement between Weyerhaeuser and the Council of the Haida Nation. On the basis of the various scenarios, harvest forecasts were produced for the entire land use planning area (Table 1).

In scenario 1, Haida Gwaii's harvest level for the decade 2004-14 was determined to be 1.88 million cubic metres, with a long-term harvest level of 1.61 million cubic metres. By comparison, scenarios 2, 3, and 4 indicated annual harvest reductions of 8 percent (1.75 million cubic metres), 22 percent (1.48 million cubic metres), and 40 percent (1.14 million cubic metres)

TABLE I   Harvest forecasts based on different management assumptions

Assumptions	Harvest level first decade (million m³)	Harvest level long term (million m³)
1 Current management	1.88	1.61
2 Current management minus Haida Protected Areas	1.75	1.42
3 Current management minus Haida Protected Areas and additional 20% retention	1.48	1.16
4 Current management minus Haida Protected Areas and additional 20% retention, and TFL 39 constraint	1.14	1.14

respectively for the first decade. In scenarios 2, 3, and 4, long-term annual harvest levels (in 250 years) were projected to decline by 21 percent (1.42 million cubic metres), 35 percent (1.16 million cubic metres), and 36 percent (1.14 million cubic metres) respectively (Cortex Consultants and Gowlland Technologies 2004, 13).[20] Whereas an 8 percent reduction in logging might be acceptable to government and industry, a 40 percent drop would certainly not be. Yet, it was the fourth scenario, which entailed a 40 percent reduction that most closely reflected the preference of the Haida and community members at the table.

A separate report examined the second-growth harvest opportunities on Haida Gwaii, an issue considered essential to understanding future timber supply and employment levels. Second-growth forests were reported to make up 39 percent of the total operable land base (Cortex Consultants and HiMark Forest Consultants 2004, 2).[21] The economic feasibility of logging them, however, was questionable due to low prices and poor markets for second-growth wood. The report suggested that improving economic feasibility would require either low harvesting costs through the use of mechanized systems or the presence of higher-value stands (such as cedar) that would help to carry the operation costs. It recommended investments in milling technology to process smaller and more uniform logs efficiently and economically, and suggested that the stumpage paid for second growth be reduced to reflect the low market prices (ibid., 26). The report concluded that "the second-growth resource will eventually become economically operable through the ongoing processes of market development, technological innovation, and industry investment" (ibid., vi).

However, it did not analyze what the benefits of logging second-growth forests might be in terms of employment and other community values.

REFORMING VERSUS TRANSFORMING

An enormous amount of ecological, social, and economic information was provided to the Community Planning Forum, which addressed a number of critical issues for land use planning. However, there were some notable gaps in the information and points of contention. At the heart of disagreements were unspoken assumptions that framed the information and analyses presented to the forum. These assumptions became increasingly visible as the table engaged in discussion.

The *Socio-Economic Base Case* (Holman and Nicol 2004), intended to provide information of most relevance for land use planning, was strongly criticized by community representatives. They argued that the report took an overly narrow economic perspective and failed to address the community's aspirations or informational needs. Critiques were laid on its failure to interpret social statistics, its misrepresentation of the island character, and its lack of alternative future scenarios. Moreover, its inclusion of sensitive social statistics without discussing why certain conditions existed was considered highly offensive.[22]

Community representatives also noted the lack of information regarding non-monetary activities such as subsistence food gathering, fishing, and hunting. These informal economic activities, which many islanders were involved with, decreased their dependency on formal employment and income generation while contributing to their quality of life. They pointed out that, unlike industry and the provincial government, islanders value their natural surroundings for much more than their monetary benefits. Their concerns encompassed broader quality-of-life issues, not just income and jobs. In the words of one community representative, the socio-economic information and analyses were "completely inadequate and meaningless."[23]

Regarding the future of logging, community representatives noted that the four-scenario timber supply analysis assumed that a reduced volume of timber would directly result in job losses. In doing so, it completely neglected the larger social and economic context of forestry and the potential for diversification. This was expressed in a document titled "Draft Islands' Declaration" (2005, 5) presented by a group of community representatives:

We know that the relationship between employment and timber volume is far more complicated than timber supply curves can predict. Over the past decade alone, the downturn in forestry was linked to a number of compounded problems: the liquidation of high value old growth, the displacement of workers by new technologies, and uncertain global markets. We have learned the painful lesson that our reliance on forestry is unsustainable and unhealthy. Yet there has been no concerted effort to evaluate economic, social and cultural opportunities for diversification on Haida Gwaii, in forestry or other resource industries.

From a more technical angle, the second-growth timber opportunities report was critiqued for calculating only the *volume* of harvestable wood while neglecting its *quality*. As old-growth forests are logged and replaced by second growth, quality becomes a significant factor because, unless second-growth wood is similar in quality to old growth, it will sell for much less. However, if second-growth forests are to attain old-growth characteristics, they must be left untouched for much longer than is generally assumed. Moreover, the uniformity of second-growth trees facilitates the use of machines to log and mill the wood, which results in reduced employment and livelihood potential. So, whereas the value of what had been logged was known, it was still unclear what the value of Haida Gwaii's second-growth forests and the basis of its future economy would be.[24]

A highly contentious issue for islanders was the fact that most of Haida Gwaii's timber was shipped off-island for processing. Although the *Socio-Economic Base Case* (Holman and Nicol 2004) did mention this point, its significance in terms of lost opportunities was not discussed. As expressed by John Broadhead (2005, para. 20): "Every log barge loaded in a single shift by a crew of five could keep fifteen people working in local mills for a year – and every forty-eight hours another barge sails." In addition, the stumpage revenues collected on trees logged on Haida Gwaii went to the provincial government rather than to the local or even regional level.

Increasing local manufacturing was seen as critically important to developing a sustainable local economy while maintaining a healthy environment. This meant addressing one of the biggest obstacles facing mills on Haida Gwaii, which, oddly enough, was the need to acquire a secure supply of timber. Solving this problem and other challenges to creating a diversified economy required innovative thinking on issues such as local control, log exports, local manufacturing, alternative economic opportunities, and governance. However, unlike the wealth of information presented on environmental conditions, community representatives stated that very little relevant social, economic, or cultural information was made available to them. Despite repeated requests for funding to carry out a locally produced economic-opportunity study for the islands, financial support was not forthcoming.

Many locals cited islands governance as a way of reversing the trend that saw the majority of benefits from the islands' resources flow in a one-way direction toward the urban centres. This concept had informed discussions among islanders since the 1970s and had been incorporated into such initiatives as the Gwaii Haanas Archipelago Management Board, Gwaii Trust Society Board, and Haida Forest Guardians. The continued call for islands governance stemmed from the view that, faced with the continuing trajectory of resource extraction, islanders had to start creating alternatives immediately, on their own terms, while there were still resources left to work with. But when discussions turned to the topic, the table was informed that governance issues lay outside the scope of the process.

From the predominant perspective of forestry and resource management, deciding how to manage land is essentially a technical exercise. For Haida Gwaii, the basic goal was to determine which areas should be protected from industrial resource extraction, placed under special management, or remain open to industry. The land use plan was to give "clear management direction and specific management objectives and strategies for a full range of values and resource uses in each planning unit or zone" (British Columbia/Council of the Haida Nation 2003a, 5). Achieving this mandate would require a massive effort to collect and analyze the relevant information and values, never mind reaching agreement on the management objectives and direction. All of this would also need to occur within a relatively short time, which, from a process management perspective, meant that discussions outside of the prescribed subject areas would have to be limited.

Consequently, although each meeting was open to input from the table, there were clear expectations regarding what could or could not be included. More significantly, certain topics of central importance to the land would not be discussed. These included existing tenure arrangements, contracts, regulations, and governance, which were to be left firmly in the hands of the Province and managed at a technical professional level. This reflected the unquestionability of Western conceptions of contract and property, and the continuing dominance of technocratic control over decision making. The details of land use were open for discussion, but recommendations would need to be made within an unaltered structure of ownership and mode of extraction.

The problem for community representatives was that the objectives and future conditions to which they aspired could not be achieved within the existing economic, regulatory, and governance framework. Their main concern was how to make the transition from high-volume logging with minimal community benefits to low-volume logging with maximum community benefits. For them, the long-term desired condition of the land and their communities was inseparable from such topics as economic diversification, local manufacturing, governance, education, social services, and local control. These issues, however, were considered outside the formal mandate for the planning process.

Rejecting the conventional economic themes of the *Socio-Economic Base Case,* a document titled *Community Sustainability* summarized many principal concerns of the community representatives. The document was jointly presented to the forum by the public interest representative, both local government representatives, and the forest-based employment representative. It was written in response to the Process Management Team's recommendations for community sustainability, which were seen as inadequately reflecting community interests.

The *Community Sustainability* document featured three principal themes: governance, community resiliency, and economic opportunities. It emphasized the concern that community representatives had repeatedly expressed – "If planning recommendations are implemented under the existing structure of governance, the underlying causes of ecosystem, cultural, social and economic degradation will persist" (*Community Sustainability,* 1). Based on forum discussions, it noted that most local residents favoured the establishment of an islands governance body that would have decision-making authority and a mandate beyond implementing an eventual land use plan.[25]

The document also underlined the importance of understanding social and cultural conditions that contribute to increased community resiliency. It recommended that central objectives related to social, economic, cultural, educational, health care, and social services be identified along with other community priorities. In addition, it suggested that the community resiliency strategy be based on the ideals expressed in the *Haida Land Use Vision* (Council of the Haida Nation 2004) and *Heritage Tourism Strategy* (Haida Gwaii/Queen Charlotte Islands Heritage Tourism Strategy Working Group 2003). This included such things as clean air, expansive spaces, ancient forests, and abundant wildlife; access to abundant fresh food provided by the land and sea; mutually supportive communities, friendships, and families; a powerful heritage shaped by the living traditions, arts, and spirituality of the Haida; and a deep connection to the land and sea of Haida Gwaii (adapted from ibid., 4-5).

It also stressed the urgent need to develop an economic diversification and stability strategy for Haida Gwaii. It emphasized the maintenance of healthy ecosystems and the simultaneous development of an islands economy that could withstand fluctuations in markets elsewhere. A number of potential growth sectors were recommended for further examination, including local forestry opportunities such as a community forest, value-added wood processing, non-timber forest products, tourism, sport and commercial fishing, ecosystem restoration, arts and culture, boat building, and a variety of food production and processing.

Islands governance became a concrete way to address the issue of control of the land without speaking directly about tenure or annual allowable cut. It became the means for articulating, outside of the structural constraints of the process, a community vision for the future and options for getting there. It drew on the vision of people such as Herb Hammond (1993, 13), who contended that eco-forestry together with forest-friendly, labour-intensive practices and value-added manufacturing could create the same number of timber-related jobs as conventional logging. When added to other potential growth sectors such as tourism, the total sustainable employment opportunities could be even greater than for conventional logging. However, as Hammond (ibid.) warned: "The longer we wait, the fewer the options."

AN ACCEPTABLE LEVEL OF RISK?

For many at the table, the environmental information was the most valuable contribution of the planning process. Nonetheless, all scientific information has its limitations. As the *Environmental Conditions Report* (Holt 2005) noted, science has a fairly good understanding of what is required to maintain biological diversity and can assess whether a species or function will persist or be lost in certain conditions. What science cannot provide, however, is a general answer to the question of how much of these elements is needed. As systems ecologist James Kay (1993, 203) put it: "We can measure and analyse changes in an ecosystem, but we can only make judgements about the integrity of that system." In other words, regardless of the amount or quality of scientific information provided, "deciding what level of risk is acceptable is a social decision and cannot be answered by science" (Holt 2005, 1-9). The challenge presented by this became clearer as the range of views and information was presented to the table.

The bulk of information and analyses presented to the forum dealt with key ecosystems and species on the islands, and made recommendations for minimizing risks to ecological integrity. Much of this information confirmed what many community members already suspected: that too much of the best timber had been taken too quickly, leaving old-growth ecosystems and the creatures dependent on them at risk. Dale Lore summed up his understanding of the information:

> It's pretty plain, if we continue [logging] at the rate we're going, we can probably go another ten years before we start having extinctions. And then we can probably have another ten years if all we care about is logging. We'll lose the goshawk, we'll lose the marbled murrelet. The people that I talk to don't think that's acceptable. They don't think we have the God-given right to deliberately make it so other things can't live here.[26]

Forestry company representatives, however, disagreed with some of the technical information. Teal-Jones forester Dale Morgan called the timber projections a lie and argued that Weyerhaeuser had thirty-five to fifty years of old-growth timber left if it were to harvest at existing levels.[27] He added that as far as logging was concerned, the amount of extant old growth was not even the main issue since vast tracts of second-growth forest were maturing very quickly, and once the market was developed for them, they too would be profitably harvested.

At a more fundamental level, industry representatives disagreed with the Coast Information Team's risk thresholds for ecosystem-based management. The team identified a 30 percent reduction of old-growth forests as the low-risk threshold for maintaining ecosystem integrity, whereas a 70 percent reduction was the high-risk threshold. However, in a presentation to the forum, Weyerhaeuser's forest ecologist and member of the Coast Information Team Bill Beese accentuated the uncertainty of these conclusions.

Considered by some to be as green as they come in the forest industry, Beese helped develop Weyerhaeuser's ecosystem-based management approach in response to the 1990s consumer boycott of wood from clearcut old-growth forests on the BC coast. Weyerhaeuser's more socially acceptable alternative to clearcutting, known as the "coast forest strategy," gave the company a social licence to operate and secure market access in Europe. Its approach, however, diverged quite sharply from that of the Coast Information Team. In a presentation to the forum, Beese critiqued the Coast Information Team's risk thresholds for hydroriparian zones (30 percent harvest for high risk, 10-30 percent harvest for moderate risk, and less than 10 percent harvest for low risk) as being unrealistic. The Coast Information Team had set the risk thresholds for forests more generally at 70 percent harvest for high risk, 30-70 percent for moderate risk, and less than 30 percent for low risk. Beese argued that a 30 percent reduction of old forests presented not a "low risk" to species and ecosystems but no risk at all. In contrast to the Coast Information Team, Beese stated that a 40 to 70 percent reduction of old forests was a reasonable goal and well within the low- to moderate-risk range.[28]

A 70 percent reduction of old forests was clearly more palatable to industry. However, it completely contradicted the findings of the Coast Information Team, which put a 70 percent reduction at the high-risk threshold, after which serious risks to ecological and conservation values would be expected. If ecosystem-based management could be reduced from a well-defined scientific consensus to a concept framed by scientific uncertainty and debate, industry would be justified in advocating a largely unaltered course. Process Technical Team member John Broadhead expressed his frustration with the situation:

> This is like all things EBM [ecosystem-based management] have fallen into. There's a round table established, all kinds of interests are brought to the table, First Nations, the Province, ministries, NGOs, etc., to discuss things. Technical help is hired. Explicit measures are required and it's all numerically defined. And when things reach a certain level, then it constrains harvesting [and ecosystem-based management is compromised].[29]

Beese's presentation earned him a public dressing-down by a prominent community representative at the forum. Shortly afterward, Weyerhaeuser pulled its two well-regarded representatives from the Process Technical Team. By this time, it had become apparent that the land use planning process would not be serving the company's interests. In addition, Weyerhaeuser was in the process of selling off its forest licences on the BC coast.

Ecosystem-based management, as it was being defined by the table, clearly did not meet the interests of the forest industry. Consequently, as the process neared its conclusion, industry representatives increasingly defended the status quo. Community representatives, by contrast, rallied behind the *Haida Land Use Vision*.

8

Land Use Recommendations and the Widening Gap

Through an eighteen-month period, the Community Planning Forum devoted forty days of public meetings to reviewing, discussing, and debating issues ranging from protected areas and old-growth retention to tourism and community sustainability. Typically, a report pertaining to a specific land use concern would be presented to the forum, concluding with a set of suggestions for consideration. Table members would discuss the information, and the Process Management Team would draft recommendations on the basis of the discussions. The ultimate goal was to generate a set of recommendations that all forum members could accept.

Although scientific data and ecological studies had received much attention, the underlying issues were unavoidably political. The fundamental incompatibility of the norms and values held by community versus industry representatives came into full view as the draft recommendations were debated. In the end, the question came down to one of power and the ways in which the values and interests of one group could be made to prevail over those of another. The collaborative process increasingly shifted to confrontation as people defended their interests.

Outside of the planning process, the Haida were strengthening alliances with other BC First Nations as well as local loggers and communities on Haida Gwaii as they prepared to defend their rights at the Supreme Court of Canada.

Draft Recommendations

A *Draft Recommendations Package* (British Columbia/Council of the Haida Nation Process Management Team 2005) was presented to the table in February 2005, the last month of meetings.[1] The report was intended to encapsulate the discussions and conclusions reached by the Community Planning Forum through the eighteen-month process. Although the goal of the process was to create a set of recommendations that all forum members accepted, many areas of disagreement remained outstanding. Given the conflicting interests at the table and the contentious nature of the issues under discussion, this was perhaps unsurprising. However, as John Broadhead (2005, para. 4) noted: "What was not so expected was how the votes stacked up, and the yawning gap between the world views they represented. Instead of the usual gray configuration of sector alliances and land use zoning schemes, this planning process had split into two options – one for the industry and one for everybody else."

The recommendations package consisted of three sections: ecosystem integrity, spiritual and cultural values, and community and economic well-being. Consensus was reached on a number of less contentious issues, but conflict arose when it came to recommendations with the potential to affect logging. The diverging recommendations were listed as "viewpoints" – viewpoint 1 represented industry recommendations and viewpoint 2 represented those of the community.[2]

Ecosystem Integrity

The first broad set of recommendations concerned ecosystem integrity and included the following nine elements: protected areas, old-growth forest representation, hydroriparian ecosystems, black bears, marbled murrelets, northern goshawks, rare and threatened wildlife species, seabird colonies, and introduced species.

The first point for consideration was the Haida Protected Areas, which covered 23 percent of the islands. Existing provincially recognized protected areas on Haida Gwaii consisted of Gwaii Haanas, at 15 percent of the land, and Naikoon, at 12 percent. In addition to these legislated protected areas, viewpoint 1 ambiguously agreed to "provide protection status for a portion of the Haida Protected Areas (areas to be included not specified)" (British Columbia/Council of the Haida Nation Process Management Team 2005, 12).[3] Viewpoint 2, by contrast, recommended protection for all fourteen Haida Protected Areas, as laid out in *Haida Land Use Vision*

(Council of the Haida Nation 2004), plus the study areas recommended by the Province's Protected Areas Strategy.

There was overall agreement on the need to maintain old-growth forests and threatened plant communities but major differences arose regarding how much should be reserved. Existing policy required that 13-19 percent of old forest ecosystems be reserved in every landscape unit. Remaining largely consistent with this, viewpoint 1 called for a minimum of 20 percent old forest retention (compared with natural or pre-1800 forest levels). Viewpoint 2 called for a minimum of 70 percent old forest retention. This target was not to be achieved immediately, as that would require retention of all existing old-growth forests. Rather, it was to be reached during the next 250 years through a combination of reserving existing old forests and allowing a portion of second growth to attain old-growth characteristics. Viewpoint 2 targeted the retention per landscape unit as follows: 100 percent for protected areas, 70 percent for areas of high biodiversity, 50 percent for areas of moderate biodiversity, and 30 percent for areas of low biodiversity.

Recommendations for hydroriparian ecosystems saw a similar divergence. Viewpoint 1 called for a fifty-metre buffer along all shorelines and held that existing management practices, as legislated in the Forest Practices Code (1995), were adequate to ensure fully functioning hydroriparian ecosystems. Viewpoint 2 called for more precautionary management, including the provision of larger riparian reserves along streams, lakes, wetlands, and shorelines (two tree lengths, or an estimated average distance of eighty metres).[4] It also advocated a maximum cut rate of 20 percent of the hydroriparian forests (compared with the natural or pre-1800 hydroriparian forest levels) over twenty years in watershed areas that were not exempted from logging. In addition, viewpoint 2 supported the restoration of hydroriparian ecosystems that had been damaged by logging.

Regarding recommendations for black bears, the main issue of contention was recreational trophy hunting. Provincial policy allowed for this, but the *Haida Land Use Vision* called for a moratorium. This issue had minimal implications for industrial forestry operations, and in the end, all but one member agreed to prohibit bear hunting. However, viewpoint 1 held that current management of riparian areas was adequate for bear maintenance, whereas viewpoint 2 called for the protection of riparian habitats deemed critical for the bear.

With regard to marbled murrelets, designated protected areas and old-growth forest reserves would retain a certain degree of suitable habitat. Viewpoint 1 deemed these areas sufficient to maintain the bird's nesting

16   "Stop the bear hunt" signage. (Gowgaia Institute)

habitats. Viewpoint 2 recommended the additional protection of all murrelet habitats identified in the *Haida Land Use Vision* (Council of the Haida Nation 2004), plus protection of all class 1 habitats (most highly suitable habitat), 70 percent retention of class 2 habitats, and inclusion of class 3 habitats within the targets for old forest retention.

Everyone agreed that all known northern goshawk nest sites should be reserved within an area of approximately two hundred hectares. These goshawk reserve areas could also contribute to old-growth forest retention targets. In addition, viewpoint 2 called for the reserve of all potentially suitable nest areas and highly suitable foraging zones as well as the restoration of second-growth forests within predicted core nest areas to increase the bird's chances for survival.

At a general level, it was agreed that strategies needed to be developed to maintain and restore habitat for rare and threatened wildlife. In addition, viewpoint 2 called for the protection of saw-whet owl and great blue heron nests, as identified in the *Haida Land Use Vision* (ibid.).

Finally, recommendations for seabird colonies unanimously called for the protection of all forty-one proposed Seabird Protection Areas. There was also full agreement on the need for a comprehensive strategy to manage introduced species, including continued support for existing initiatives. In both cases, agreement was facilitated by the fact that potential impacts to logging were largely negligible.

Spiritual and Cultural Values

Recommendations for cedar and culturally important plants were listed under the heading of "Spiritual and Cultural Values." The conflicting priorities of the logging industry and local community representatives again arose around cedar. Viewpoint 1 maintained that future cultural requirements for cedar were adequately addressed through the protected areas and old-growth forest reserves, and suggested that current legislation and policy were sufficient to protect culturally modified and archaeological cedars. Viewpoint 2, however, called for the reserve of all the archaeological and cultural cedar areas identified in the *Haida Land Use Vision* (ibid.) and supported the Council of the Haida Nation's thousand-year cedar strategy for the protection and management of cultural cedar.

Regarding culturally important plants, only a viewpoint 2 was presented. Although this might suggest disagreement on recommendations, no alternative was given. Viewpoint 2 called for the implementation of Haida Cultural Value Surveys across the land base, with priority accorded to areas slated for logging. The Haida had recently employed these surveys as a tool to identify and preserve areas containing important cultural values.[5] In addition, the viewpoint recommended that rare cultural and medicinal plant sites be reserved, and that commercial harvest of Haida medicinal plants and yew be prohibited.

Community and Economic Well-Being

This section covered six topics: community sustainability, tourism and recreation, visual management, non-timber forest products, timber resources, and minerals. Overall, recommendations concerning the first four had a high degree of agreement, but viewpoints again diverged when it came to timber resources and minerals.

The recommendations for community sustainability agreed that various studies should be undertaken, most importantly a comprehensive economic opportunities study to assist transitional planning for island communities. There was also consensus on potential areas for economic growth and the need to maintain local opportunities for food gathering and resource harvesting. There was even agreement that a resource management board should be established. However, the viewpoints differed regarding its role. Viewpoint 1 held that the board should be advisory and restricted to issues related to the land use plan. Viewpoint 2 stated that it should have decision-making power in island land issues more generally. A third viewpoint took an intermediate position, recommending that the board initially play an advisory role and evolve to a larger decision-making role in prescribed areas to be determined later.

Recommendations concerning tourism and recreation met with full agreement. They included support for implementation of the Heritage Tourism Strategy, management of key trails and boat anchorages, development of a sports-fishing strategy, and promotion of local tourism development opportunities. There was also consensus on visual management recommendations and strategies to preserve high-quality viewscapes.

Agreement was also reached on recommendations for non-timber forest products. They included establishing an advisory board to oversee the harvesting and marketing of these products, in a manner respectful of Haida cultural values, maintaining and managing opportunities to harvest on the islands, and exploring potential opportunities to market other non-timber forest products.

A number of general objectives were accepted for timber resources, including improving communications between competing interests, respecting and protecting forest values other than timber, and maintaining a sustainable forest resource on the islands. There was also consensus on generating opportunities for local processing and forest-based employment. However, differences arose regarding forest certification, annual allowable cut, labour-saving technology, and tenure allocation. Viewpoint 1 suggested that current practices be maintained in all these areas, apart from pursuing some form of forest certification. Viewpoint 2 recommended that higher-level forest certification be pursued for logging activities and that ecologically appropriate rates of harvest be used to determine the annual allowable cut. Viewpoint 2 also called for the use of employment-maximizing forest practices wherever possible and for adjustment of forest tenures to optimize the achievement of community benefits and environmental objectives.

Finally, recommendations for minerals were not approved by forum members at the last meeting, due to time constraints. For this reason, the *Draft Recommendations Package* (British Columbia/Council of the Haida Nation Process Management Team 2005) characterized them as "perspectives" rather than "viewpoints." At a general level, it was agreed that mining should respect Haida and local values, and should provide local benefit. However, perspectives diverged on the question of consultation and access. For perspective 1, a process that *sought* local consensus was sufficient, whereas perspective 2 held that exploration and development plans must be *approved* by the local community prior to commencement. On the topic of access, perspective 1 called for access to exploration in all areas outside of protected areas (which was consistent with provincial policy). Perspective 2 advocated the restriction of mining-related activities in ecologically sensitive reserves and watersheds with important fish values, and it recommended a number of additional procedures to minimize potential environmental impacts.

The key recommendations of the two viewpoints are summarized in Table 2.

In the end, all recommendations put forward by the community were fully consistent with the *Haida Land Use Vision* and followed the Coast Information Team's recommendations for ecosystem-based management. By contrast, industry's recommendations followed neither the *Haida Land Use Vision* nor the recommendations for ecosystem-based management. After the nearly two-year process, positions were now more refined but just as polarized and perhaps even more entrenched than before.

Industry representatives seemed relatively comfortable with the *Draft Recommendations Package.* In general, they maintained that land use planning was best left to forestry professionals and elected government. Teal-Jones forester Dale Morgan commented: "I thought it was good we had two options. Then I hoped we would have government-to-government discussions and that industry would be involved in ... modelling how much volume [of timber] would be left. Then there would be a serious look at the recommendations with the provincial government making the final decision."[6] Accustomed to influencing forestry decisions, industry expected its professional data to trump the recommendations of the community. This sentiment was not shared by the majority of the table.

A Vote for Change

When a preliminary version of the land use recommendations was presented to the table in December 2004, the reception was less than enthusiastic. Guujaaw, president of the Council of the Haida Nation, stated unequivocally that including recommendations that compromised the *Haida Land Use Vision* was unacceptable. He concluded that the Province had "no real

TABLE 2 **Summary of recommendations and viewpoints**

Land use concern	Viewpoint 1	Viewpoint 2
Protected areas	Unspecified "portion" of Haida Protected Areas	All Haida Protected Areas and Provincial Study Areas
Old-growth retention	Minimum 20% island-wide	Minimum 70% island-wide
Hydroriparian ecosystems	Maintain current management; 50 m riparian reserves on all shorelines	Two tree lengths (80 m) riparian reserves on headwater streams, valley-bottom transport and deposition streams, lakes, wetlands, and shorelines
Black bears	Hunting permitted;[a] maintain current riparian management	Hunting prohibited; reserve critical riparian habitats
Marbled murrelets	Needs addressed through protected areas and old-growth reserves	Reserve habitats identified in *Haida Land Use Vision* plus all class 1 habitats, 70% retention of class 2 habitats, and inclusion of class 3 habitats in old-growth targets
Northern goshawks	Reserve all nest sites (200 ha)	Reserve all known and potentially suitable nest areas and highly suitable foraging areas; restore second growth in predicted core nest areas
Rare and threatened wildlife	Develop strategies to maintain and restore habitat	Same as viewpoint 1 plus reserve known saw-whet owl and great blue heron nests
Seabird colonies	Protect all Seabird Protection Areas	Agreement
Cedar	Addressed through protected areas and old-growth reserves	Reserve all archaeological and cultural cedar areas identified in *Haida Land Use Vision*
Culturally important plants	No recommendations	Implement Haida Cultural Value Surveys across land base; reserve rare cultural and medicinal plant sites; prohibit commercial harvest of Haida medicinal plants and yew

▶

◄   **TABLE 2**

Land use concern	Viewpoint 1	Viewpoint 2
Community sustainability	Undertake economic opportunities study; maintain local food-gathering and resource-harvesting opportunities; establish resource management board with advisory role	Same as viewpoint 1, but establish resource management board with decision-making power on land use issues more generally
Tourism and recreation	Support Heritage Tourism Strategy; manage key trails; promote local tourism	Agreement
Visual management	Agreement on scenic areas and strategies for maintaining visual quality	Agreement
Non-timber forest products	Establish advisory board; explore market opportunities	Agreement
Timber resources	Agreement on various general objectives; maintain current procedures apart from pursuing forest certification	Pursue higher-level forest certification; determine allowable annual cut using ecologically appropriate rates; use employment maximizing forest practices; adjust forest tenures
Minerals	Consultation process to seek local consensus; access to all areas outside protected areas	Approval of plans by local community prior to exploration; mining restriction in protected areas, ecologically sensitive reserves, and important fish-bearing watersheds

a Bear hunting was supported by only one member of the forum.

interest in dealing with the Haida properly" and asserted that its real intention was only to "settle things down for a while" until the next five-year cut could be established.[7] Council of the Haida Nation representative Gary Russ described the table as "self-serving for government and industry." Cultural heritage tourism representative Vince Collison added: "The people have said in no uncertain terms that the status quo is not good enough and has to change. This has to be reflected in the plan, or the Haida are not willing to sign it."

In addition, many forum members were frustrated and angered when the major forest licensees rejected recommendations put forward for ecosystem-based management without providing any workable alternatives. They demanded that licensees be required to provide constructive solutions rather than simply rejecting their proposal. For the forum's final month of meetings in February 2005, the licensees' recommendations for ecosystem-based management were inserted directly into the *Draft Recommendations Package,* alongside the community recommendations, without ever having been discussed at the table. In addition, industry's recommendations were listed as "viewpoint 1," which for some members implied that it was the preferred option. The community's priorities appeared patronized and the guiding documents trivialized.

Outraged, community representatives demanded to know how the industry option, which followed neither the *Haida Land Use Vision* nor the *Ecosystem-Based Management Framework,* could be given equal footing with the community's recommendations. Husby Forest Products vice-president Bob Brash stated that their forestry professionals had some major concerns with the community recommendations and that he did not want to discuss certain technical issues with "non-experts." Hereditary chief Allan Wilson responded: "I've also consulted with my experts – my parents, grandparents, uncles and aunts – and they know *exactly* what they're talking about."[8]

The table had previously agreed not to vote on subjects under discussion, but community representatives now requested that votes be taken to show the broad support for the community recommendations. The results showed that viewpoint 1 (industry recommendations) was supported by an average of three votes.[9] By contrast, viewpoint 2 (community recommendations) was supported by an average of thirteen to fourteen votes.[10] Industry representatives insisted that community members did not understand the immense socio-economic impacts of viewpoint 2. It appeared, however, that community representatives had chosen to vote against what they knew to be the socio-economic impacts of the status quo.

The task of turning forum deliberations and debate into draft land use policy recommendations had been left primarily in the hands of the provincially appointed managers for the process. Their job was to sort, prioritize, and translate the input from forum discussions to create recommendations with technical planning functionality. This inevitably involved engaging their expert knowledge and rationality, which was attuned to techno-scientific analysis and expert modes of reasoning. With this professional bias, it might be expected that some priorities, values, and meanings expressed by community members would be lost in translation – and there were frequent complaints to this effect. But a more significant constraint was the Province's legal, administrative, and institutional framework, which was based on and geared toward dominant forms of knowledge, valuing, and reasoning. Industry's recommendations readily fit within this broader framework; the community's did not. Thus, regardless of goodwill or reflexivity to promote an alternative agenda, provincial planners were faced with the disciplinary power of the dominant knowledge discourse, legal and administrative frameworks, and government priorities.

Similarly, the Haida-appointed process managers were at a disadvantage when it came to influencing the process. Puzzled by the angry response to the *Draft Recommendation Package,* a provincial representative pointed out that the process had been co-managed by the Haida Nation and that the Haida had reviewed every section of the report.[11] A Haida representative, however, explained the situation differently:

> We tried to work and make it a co-managed process, but it was a fight along the way. The government team we worked with had already worked on a lot of these plans before. They had a set of expectations of what worked and what didn't, and they really weren't going to budge from what their expectations were ...
>
> It came out like it did in the last meeting because the Province allowed industry to put forward that option, and it didn't follow EBM [ecosystem-based management] or the HLUV *[Haida Land Use Vision].* That's what we kept saying, "Why are we allowing [industry] to have this in here when it's not EBM?" And they said, "We're just allowing both parties to put their positions forward, like having book ends."[12]

Even before the report was completed, a group of community representatives predicted that it would not adequately reflect their interests. In response, they developed their own document, titled *Draft Islands Declaration*

(2005), to express, without translation, the community's recommendations. A starting assumption of the twenty-nine-page document was that tough decisions were inevitable and that "if we do not make them now, they will be made for us in another decade when those forests are gone" (ibid., 1). It emphasized the imperative to "meet the needs of the islands' communities" by optimizing benefits accruing to local communities from local resources, implementing strategies to minimize short-term impacts on forestry employees, and identifying opportunities to diversify the island economy (ibid., 3). It reiterated the recommendations for old-growth forest and hydroriparian ecosystems put forward by community ecosystem representatives. Finally, it laid out a proposal for implementing local governance through an Islands' Community Council. The stated intention of the document was to strengthen the position of community recommendations in upcoming government-to-government negotiations.

The *Draft Islands Declaration* made a strong statement on community values, visions, and aspirations, further consolidating the community's unified stance. However, in its effort to speak on behalf of all community representatives, it incorporated aspects of the *Haida Land Use Vision* without involving any Haida individuals. This made it somewhat problematic, since, as one Haida person commented: "I don't like anyone speaking on my behalf, whether it's my friend or the government. You never give your voice away ... It's like giving your power away."[13] The Haida stated that their interests were already clearly expressed through the *Haida Land Use Vision* and suggested that if the communities wished to generate a statement, they should do so on their own behalf.[14] Nevertheless, the Council of the Haida Nation acknowledged the value of the document and expressed interest in pursuing it further with its authors.

As the forum drew to a close, key forestry issues remained unresolved. It had previously been agreed that outstanding conflicts would be resolved through government-to-government negotiations between the Council of the Haida Nation and the Province. In an attempt to strengthen the position of the community's recommendations, several motions were made at the final forum meeting. These included that the land use plan be grounded in the *Haida Land Use Vision;* that a locally defined form of ecosystem-based management be rooted in the *Haida Land Use Vision;* and that, until a final land use plan was completed, a logging moratorium be established in areas designated for protection by the *Haida Land Use Vision.*

These motions received overwhelming community support, but the Province was not obligated to move on any of them. In fact, the recently amended Forest and Range Practices Act made it increasingly difficult for the Province to take any alternative course of action. The new Land Use Objectives Regulation (British Columbia 2005, s. 2(2)(b)) stated that a minister who wished to significantly amend a land use objective "must be satisfied that ... the importance of the land use objective or amendment outweighs any adverse impact on opportunities for timber harvesting or forage use within or adjacent to the area that will be affected." This under-lined the prevailing culture of corporatist dominance and "the propensity of British Columbia governments of all political stripes ... to find ways of accommodating the requirements of global capital through lower operating costs, weakened unions, and 'open for business' investment strategies" (Salazar and Alper 1996, 386).

The Haida would also face another disadvantage in negotiations. No agreement had been reached on interim forestry measures that would temporarily protect certain areas from logging until a land use plan was finalized. Apart from the Haida Protected Areas, which had been un-officially set aside since early 2000, the Province maintained that existing policy and legislation would continue to govern logging until a land use plan was in place. However, now that proposed areas for protection were clearly laid out, it made sense from an industry perspective to log them while they were still open for business. And when logging companies ap-plied for cut-block approvals in these contentious areas, provincial policy dictated that the local Ministry of Forests office had to approve them. The effect was to pressure the Haida into agreeing to a land use plan if they wished to avoid an extended talk-and-log scenario. This behaviour was inconsistent with the recent Supreme Court of Canada ruling, which legally obligated the Province to meaningfully consult and accommodate Haida interests in decisions affecting the land. However, the Province had yet to take that ruling seriously.

MAKING A MOCKERY

Considering the contentiousness of logging on the islands and the recent court rulings in favour of the Haida, the government's response to the concerns of islanders seemed short-sighted. At the same time, it was con-sistent with the radical deregulation that was occurring simultaneously with the planning process. In a move labelled by environmentalists as unprecedented in modern democracies, a barrage of amendments and re-peals to the Forest Act and Forest Practices Code were made between 2002 and 2004. These changes gave forestry companies an unprecedented degree of control, while legislating provincial authority out. Measures to protect the environment could be applied only "without unduly reducing the supply of timber," keeping in line with the government's emphasis on a "vigorous, efficient and world competitive" industry (British Columbia 2004a, ss. 5, 7, 8, 9; British Columbia 2004b).

In addition, government consent was no longer required when Crown tenures (rights to log on public and indigenous land) were sold or transferred. This eliminated an important tool available to First Nations to ensure that new licence-holders accommodated their Aboriginal rights and interests prior to purchase, or even returned some lands to First Nations. The new legislation also allowed logging companies to remove private lands from a tree farm licence, thereby exempting them from certain requirements. Companies were originally given access to Crown forest lands and granted tax exemptions and subsidies on the condition that their private lands would be managed under the same rules as the rest of the tenure. Extracting private lands from Crown tenures allowed not only for the removal of such things as cut controls, silviculture obligation, and restrictions on log exports, but also for the subdivision of the more idyllically situated areas, which could then be sold as real estate for enormous profits.

In response, First Nations throughout the province formed the Title and Rights Alliance to prevent infringements of their Aboriginal title and rights arising from the recent amendments. In May 2004, over 2,400 First Nations members and supporters rallied at the BC legislature, demanding fair negotiations and accommodation of their interests and rights. Nevertheless, two months later, Weyerhaeuser received approval to remove almost ninety thousand hectares of private lands from their coastal tree farm licences, including some twenty thousand hectares from tree farm licence (TFL) 39 on Haida Gwaii. Affected First Nations and communities were not consulted. On Haida Gwaii, the announcement prompted a march on the Ministry of Forests office to denounce the removal of the private lands and to demand a halt to excessive logging on the islands.

In March 2004, the Haida were back in court with the TFL 39 appeal. Previously, the BC Supreme Court had found that the government had a moral but not a legal duty to consult with the Haida on logging in TFL 39. The BC Court of Appeal reversed the ruling, finding that both the government and Weyerhaeuser had a duty to consult with and accommodate the Haida regardless of the fact that their title claim was not yet legally proven. This time, the Supreme Court of Canada was to decide whether the Province and Weyerhaeuser were obligated to consult and accommodate Haida interests in the transfer of TFL 39. The new hearing brought an unprecedented development, when the village of Port Clements, with Dale Lore as mayor, requested intervenor status on behalf of the Haida.

For Lore, the turning point came when he saw the Ministry of Forests' projections, which showed that, if current management of the forests continued, the timber that his community relied on would be gone by 2027 and no new logging would take place for twenty years. This was the so-called "falldown" effect, the decline in timber supply associated with the time between the depletion of old-growth forests and the commercial viability of second-growth forests. It was not rocket science for Lore to see that his forestry-dependent community would collapse during twenty years without logging. He urged the government to act but was brushed off. "You're the mayor of a small community," he was told. "What are you going to do about it?" He realized that his first priority as mayor was to ensure that the land could provide for his community into the future – and he could see only one way out of the predicament.[15]

Lore was well versed in the politics of land and title on Haida Gwaii. As a new councillor, he had attended a 1992 Union of British Columbia Municipalities meeting and had publicly pressed the premier into assuring him that he would not be excluded from future land claim discussions that might affect his community. This soon led to a showdown between Lore and the Haida, when Lore arrived unannounced and uninvited at a meeting between the Haida, the Province, and select environmentalists. Determined to take his place at the table, Lore challenged the Haida to work with island communities instead of with a government that had repeatedly demonstrated its lack of credibility. When he obstinately refused to leave, the Haida made him a private proposition: if Lore would voluntarily leave the meeting, he would be allowed to observe future negotiations. Lore conceded and the Haida honoured their promise.[16]

Now, two days before the 2004 court hearing, the Haida were holding a *How'aa* (meaning thank you) feast in Port Clements, the first Haida feast to be hosted in a non-Haida village. More extraordinary was the agreement that was signed that night. The old conflicts between loggers and Haida seemed a thing of the past as the Council of the Haida Nation and the villages of Port Clements and Masset signed the groundbreaking *Protocol Agreement* (Council of the Haida Nation and the Municipalities of Port Clements and Masset 2004). In it, Port Clements and Masset recognized Haida title, and, in return, the Haida Nation guaranteed individual property rights and shared islands governance.[17] The agreement reconciled injustices of a colonial past while at the same time providing assurances of a shared future for all islanders, Haida and non-Haida alike. For Dale Lore, this was a prerequisite for his support of the Haida at the Supreme Court of Canada. Guujaaw explained the situation further: "If there was no such thing as Aboriginal title, each community's fate would be in the hands of the Crown. These logs would continue to go out as they have been, and they'd have no qualms about shutting down communities. Haida title has empowered the whole island community to push back."[18]

The presiding judge for the hearing was Chief Justice Beverley McLachlin, the first female chief justice in the history of the Supreme Court of Canada. In a radio interview shortly after her appointment, she was asked how she would be different from previous chief justices. Her answer was clear: she would consider not only the law but also the consequence of her decision. This was the most important clue for the Haida in the lead-up to the hearing. It meant that the opinions and perceptions of the broader society mattered, and support by the non-Haida communities was critical.[19]

At the Supreme Court, the Province and Weyerhaeuser (a huge multinational forestry company) set out to convince the court that the world would collapse if they ruled in the Haida's favour. Acting as intervenors for them were nine provinces, the BC Chamber of Commerce, the BC Chamber of Mines, the Cattlemen's Association, and many others. In their presentations to the court, they stressed that economies would fail and thousands of livelihoods would be ruined if they were required to consult and accommodate First Nations on every decision that might affect Aboriginal rights.

On the Haida's side were Kitimaat Village, the First Nation Summit, and the mayors of Port Clements and Masset, the only two incorporated municipalities on the islands at the time. The Port Clements intervenor statement made a powerful case for the greater public interest of Haida Gwaii in requesting that Weyerhaeuser's appeal be dismissed. The essence of its argument was that Port Clements believed that the Haida were more capable than the Province of sustainably managing the forest:

> The resolution of the question before the Court goes to the continued existence of Port Clements as a community. While the residents of Port Clements are dependent on logging operations for their livelihood, they are also socially and economically integrated into the local Haida community. The members of these communities live and work together and share much

of the same long-term vision of sustainability of the forest and the future of Haida Gwaii ...

The future of Port Clements depends on finding local, workable accommodations. Neither the province nor Weyerhaeuser share the aspirations or concerns of Port Clements.

Port Clements submits that, if Haida interests are protected through workable accommodations, the island community would be better served than the status quo is providing. There is also far greater likelihood that the public interest which Port Clements represents will be protected.

In contrast to the position taken by the Appellants [Weyerhaeuser and British Columbia] and their supporting intervenors, Port Clements submits that the concerns, interests and objectives of the Haida and the local non-aboriginal community are compatible and complementary. The Haida have pursued this issue because of their concerns about the rate of logging, the method of logging and the environmental effects of logging in T.F.L. 39 Block 6   Port Clements has the same concerns. Furthermore, Port Clements submits that these concerns are not being addressed by the province or industry. ("Village of Port Clements Intervenor Statement" 2004, 3)

In November 2004, the court handed down its groundbreaking decision. It upheld the previous BC Court of Appeal ruling confirming that the provincial government was indeed obligated to consult with First Nations prior to making decisions that might adversely impact their Aboriginal rights and title. The duty was always engaged and did not require a treaty or court ruling on title. However, the 2004 decision differed from that of the appeal court in that Weyerhaeuser was not under the same obligation to consult; the responsibility rested with the Province to direct industry. In the words of the Supreme Court decision:

The government's duty to consult with Aboriginal peoples and accommodate their interests is grounded in the principle of the honour of the Crown, which must be understood generously ... the Crown, acting honourably, cannot cavalierly run roughshod over Aboriginal interests where claims affecting these interests are being seriously pursued ... The foundation of the duty in the Crown's honour and the goal of reconciliation suggest that the duty arises when the Crown has knowledge, real or constructive, of the potential existence of the Aboriginal right or title and contemplates conduct that might adversely affect it. (*Haida Nation v. British Columbia [Minister of Forests]* 2004, para. 27)

First Nations across British Columbia hailed the ruling as a major victory that would end the Province's long-held position that it was not required to accommodate First Nations interests until title claims were legally proven. First Nations Summit political executive member Dave Porter described the ruling as "a tremendous victory felt throughout the indigenous world" and "a wakeup call for the government of British Columbia and Canada."[20] Guujaaw's assessment was more cautious: "We can be sure the victory won't be known unless we go out there and get it" (quoted in "Supreme Court of Canada Ruling ..." 2004, 11).

Three months later, Guujaaw's remark proved prophetic, when, just a week before the Community Planning Forum was to hold its final meetings, Brascan Corporation announced that it had reached a deal with Weyerhaeuser to acquire its coastal "assets," including TFL 39 on Haida Gwaii. The Province's decision to permit the removal of Weyerhaeuser's private lands had been a critical factor in the lucrative $1.2 billion deal with Brascan, an industrial conglomerate with interests in real estate. Once again, the Haida were not consulted, and their interests were not accommodated despite three court rulings in their favour. For its part, the Province now claimed that it had no authority over the licence transfer. In fact, it had conveniently legislated itself out of the duty to approve transfers while the TFL 39 case was making its way through the court system. This had not gone unnoticed by Chief Justice McLachlin, whose ruling stated that the Province was to use legislation to fulfill rather than avoid its obligation to First Nations (*Haida Nation v. British Columbia [Minister of Forests]* 2004).

The final blow came when, only days after the final Community Planning Forum meeting, the Province authorized Husby Forest Products to log in areas designated for murrelet protection. Guujaaw charged the government with making a mockery of the land use planning process. Reflecting on the situation, he commented: "There is a pattern in tying people up in process while, at the same time, the Crown puts itself in a box where bureaucrats have no ability to do anything but say yes to industry."[21]

In the end, despite the extensive procedural design and sincere efforts by process managers and coordinators of the Community Planning Forum to create a bottom-up participatory process, politics and power relations remained problematic. Relations of dominance within the broader legal frameworks, policies, and rules penetrated the process and restricted the extent to which alternative knowledge, values, and rationality were able to influence decisions.

9

Uprising

H aida and community representatives had put their best efforts into promoting new meanings and creating change through the collaborative planning process. However, it now became clear that the Province had no intention of acting on their recommendations. Despite the theoretical intentions of deliberative planning, the reality remained: if a new meaning threatens dominant interests, it will be delegitimized by the existing social order. In such circumstances, if the new meaning is to proceed toward social change, a major collective action is likely required. As collaborative planning reached its limit, Haida and community members prepared to take their stand to the road.

This chapter examines the logging blockade that was launched to oppose the actions of Weyerhaeuser and the Province. It highlights the discursive framework that the Haida and their community allies developed to explain and legitimize their actions. This is contrasted with the counter images that arose as a new direction for land use began to emerge on the islands. The chapter explores the discourses, strategies, and tactics used to shift power dynamics, both during and after the blockade. It underlines the important roles played by planning, scientific knowledge, negotiation skills, and leadership in the final outcome.

Enough is Enough

When the Province demonstrated its intent to ignore both the court rulings and the community recommendations for land use, the time had come to change gears. The Haida Nation made their decision to blockade. However, unlike twenty years ago at Lyell Island, when only Haida people were to take a stand, this time all islanders were invited to stand with them. John Broadhead remarked: "The local willingness and readiness to go to the barricades, go on the road, is back in a way it was in the mid-eighties ... People see that some emphatic statements have to be made. Positions have to be taken because the Crown has no honour."[1]

Islanders knew full well that protest action could be effective. As Gowgaia Institute co-director Simon Davies stated: "The gains we've been making here have not been through legislative processes or following a plan that the Crown may have in mind. The gains we've made were outside the system through pressuring and changing things in other ways ... The legislation isn't our problem, it's the Province's."[2]

At the same time, even though the Lyell Island blockade had been a huge success, blockades more commonly ended with court-ordered injunctions affably granted to resource-extracting companies and a quick return to business-as-usual, with protesters escorted out of the way. In addition, a blockade would invariably deprive some forestry workers and community members of their immediate livelihood, which raised the spectre of local opposition and condemnation. Industry supporters, moreover, could be relied on to denounce the action as misguided and harmful to long-term community interests. Thus, a decision to launch a blockade required strong justification as well as a reasonable expectation of success.

The current situation, however, presented an interesting set of circumstances. The provincial government was in a legally precarious situation: it had neglected to consult with the Haida Nation regarding the latest transfer and renewal of tree farm licence (TFL) 39, despite the Supreme Court decision that obligated it to do so. In addition, it had shown little regard for the community consensus as expressed in the land use planning process. Perhaps most importantly, the government was entering an election campaign and wanted desperately to avoid bad publicity involving conflict with disgruntled Natives and communities. This was especially true, given that the premier had recently committed with great fanfare to developing a "new relationship" with First Nations, which would be based on respect, recognition, and reconciliation of Aboriginal rights and title.[3]

Weyerhaeuser's situation was also unique. The company was on the verge of closing its $1.2 billion deal with Brascan Corporation and in many ways was on its way out of the scene. However, the Council of the Haida Nation was accusing Weyerhaeuser of breaching five points of the six-point agreement it had made with the Haida Nation and Forest Workers

Association in 2002. The company was charged with adding two mechanical harvesters after agreeing not to acquire more, failing to support maximum employment for islanders, refusing to safeguard cedar for Haida cultural use, and generally lacking respect for cultural, community, and environmental values.

The Haida also contended that Weyerhaeuser had accelerated its cutting of the finest old-growth cedar while it negotiated its deal with Brascan. The company now had approximately sixty days to liquidate this valuable timber before the deal with Brascan would be complete. If the deal went through, Brascan would be looking for quick returns on its investment, and residents feared that this would mean a faster rate of logging with little hope for improvement. Even if the tree farm licence were to be acquired locally, as the Haida hoped, months of engineering and millions of dollars in operational costs would be expended before they cut their first saleable piece of timber. However, if Weyerhaeuser's operations were stopped now, the cut timber would remain where it was, and business could profitably be picked up by a local owner tomorrow.[4]

For all these reasons, the timing for a blockade seemed both critical and favourable. Although there was a risk that an injunction could shut the blockade down, the Haida leadership felt compelled to take action. Guujaaw was confident that the Crown would not be able to convince any court that it acted honourably. Given the Province's indifference to the Supreme Court decision, he remarked that it "would be embarrassed to go before the courts for an injunction at this point."[5]

A place-centred ideology now united a large number of islanders. Threatened by the prevailing economic and political system, they shared a connection with the land, a concern for the well-being of the forests and stability of their communities, an attachment to a unique way of life, and an emerging consensus around respect for Haida title and shared local control. Their experience of resource industrialization was in sharp contrast to the official ideology that promised benefits to all. Instead they saw their future severely compromised by the forest industry and a government that had repeatedly demonstrated its lack of accountability.

Shortly before the blockades went up, the Haida Nation received a letter from the Ministry of Forests, responding to its concerns regarding the lack of consultation in the Weyerhaeuser deal. The ministry defended its position, maintaining that, under the new forestry regulations, the Crown had no authority over the licence transfer and therefore was not obligated to consult with the Haida. Subsequently, the Haida wrote to the governor general, Adrienne Clarkson, asking her to intervene in the situation and

restore the honour of the Crown.[6] Public meetings were then held in the
reserve village of Skidegate and in Port Clements to inform islanders of
the plans for the blockade. In Port Clements, residents argued that the
real problem was the barging of raw logs rather than logging per se. Such
was the dissatisfaction with Weyerhaeuser that resident loggers were willing
to support the blockade if organizers agreed to shut down the barges.[7]

A website for the action was also created and its first bulletin read as
follows:

> We have made alliances and partnerships and entered processes in good
> faith in attempts to balance the interests of the land and culture with an
> economy. We have also shown that the "Island Community" is compatible
> with Haida Aboriginal Title during this time and have presented jointly
> supported solutions for resolve.
>
> In the past two years, the province has taken the approach of getting out
> of the way of industry, and practically handed all management responsibility
> and accountability to the companies. Never in the history of the province
> has a government been so weak in its ability to manage and regulate natural
> resource industries.
>
> After an 18-month "Land Use Planning" process and strong consensus
> among the Island people, the BC Ministry of Forests continues to com-
> promise the outcome through approval of logging inside of areas cited for
> protection.
>
> Weyerhaeuser has shown no respect for the land, the culture, or the
> people who have worked for them. Weyerhaeuser has also shown no respect
> for its own word. In commitments made to the CHN [Council of the
> Haida Nation], the communities and the people who work for them, five
> of the six commitments have been violated. Now the company is poised
> to sell its interests and in its final hours is attempting to strip all that it can
> from this land.
>
> The opportunity to design a future that maintains the land and culture
> while providing for a sustainable economy is in our hands. The next genera-
> tion will not have the same chance if the forest industry is allowed to strip
> our lands in the next few years. (Council of the Haida Nation 2005a)

On 22 March 2005, the barricades went up. Guujaaw asserted that when
reason and diplomacy fail, the spirit rises. This reflected the name chosen
for the blockade, Islands Spirit Rising.[8] Two public roads were obstructed
to prevent Weyerhaeuser from accessing its logging operations and the BC
Forest Service from entering its offices. Other traffic, however, was allowed

17 Blocking the road to Weyerhaeuser's log sort. Front row, kneeling, left to right: Aaron Riis, Ryan Smith, Todd DeVries, Beau Dick, Terri Russ, and Jaalen Edenshaw. Standing, left to right: Gwaai Edenshaw, Shawn Peacock, Owen Jones, Dwight Russ, Ernie Swanson, Brodie Swanson, Leo Gagnon, Nate Jolley, Sue Cowpar, Arnie Bellis, Richard Watts, Rodney White, Wilson Brown, Allan Wilson Jr., James Wilson, Matthew Brown, Jana Braman McLeod, and Floyd Young. (Joanne Mills)

18 Checkpoint on Highway 16 in Queen Charlotte. Left to right, Allan Wilson Jr., Matthew Brown, Elliot Jones, Richard Watts, Terri Russ, and Sue Cowpar. (Robert Mills)

to pass, warranting the term "checkpoints" rather than "blockades" for these sites. Staffed around the clock by both Haida and non-Haida community members, the checkpoints prevented more than a hundred loggers from going to work. At Weyerhaeuser's log-sorting facilities, hundreds of valuable cedars waited to be shipped out, but no barge came or left. Even if a barge had managed to evade the local fishing boats that held watch over the inlet, there would be no workers at the dock to load it.

On the second day of the blockade, the Haida Nation placed seizure notices on logs that Weyerhaeuser had recently cut, which were estimated to be worth $5-10 million.[9] The Haida announced that they had seized the logs in response to Weyerhaeuser's breach of contract. The news hit the national media. A team of well-connected people took charge of media relations on Haida Gwaii, with Gilbert Parnell of the Council of the Haida Nation, Port Clements mayor Dale Lore, and Haida Nation president Guujaaw acting as lead spokespersons. Guujaaw declared that the money from the sale of the logs would provide much-needed support to the underfunded schools and hospital on the islands, as well as to youth and cultural programs. The money could provide a huge boost to the local economy, although it translated to only about five barges of timber – a small fraction of the 250 or so barges that went out during some years.[10]

Standing at the barricade, Guujaaw's son Gwaai Edenshaw commented: "We are not against people trying to eke out a living from the resources – we are against corporations making a money grab ... I have seen what the corporations have been doing here all my life. Things are just getting worse. This blockade is something we have been waiting for practically all our lives" (quoted in Hearne 2005).

Thanks to the land use planning process, allegations that logging firms and the Province had disregarded the needs and wishes of the communities were now supported by detailed maps and analyses with concrete figures for logging rates, endangered species, dwindling habitats, and risks to ecosystems. At a time when biodiversity research was facing severe cuts across Canada, the planning process had provided substantial funding for this critical research. The assertions of the Haida and environmentalists, once labelled as parochial or exaggerated, had now been validated by an independent team of research scientists. Moreover, the process had strengthened relationships and mutual trust between islanders, which allowed them to put forward a collective community vision that was firmly rooted in the *Haida Land Use Vision*.

Despite the inherently confrontational nature of a blockade, the atmosphere at the checkpoints was amiable, with those staffing the checkpoints

19   Seizure notice on logs cut by Weyerhaeuser. (Mare Levesque)

and those driving through them generally knowing each other by name. Most islanders acknowledged that the status quo could not persist, even if they did not support the blockade per se. The people at the checkpoints varied from a few overnighters to sometimes more than a hundred during the day. Food was provided by guests, community members, and local businesses, and an account was set up for donations to cover other expenses. Islanders from all walks of life, including loggers and ex-loggers, began discovering common ground as they chatted around the fires.

At the Yakoun River checkpoint, organizers constructed a permanent cabin so that elders could more comfortably visit the site. In the Yakoun camp, Haida artisans undertook a variety of projects, including weaving cedar hats from traditionally prepared bark strips and carving cedar masks and argillite sculptures. Haida carver Christian White remarked that the blockade had become a part of the Haida's cultural reawakening (McCullough 2005). Acclaimed Kwakwaka'wakw artist Beau Dick joined the team of carvers who were working on a multi-person drum, two eighteen-foot cedar canoes, and an impressive thirty-six-foot cedar canoe. All three canoes were constructed from trees that had blown down – a common phenomenon when forests are logged and the remaining adjacent trees are exposed to strong winds ("Story from the Yakoun No. 4" 2005).

20   Discussing around the fire. Standing: Dale Lore and Guujaaw. (Roberta Aiken)

In the evenings, people gathered around a bonfire for drumming, singing, and storytelling. Distinguished Haida artist Robert Davidson emphasized that the action was not about winning – it was about who they were becoming (Council of the Haida Nation 2005c).

However, not all islanders were happy about the blockade. Of the hundred or so forestry employees who were prevented from working, about half were from Port Clements. Although most loggers agreed that the forestry situation needed to be resolved, many were skeptical about a solution that put them out of work. At a public meeting held at Port Clements the day before the blockade began, one logger demanded: "Why are you stepping on us?" (quoted in Rinfret 2005c, 9). Many loggers already felt financially stretched; they had had only a couple of weeks of work that year on top of a poor work year the year before. Now, just as Weyerhaeuser was about to call them back, the blockade had put them out of work. Guujaaw responded: "We are not recklessly making an action ... to hurt the people here. We want to kick Weyerhaeuser in the butt on their way out the door and slam it before the other guy gets in" (ibid.).

21 Robert Davidson addressing the crowd at the Queen Charlotte checkpoint. Foreground facing, left to right: Captain Gold, Sara Eaton, Robert Davidson, and Cindy Boyko. (Roberta Aiken)

Few islanders could disagree with the goal of greater local control. Another logger conceded: "Short-term it's tough, but long-term it could be the solution" (ibid.).

Whereas community activists framed the blockade in terms of an urgent need to maintain environmental, community, and cultural values, logging companies argued that the demands had little to do with sustainability and everything to do with the Haida title case. Teal-Jones forester Dale Morgan stated,

> We [licensees] all agree that the dispersed pattern and scope of the [proposed protected areas] are a clear way to stop harvesting or make it very, very difficult for operations to continue. If I was thinking about a way ... to stop harvesting, this is the way I'd do it. That sounds like a conspiracy theory, but unfortunately I think that's the reality of it ...
>
> From where the Haida want to be, it makes total sense, and I actually respect them a lot for that. They have some clear rights, and they're going

to try and assert those rights and push it as hard as they can ... As a licensee, and for all licensees, that's the way we see it. They're going to try and take [the timber] away from us. But we have some rights as well, because we've been paying for these rights for a long time, and we have the right to harvest in certain areas. So it's also our obligation as licensees to push the issue so that we can harvest that timber right. That's where we're coming from, and I think the Haida, for the most part, understand that. It's not a personal thing. But we have an agenda and they have an agenda.[11]

Weyerhaeuser strongly refuted the allegations made against it. Its corporate attorney, Anne Giardini, asserted: "Every single stick that has been cut has been cut with Haida involvement" (quoted in Shukovsky 2005). Weyerhaeuser's vice-president of Canadian forest lands, Tom Holmes, insisted that the company had "extended itself to accommodate the Haida in numerous ways, including an offer to share ownership in the license," and suggested that the Haida were protesting the sale only to raise the profile of their title case (ibid.). In Weyerhaeuser's view, the company was simply caught in the middle of "an epic legal battle between two sovereign powers – the Haida and the BC government – over who controls the forest" (ibid.).

The minister of forestry operations, Roger Harris, also declared that the Province had tried to consult and accommodate the Haida, particularly noting its 2003 treaty offer. The islanders' issues were partially acknowledged by their MLA, Bill Belsey, who affirmed: "The challenges they've had [on Haida Gwaii] for years and years and years is the export of logs off the islands. I sympathize with them, I recognize that as being a major problem ... The returns to the islands at times are very limited" (quoted in Vassallo 2005b). Belsey also believed that the provincial and federal governments would be willing to work with the Haida to establish a "home-grown" forest industry and added that the Haida could potentially purchase a forest tenure and control forest activities on the islands. However, he maintained that the Province had no obligation to consult with them on Weyerhaeuser's sale of TFL 39 (ibid.).

Despite their strong objections, it soon became clear that neither the Province nor Weyerhaeuser would file for an injunction. Their case would be uncertain at best, considering the allegations against the Province for contempt of court and Weyerhaeuser for breach of contract. Moreover, the fortuitous timing of the blockade, with a provincial election around the corner and the Weyerhaeuser deal about to close, meant that too much was at stake for either the Province or the company to risk an escalating conflict.

22 Witnessing Islands Spirit Rising. (SpruceRoots, Gowgaia Institute)

As news of the blockade spread, so did its support. After two weeks, the Islands Spirit Rising website, which posted regular bulletins and commentaries, had had over eighty thousand hits. By the third week, a province-wide coalition of forty-nine non-governmental organizations, labour unions, and indigenous peoples associations, known as the British Columbia Coalition for Sustainable Forest Solutions, had thrown its support behind the Haida and the communities of Haida Gwaii. In an open letter to the premier, the coalition urged the Province to deal honourably with the Haida and other First Nations, and to fundamentally rethink recent changes to forestry and environmental laws (British Columbia Coalition for Sustainable Forest Solutions 2005).

These sentiments arose not only from the recent events on Haida Gwaii, but also from an expanding global discourse that increasingly emphasized the rights of indigenous people, the destructive impacts of deforestation, the urgency of environmental issues, and the strong connection between indigenous communities and their natural surroundings. With the provincial election looming, the Province could not afford to be seen on the wrong side of such issues.

VICTORY ON THE LINE

By the first week of the blockade, organizers had already generated a proposal they said would "help the province save face" and bring an end to the conflict (Vassallo 2005a). Their plan called for greater local control of resources and a shift to sustainable logging. Former Council of the Haida Nation vice-president Gilbert Parnell (2005) told a CBC Radio talk show: "The people here would like to see the work that we've done in the land use planning process, a joint process between the province and the Council of the Haida Nation ... implemented. And what is found in that process is a common vision by Islanders from a variety of interests for sustainability into the future."

The Province soon agreed to hear their proposal. As the blockade entered its third week, serious negotiations got under way. A delegation of Council of the Haida Nation executives and hereditary chiefs met with representatives from the Premier's Office, led by Deputy Minister to the Premier Jessica McDonald. Port Clements mayor Dale Lore was also among the negotiating team, but the Province barred him from the meetings. Apparently, although the blockade was a joint effort by Haida and non-Haida residents, the Supreme Court of Canada ruling obligated the Province to consult only with the Haida. Moreover, the Province had no interest in validating a mayor who allied himself with the Haida Nation against the government that purportedly represented his interests.[12]

The Ministry of Forests was brought in for technical advice, though its view of how to proceed did not necessarily correspond with that of the Premier's Office. On several occasions, negotiations were almost cut short when agreements reached between the Premier's Office and the Haida appeared altered after they were passed on to line ministries for processing.[13] The situation was indicative of the decades-old conflict between islanders and the Ministry of Forests. The Premier's Office, however, was pursuing a different agenda, which was to clear up the conflict and ensure that no glitches would mar the election campaign.

After four days of intense talks, the Province and the Haida reached a tentative agreement. The memorandum of understanding (Understanding Arising from April 22 2005 Discussions) included interim protection for all fourteen Haida Protected Areas, cultural and archaeological cedar stands, and bird-nesting habitat, as identified in the *Haida Land Use Vision*. Approximately 20 percent of the islands, or 230,000 hectares, was placed under temporary protection from logging while negotiations took place. The Haida were also offered a volume-based forest tenure of 120,000 cubic metres per year and $5 million as preliminary compensation for resources extracted from the islands. In addition, the parties agreed to review options for ending commercial and recreational bear hunting, and to reconvene the land use planning forum for another six months to address the neglected issues of economic transition and community stability.[14] Moreover, whereas the agreement itself was acknowledged as fulfilling the Province's obligation to consult with and accommodate the Haida on the TFL 39 licence transfer, it did not require the Haida to halt legal proceedings related to past infringements of their rights and title.

The Haida negotiating team brought home the news of the agreement to a Unity Dance, which was organized to raise money for families that were experiencing financial hardship due to the blockade. Guujaaw told an enthusiastic crowd that Victoria had agreed to respect the wishes of the island communities and put their interests ahead of the provincial economy. He characterized the agreement not so much as a major victory but as preventing Weyerhaeuser from doing more damage, adding: "We know that there is still an opportunity to create a future that includes culture and a sustainable economy" (quoted in King 2005). Hereditary chief Allan Wilson expressed his delight with the agreement: "It seems we have about 450 horsepower and we are moving full-tilt in sixth gear ... This started over twenty years ago on Lyell Island" (ibid.).

The memorandum of understanding was signed two weeks later, on 11 May 2005. It contained many hopeful features for the Haida, though numerous details were still to be resolved. It gave the parties thirty days to develop a consultation protocol that would govern operating lands outside the protected areas, determine the status and boundaries of the protected areas themselves, and continue work on a series of broader interim agreements regarding land, revenue sharing, fishing, economic development, shared decision making, and consultation. Discussion of these matters, however, would extend well beyond the thirty days.[15]

BACKLASH AND COUNTER IMAGES

As land use negotiations got under way between the Province and the Haida Nation, a growing backlash developed, particularly in the logging community of Port Clements. Lost wages had sparked resentment, and local forestry-based manufacturers feared that placing additional areas under interim protection would further limit their access to timber. Moreover, some residents were furious that their mayor not only supported the agreement but had been at the forefront of the events that created it.

Dale Lore returned from the blockade negotiations to a petition demanding that he stop representing Port Clements on forestry issues. Initiated by a group of forestry-based business owners and signed by about 160 of the 240 voters in his community, the petition read: "[Dale Lore] has not fairly represented the view of the majority of residents and has pursued his own agenda as they [sic] related to recent developments surrounding forestry issues that have negatively impacted our community and caused undue hardship" (quoted in Rinfret 2005b, 4).[16] The petition called for the local village council to immediately set up an economic development committee that would "make sure that the positions council takes are in line with what residents want" (Larry Brealey, quoted in ibid.). Some council members argued that the interests of Port Clements were better served with Dale Lore at the negotiations, but petitioners expressed their strong disapproval of the closed-door talks and lack of communication.

The blockade checkpoints remained in place while negotiations dealt with the details of the memorandum of understanding. Although traffic had been allowed to pass since the negotiations began, Weyerhaeuser did not call its employees back to work, unwilling to risk having them blockaded again.[17] Even a month after the memorandum was signed, Weyerhaeuser loggers were still off the job. And the longer they stayed off the job, the angrier they became. The $11,000 that the Unity Dance had raised for families in need was a great community gesture, with thousands of dollars in Haida art donated for auctioning. But requests for financial assistance continued long after this money had been distributed.[18] Indeed, the $11,000 raised was roughly comparable to the lost wages of one logger. Weyerhaeuser employees remained off the job for almost three months before finally being called back to work. When they returned, Dale Lore was not among them. As a long-time forestry worker, he had often walked the line between what the company would and would not tolerate. This time, it seemed he had crossed the line – his career in Haida Gwaii's logging industry was over. Nevertheless, his commitment to building a sustainable island economy would continue.[19]

On 29 May 2005, Brascan officially took over Weyerhaeuser's coastal forestry operations. The timberlands were immediately divided between two new Brascan-controlled companies. The recently removed privately held lands became Island Timberlands, and the remaining Crown tenure was named Cascadia Forest Products. Brascan's managing partner, Reid Carter, confirmed that the purchase was made specifically to acquire the private lands (Hamilton 2005).[20] Brascan's CEO described the deal as furthering its "strategy of investing in high quality assets that generate long term, sustainable cash flows and increase in value over time" (quoted in Prudham 2007, 258). However, now that the profitable private lands had been removed from the licence, the poorer-performing public lands would need major restructuring if they were to be economically viable. As to the nature of this restructuring, Carter said only that the necessary changes were expected to produce controversy and resistance (Hamilton 2005).

As negotiations continued between the Province and the Haida, some non-Haida residents became increasingly frustrated regarding their exclusion from the talks. One Port Clements resident accused the Province and the Haida Nation of violating the Charter of Rights and Freedoms "in that an agreement that affects all citizens has been negotiated without representation from the majority of the population" (Brealey 2005, 7). The Council of the Haida Nation had held several public meetings in both Haida and non-Haida communities to inform people of the state of negotiations and to generally consult with them. But though the council was open to hearing everyone's view, it was mandated to take direction from the Haida people only.

Major forest licensees were also concerned about the direction of talks, and, much to their chagrin, they too were excluded from them. They had expected the Haida Protected Areas to be removed from the forestry land base, but they were alarmed to see that cedar and wildlife habitat areas were also on the table. The three major forest licensees, Teal-Jones Group, Husby Forest Products, and Cascadia Forest Products (formerly Weyerhaeuser), responded by placing a full-page ad in the local paper. Written in the form of a letter to residents, it contained the following:

> It is important to understand that while the potential impacts to our businesses could be severe these impacts will be equally severe to the economic stability of the Islands, its businesses, as well as its infrastructure and facilities such as hospitals, schools and other public institutions. The total annual harvest impacts and reductions could be in the magnitude of 50 percent-80 percent of the allowable annual cut in the region if all land use and land management recommendations, as we understand them today, are implemented. Considering that forestry is the dominant employment and income sector on the Islands, this means the short-term effects you felt during the

recent blockades would be appreciably magnified as a consequence of these negotiations. Any significant reductions will permanently impair commercial forestry on the Islands, resulting in destruction of the economic base for local communities. (Dear Residents of Haida Gwaii 2005, 20)

Many islanders dismissed the ad as fear-mongering, restating their vision for a locally controlled forest industry with sustainable logging, on-island processing, and greater community benefits. However, a group of local loggers voiced similar concerns about the closed-door negotiations and negative impacts of possible cut reductions. Organizing themselves into the Haida Gwaii Working Forest Action Group, they called for "a middle ground" between the demands of the Haida and the forest licensees. One member, a local Haida logger, told the media: "I stood on the line with everybody and showed support. I wasn't supporting the fact we would be out of work ... I feel like we were used" (Randy Tenant, quoted in Rinfret 2005a, 1). Repeating industry's prediction of a possible 80 percent cut reduction, the group's acting spokesperson, Phil Shiels (2005), wrote to the local newspaper:

> Our greatest fear is that the leadership of the [Council of the Haida Nation] is on an environmental crusade to eradicate our livelihoods from the Islands and that the provincial government either wants peace at any cost or simply no longer cares about the diminishing population of workers on the Islands ... It is a fairly sad commentary on this situation that the group has been formed not so much to try and sway the politicians from their course of action as it was to group together parties that will be impacted by those actions into a legally definable entity for the purposes of seeking compensation through the courts for those impacts.

In response to local concerns, Guujaaw stated: "We are going to do our best in negotiations. The last thing we want to see is islanders suffer and big business walk away with more money in their pockets" (quoted in Rinfret, King, and Ramsay 2005, 9). At the same time, he maintained that the current hardship was ultimately the result of many years of overlogging, not the new agreement.

By November 2005, TFL 39 had changed hands yet again. This time, Western Forest Products announced its purchase of Cascadia Forest Products, making it the fourth company in six years to own the licence. The quick transfers between MacMillan Bloedel, Weyerhaeuser, Brascan, and now Western Forest Products highlighted the nature of the multi-national forest industry, in which faceless executives cement their deals, oblivious of the communities affected and with just one goal in mind – profit.

Brascan retained the profitable private lands (Island Timberlands) and sold the less lucrative public forest tenure to Western Forest Products, which, incidentally, was itself nearly one-third owned by Brascan. Following this deal, Western Forest Products received government approval to remove private lands from three of its other tree farm licences. The justification for it was that the company was suffering financially and in need of assistance with its debt load. This reasoning conveniently ignored the fact that its own main shareholder, Brascan, was its major creditor. The value of just 120 square kilometres of waterfront land released from Western Forest Products' Crown tenure on Vancouver Island was estimated at $3.5 billion (Horter 2008).[21]

Back in Port Clements, Dale Lore lost his seat as mayor during a November 2005 election and was replaced by Cory Delves, the contract supervisor for Cascadia. The new council was composed almost entirely of forestry-based small-business owners who had opposed the blockade. Among its priorities was reconsideration of the 2004 *Protocol Agreement* that had been signed with the Council of the Haida Nation and was credited, in part, to the strong relationship between Guujaaw and Dale Lore. Local critics viewed its recognition of Haida title in exchange for shared islands governance as both risky and foolish. For Lore, the matter was quite the opposite: "I got an agreement that my people are allowed to grow and prosper. You want to rip it up? You're just ripping up your side."[22]

Despite the abrupt turnover in council leadership and politics, it soon became apparent that the earlier cooperation between Port Clements and the Haida Nation would be maintained. Within six months, not only did the new council agree to uphold the *Protocol Agreement*, but Mayor Delves declared that he wanted to make it work. When challenged by a local resident who argued that the non-Haida never came out ahead and had "no bargaining chips," Delves responded: "[There are] a lot of common items between all communities, native and non-native ... I'm very optimistic that there's going to be positive things come out of [the agreement]" (quoted in Rinfret 2006). Evidently, shared islands governance by way of Haida title was a vision beyond personal agendas. However, the importance of trust and strong relationships to the success of the protocol would become quite evident.

Meanwhile, land use negotiations between the Province and the Council of the Haida Nation were moving very slowly. It was becoming clear that Victoria hoped to dilute its post-blockade agreements, whereas the Haida were determined to see them upheld. By this point, the Province had appointed its fourth chief negotiator, Attorney General Geoff Plant. Two separate but related talks were under way: one to work out the details of the memorandum of understanding that had resulted from the blockade, and the other to finalize the land use plan. Final boundaries around the protected areas were almost in place, but discussions had stalled regarding the Haida forestry tenure and the consultation protocol for operating lands outside the protected areas.[23] The memorandum of understanding called for shared decision making, but Guujaaw contended that the consultation protocol offered by the Province resembled what had been already in place before 2004 and deemed unacceptable by the courts.

The Aboriginal tenure promised to the Haida was also the focus of controversy. The parties had agreed that once the final land use plan was accepted and the new annual allowable cut for the islands was established, the harvest levels of all forestry companies would be reduced proportionally to spread the burden equally between them.[24] The Province now argued that the Haida tenure should also be dropped proportionally, the same as the others. Determined to retain the originally agreed volume of 120,000 cubic metres, the Council of the Haida Nation refused to accept the Aboriginal tenure until after the land use plan was finalized and the cut reductions distributed among the existing operators. Even the bear hunt was continuing, despite the Province's commitment to finding ways of ending it. Guujaaw maintained that once the provincial election was over and the dust had settled from the blockade, the Province was acting as if the memorandum of understanding were nonbinding.[25]

In June 2006, after more than a year of post-blockade negotiations, the Province released a controversial report titled *Socio-Economic and Environmental Assessment of Haida Gwaii/Queen Charlotte Islands Land Use Viewpoints: Summary* (Pierce Lefebvre Consulting 2006). It outlined two logging industry scenarios for the coming decade, based on the two viewpoints presented in the *Land Use Plan Recommendations Report* (British Columbia/Council of the Haida Nation Process Management Team 2006) (Table 3). The socio-economic and environmental assessment report had been commissioned by the Province while the blockade was under way, and unlike other documents prepared as part of the land use planning process, it was written and released without any Haida involvement.

TABLE 3   Forestry projections under viewpoints 1 and 2

Category	Current reality	Viewpoint 1	Viewpoint 2
Legislated protected areas	22%	38%	42%
Forest area protected under all designations[a]	32%	58%	83%
Harvest level (m³)[b]	1.14 million	1.6 million	549,000
Islanders employed in forest sector	445	620	215
Total population	5,220	5,660 (+440)	4,655 (−565)
Forestry annual net economic value	$20 million	$30 million	$10 million

a This includes legislated protected areas plus other designations such as wildlife
   habitat, old-growth areas, and riparian reserves.
b The estimate was for the actual current harvest level (versus annual allowable cut) and
   the projected harvest levels in the first decade under the two viewpoints.
Source: Pierce Lefebvre Consulting 2006, iii, 7.

For the first time, the report revealed that viewpoint 1 (the industry
option) would agree to set aside twelve of the fourteen Haida Protected
Areas. When existing areas were added to this, viewpoint 1 protected
37.7 percent of the islands. However, additional reserves for other values
such as cultural and archaeological cedar were deemed unnecessary. When
all other designations that protected portions of forested areas from
timber harvesting (such as wildlife habitat, old-growth zones, and riparian
reserves) were included, viewpoint 1 protected 58 percent of the forest from
logging.

By contrast, viewpoint 2 (the community option) included all fourteen
Haida Protected Areas as well as those recommended by the Province's
Protected Areas Strategy, or an estimated 42 percent of the islands. When
added to all other designations, it called for 83 percent of the forest area
to be protected from logging.

On the basis of these statistics, the report predicted that the application
of viewpoint 1 would result in a 40 percent increase in forestry employment (from 445 to 620 full-time jobs), whereas viewpoint 2 would lead
to a 50 percent decline (from 445 to 215). If the job losses under viewpoint
2 were to be offset, activity in all other sectors (sports fishing, guided
hunting, tourism, and non-timber forest products) must be doubled – a

scenario that the report considered highly unlikely in the next ten to twenty years. Viewpoint 2 had emphasized the importance of expanding local manufacturing to develop a sustainable economy, but the report foresaw no additional job creation from local wood processing or niche product manufacturing under either viewpoint 1 or 2 and predicted that the potential number of jobs in this area would remain constant at 25.

Extending to the implications for population trends, viewpoint 1 was forecasted to increase population by 8 percent (rising from an estimated 5,220 in 2004 to 5,660), whereas population was predicted to drop by 11 percent under viewpoint 2 (down to 4,655). In terms of annual net economic value of forestry, viewpoint 1 was forecasted to net $30 million during the first decade versus only $10 million under viewpoint 2. The report acknowledged that negative "externalities" should be set against raw net economic values, but it did not quantify their potential value.[26]

The overall message of the report was clear: viewpoint 2 was more consistent with the *Haida Land Use Vision* and would have certain environmental benefits lacking in viewpoint 1, but its economic and social costs would be devastating. It concluded that viewpoint 2 presented "a high-risk scenario from a community stability perspective that could exacerbate the economic hardship currently experienced" on the islands (Pierce Lefebvre Consulting 2006, 9). At the same time, it acknowledged that viewpoint 1 was not endorsed by local communities and thus "would diminish the positive social impacts one would expect to gain from a consensus land use plan" (ibid.).

The Council of the Haida Nation immediately dismissed the report as "so fatally flawed it shouldn't be released" (Bill Beldessi, quoted in "Provincial Report Badly Flawed" 2006). Guujaaw called the report "more mischief" and characterized its findings as "clearly misleading," noting that the Province had chosen to release the report despite the fact that significant errors had been identified ("Provincial Report Is More Mischief" 2006, 1, 36). Process Technical Team member John Broadhead stated that, unlike all other technical reports produced for the land use planning process, this one had not been peer-reviewed by the team. He also pointed to major errors in employment calculations and provincial revenues, and added that the Process Technical Team had previously rejected its assumptions and methods as "liable to produce results biased against local aspirations for community stability and cultural sustainability" (ibid., 36). Guujaaw concluded that the report was released "either to strengthen a negotiating position" or to "drive wedges between the communities" (ibid.). Indeed, the report prompted some community members to condemn viewpoint 2.

As one local remarked: "There is no way in hell's good acres that I can support viewpoint 2. You can't sustain a society living on welfare" (Carole Wagner, quoted in Ramsay 2006, 9).

The controversial report caused a setback for negotiations between the Province and the Haida Nation, and its author was asked to leave the table. The situation declined further when evidence suggested that chief negotiator Geoff Plant's assistant, Jose Villa-Arce, had undermined the process by encouraging a local forestry employee in a "letters to the editor" campaign. He too was forced to withdraw from the table.[27] Guujaaw maintained that Plant's singular aim was to water down the agreement made between the Haida and Deputy Minister Jessica McDonald.[28] Arguing that Plant was wasting their time, the Haida refused to have him back in negotiations. As talks stalled, and much of the provincial team was dismissed, Minister of Agriculture and Lands Pat Bell stated that, if an agreement could not be reached, he himself might be obliged to unilaterally impose a land use plan ("Land Use Plan Possible" 2006). To the Province's mantra that "There will never be a deal with the Haida," Guujaaw's response was "There will never be a *bad* deal with the Haida."[29]

In contrast to the government report, other actors were framing the issue quite differently. The locally based Gowgaia Institute had produced an animated logging history of Haida Gwaii, based entirely on forest service data, showing the extent and pattern of logging during the past century. It was a running timeline, about five minutes in length, which gradually highlighted a satellite image of Haida Gwaii to mark the places where logging had occurred between 1900 and 2004.[30] Shown at a community information meeting held by the Council of the Haida Nation, it painted a reality that was hard to deny – so much of the old-growth forests had been cut so quickly. Reflecting on the graphic model, John Broadhead commented: "The quickest and most effective way to change a paradigm is to model it. If you do it effectively, people withdraw from it and see a pattern they couldn't see when they were in it. That can be a huge 'aha' moment."[31] The timeline's implications were clear. As Broadhead (2007) stated: "If the industry owners had cut less and cared more about community stability, we probably wouldn't need a land use plan like we do now, or in any case the changes that must be made might not seem as catastrophic as they do for some."

British Columbia's four big environmental groups (ForestEthics, Greenpeace, Sierra Club of British Columbia, and Rainforest Action Network) had also produced a report, which supported an alternative socio-economic future for Haida Gwaii. Titled *Revitalizing British Columbia's Coastal*

Economy: A New Economic Vision for the North and Central Coast and Haida Gwaii (Pacific Analytics and Don Harrison 2004), it noted that the world was awash in wood from much cheaper sources than Canada and contended that the coastal timber industry would slowly decline if the business-as-usual approach continued. On the other hand, cutting fewer trees, using certified ecosystem-based management practices, and processing the wood locally could increase job security while ensuring that coastal timber products remained marketable in an increasingly ecologically sensitive world. The report noted that tourism would greatly benefit from added environmental protection and that emerging industries consistent with ecosystem-based management, such as shellfish aquaculture and non-timber forest products, could attract socially responsible investment. Its conclusion differed starkly from that of the Province's report – ecosystem-based management, combined with the protection of 45 percent of Haida Gwaii, was a rational economic choice that boded well for the future, even without taking into account the globally significant conservation values that would be preserved.

These findings concurred with community aspirations that were now being pursued through the Community Viability Strategy, which the Haida had negotiated for during talks to end the blockade. Its aim was to create an island-wide economic development strategy to help communities build a sustainable and diversified future that was consistent with viewpoint 2 as laid out in the *Land Use Plan Recommendations Report* (British Columbia/ Council of the Haida Nation Process Management Team 2006). Research for the strategy was overseen by a steering committee composed of elected leaders from every island community, and it included individual and group consultations with hundreds of locals. The new strategy allowed community leaders and community forum members to re-engage in a process to envision a locally determined and controlled future.

A strategic plan for economic transition was publicly presented in March 2007. As the main product of the Community Viability Study, it included a three-year action plan for five main areas: infrastructure development (transportation, utilities, and land), sector development (forestry, tourism, fisheries, agriculture), community marketing, human resource development, and implementation. Among the top goals were establishing more local control over resources, expanding the job base through increased processing of local resources, and improving infrastructure. The report (Lions Gate Consulting, Westcoast CED, and Peak Solutions Consulting 2007) noted that the present level of cooperation between communities could not address the regional nature of most economic barriers and opportunities that they faced.[32] It also identified an extensive range of opportunities for island communities, from research, advocacy, fundraising, brokering, and capacity building to specific opportunities in tourism, community forestry, manufacturing, craft industries, and the arts. Above all, it stressed the critical importance of generating a regional economic development strategy through a cohesive and collaborative effort by all communities on Haida Gwaii. To facilitate this coordinated approach, it recommended that an all-islands economic development agency be established. The desired outcome would be new opportunities for locals, long-term community stability, and a more respectful approach to land and resource use.

Meanwhile, talks between the Province and the Council of the Haida Nation were getting back on track, with Minister of Agriculture and Lands Pat Bell taking on the role of Victoria's chief negotiator in October 2006. At this point, the parties agreed to focus on reaching a strategic land use agreement. With a certain amount of face saving required on behalf of the previous provincial negotiators, Bell put his two top advisors, Lindsay Jones and John Bones, onto the file.

To placate cabinet's growing frustration with the extended planning process, Bell proposed that the same Ecosystem-Based Management Framework used on the central coast be employed for Haida Gwaii. This initially seemed out of the question for the Haida, since the recommendations of the Haida Gwaii Community Planning Forum were far more environmentally stringent than those applied on the central coast. However, even though the basic principles were to be the same, the parameters of the ecosystem-based management framework could be adjusted.[33] This meant that, with a little creative thinking, the situation could become workable.

This creativity was demonstrated in connection with risk management. Under the Forest and Range Practices Act, forest licensees who wished to deviate from the default parameters of an environmental objective could under certain circumstances propose their own parameters and assume responsibility for "managing" any resulting risks. In the name of efficiency, as long as the risk proposal was vetted by a professional forester, the government typically approved it. This form of risk management, which was written into every clause of the central coast land use agreement, was a non-starter on Haida Gwaii. However, retaining the principle of risk management, it was agreed that a licensee was free to propose a risk management target – not to the Ministry of Forests, but to the Province *and* the Haida, who would *together* decide whether the issue warranted the allowance for risk management.[34]

Another example was riparian forest retention. On the central coast, riparian forests were allocated a one-tree buffer zone. On Haida Gwaii, negotiations focused on *identified* high-value fish habitat and thus a two-tree riparian buffer was accepted. On the central coast, high-value fish habitat had never been identified and was therefore open to future debate. However, on Haida Gwaii, the Gowgaia Institute had already modelled eighty thousand data points and produced a riparian forest map of high-value fish habitat. The map had been presented at the Community Planning Forum, but the current provincial negotiators were apparently unaware of it. It was not until after the Province declared a lockdown on riparian forest negotiations that they learned of the riparian forest map and the extent of identified high-value fish habitat that they had just agreed to. According to John Broadhead, who carried out technical reviews for both parties during the negotiations, agreement on this point alone meant that an additional 8 percent of the land would be protected.[35]

Once the Province had abandoned its hardline stance, and its negotiating team had the authority to make difficult but necessary concessions, progress was finally being made. Six months after Pat Bell took charge of the provincial side, a land use agreement was all but finalized.

Toward a Transformative Agreement

A draft *Strategic Land Use Agreement* was finally initialled by the Council of the Haida Nation and the Province on 28 May 2007. This unprecedented agreement proposed more than doubling the amount of protected areas and temporarily reducing the annual cut by nearly half. However, before it could be ratified, the timber harvest opportunities under the draft agreement were to be analyzed, communities were to be consulted, and more detailed strategic planning was to determine precise targets for ecosystem-based management.

Two weeks later, elected leaders from the islands' communities met with Pat Bell, several deputy ministers, and the Council of the Haida Nation to express their support for the agreement.[36] With more certainty in their future, they could assess their opportunities and challenges, and more accurately frame the task of building a sustainable economy. At the meeting, the community leaders also requested additional resources from the Province to implement the Community Viability Strategy, which they hoped would form part of the final *Strategic Land Use Agreement*.

Two months later, the Council of the Haida Nation informed residents that it was negotiating with Western Forest Products to buy TFL 39 (block 6) on Haida Gwaii (Rinfret 2008). To finance the deal, the Haida were exploring the possibility of using the Gwaii Trust Fund. The federal government had established this regional economic diversification fund, originally worth $38 million, when Gwaii Haanas National Park Reserve and Haida Heritage Site was created. Part of the interest from the fund had since been used to finance various projects on the islands. Guujaaw noted that the fund could be used as the community wished, since it belonged to islanders collectively, with no strings attached from the federal or provincial governments. He contended that borrowing from the fund to purchase the forest licence made good sense, as the interest paid back on the loan would benefit islanders instead of the banks (ibid.).

Soon, the analysis of the timber harvest opportunities was completed by forestry consultant and local resident Keith Moore, overseen by the Province and the Council of the Haida Nation. The focal point was to assess whether an annual allowable cut of 800,000 cubic metres, as laid out in the draft *Strategic Land Use Agreement,* was feasible when the protected areas, cultural and heritage objectives, and ecosystem-based management objectives were taken into account. According to Guujaaw, the report concluded that harvesting 800,000 cubic metres would be physically possible but might not be economically advisable (quoted in Hamilton 2007b). However, the key factor would be putting ecosystem-based management into practice. Minister Pat Bell noted that aggressive objectives for ecosystem-based management could bring the annual allowable cut down to 300,000 cubic metres, whereas more relaxed objectives might allow for over 1 million cubic metres (King 2007b).

The report prompted Teal-Jones Group (2007), one of the three major forest licensees on the islands, to generate a news release, which warned that "the proposed *Strategic Land Use Agreement* for Haida Gwaii ... will have devastating impacts on the coastal forest industry and the communities that depend on the forest industry operating on Haida Gwaii." Coast Forest Products Association president Rick Jeffery emphasized: "The impacts of these cuts will be felt not only in the Queen Charlottes but downstream in communities with sawmills on Vancouver Island and the Lower Mainland" (quoted in Hamilton 2007a, D3). Husby Forest Products vice-president Bob Brash said that harvesting levels for his company could drop by 60 to 75 percent even as costs could increase by 20 to 25 percent, and concluded that "it all adds up to a bleak business picture" (ibid.).

In an interesting show of solidarity, Pat Bell responded: "The islands have had a huge amount of forestry going on up there historically over the decades. I was very surprised as to the volume of timber that has come off the islands and the number of clear cuts I saw when I was up there" (ibid.). Bell acknowledged that everyone's concerns would need to be taken into consideration but added: "There are people who have financial interests on the islands that don't live here. I always think that my first responsibility is to on-island residents, the people that live here, the people that have made their living here over the years, the people that intend to continue living here for a long time" (quoted in King 2007b). This new attitude was indicative not of a change in government, but of a new relationship between the Province and the Haida. Guujaaw summed it up as follows: "What it boiled down to was that the Province just decided they wanted us out of the fight."[37] He remarked that by the end of the process, he and Premier Gordon Campbell were even "hitting it off pretty good."[38]

On 12 December 2007, nearly seven years after the first agreements for the planning process were signed, and almost three years since the start of the post-blockade negotiations, the *Haida Gwaii Strategic Land Use Agreement* (British Columbia/Council of the Haida Nation 2007) was signed. Fully consistent with the *Haida Land Use Vision*, it incorporated many of the community's recommendations for ecosystem-based management. Under the agreement, protected areas and ecosystem-based management reserves encompassed 52 percent of Haida Gwaii; of this, existing protected areas accounted for 23 percent, new protected areas made up another 25 percent, and ecosystem-based management reserves added the remaining 4 percent. To accommodate the newly designated protected areas and ecosystem-based management objectives, the annual allowable cut was dropped from the pre-blockade level of 1.7 million cubic metres to 800,000 cubic metres.[39] Of this, 120,000 cubic metres were to be allocated to the Haida Nation's Aboriginal tenure.

For lands outside the protected and special value areas, various ecosystem-based management objectives were outlined. In many cases, setting concrete targets would require further analysis and planning, but the general direction was clearly in line with the *Haida Land Use Vision*. The objectives for ecosystem-based management included the following:

- maintenance of traditional forest resources and Haida heritage features
- maintenance of monumental cedar and monumental cedar stands
- 100 percent retention of yew
- 100 percent retention of culturally modified trees and tree areas

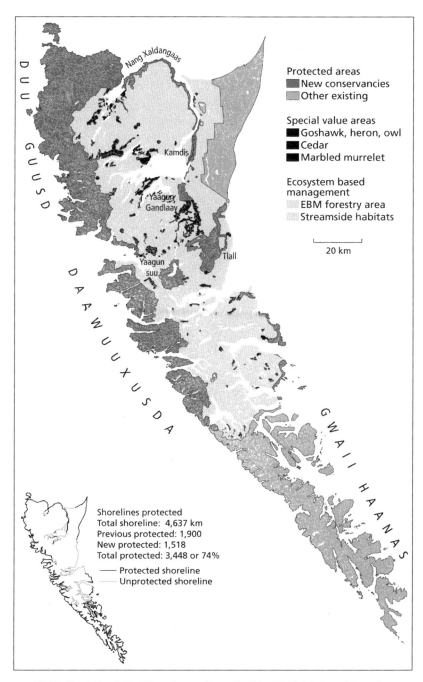

Protected areas
■ New conservancies
□ Other existing

Special value areas
■ Goshawk, heron, owl
■ Cedar
■ Marbled murrelet

Ecosystem based
management
▦ EBM forestry area
▦ Streamside habitats

20 km

Shorelines protected
Total shoreline: 4,637 km
Previous protected: 1,900
New protected: 1,518
Total protected: 3,448 or 74%

—— Protected shoreline
—— Unprotected shoreline

23   Haida Gwaii Land Use Plan. *Source:* Council of the Haida Nation. Adapted
by Eric Leinberger

- 80 percent forest retention in sensitive watersheds
- 100 percent retention of riparian forests within two tree lengths of high-value fish habitat
- 70 percent minimum forest retention in old forest ecosystems with high biodiversity
- 30 percent minimum forest retention in old forest ecosystems with low biodiversity
- 100 percent retention of red-listed (endangered) and selected blue-listed (threatened) plant communities
- 100 percent protection of black bear den sites
- maximum 10 percent alteration of most suitable (class 1) marbled murrelet habitat
- 100 percent protection of goshawk nesting sites.

Guujaaw described the landmark agreement as providing the Haida with a good foundation "to work on some real reconciliation" with the Province (quoted in King 2007a). Indeed, the agreement resolved so many central conflicts between the Haida and the Province that Guujaaw suggested they were "running out of things to fight over." However, options remained open, because, unlike government agreements in the past, this one did not prohibit the Haida from proceeding with future legal actions. At a celebration to mark the agreement, BC premier Gordon Campbell echoed Guujaaw's sentiments, calling the agreement a first step toward reconciliation and adding: "The Haida are true leaders across British Columbia and across Canada. You are demonstrating the ability to find agreement to build an economy like no others" (quoted in King 2008a).

After decades of resistance, strategic manoeuvring, and radical planning by the Haida, local environmentalists, and allied community members, the future now holds enormous potential for greater control over the land and their destinies. Despite the magnitude of the challenge that lies ahead to make ecosystem-based management and community-based forestry work, Guujaaw remains confident: "The interesting story is yet to come. How do we make this work? How do we create that ecotopian view of the world? I think we can do it. I think the world needs these little places to start turning the tide. I think we have a good chance to set an example for the rest of the world" (quoted in King 2008b).

10

New Political Landscape

While our people enjoy a good fight, peace time provides even greater opportunities. Through reconciliation we will be able to focus on the wellbeing of the people, culture and the proper management of our lands.

— Guujaaw, August 2013

Since the signing of the *Strategic Land Use Agreement,* things have moved at lightning speed on Haida Gwaii. Metaphorically capturing the scope of the transformation, an unprecedented name-changing ceremony was held on 17 June 2010. In a hall packed with emotion, a traditionally crafted bentwood box was held out to the crowd of seven hundred who had come to witness the event. Their collective shout of "Queen Charlotte Islands" was captured in the box, which was danced through twenty hereditary chiefs, each ceremonially touching it in a gesture of final farewell. The box, with its symbolic contents, was then presented to Premier Gordon Campbell, who held it high in the air amid climactic chants of "Haida Gwaii, Haida Gwaii."

The ceremony marked the respectful return of the name "Queen Charlotte Islands" to the Crown and welcomed "Haida Gwaii" as the new officially recognized name for the islands.[1] In the words of the event organizer, Vince Collison, "We're not taking back a name ... We've always known it to be Haida Gwaii" (quoted in "Name-Change Ceremony" 2010). Amid a jubilant crowd, the premier unveiled the first official globes

24 "Giving the Name Back with Respect" ceremony. Front row, left to right: Ginaawaan, Dayaang, George Abbott (then Minister of Aboriginal Relations and Reconciliation), Gaahlaay, Gordon Campbell (then Premier), Iljuuwaas, Gidkun, and Ihldiinii. Back row, left to right: April Churchill-Davis, Guujaaw, John T. Jones, 7idansuu, Nang Jingwas, Sdiithladaa, Sgaann 7iw7waans, Giteewans, Gidkinjuwaas, and Robert Mills. *Source:* Haida Laas, Council of the Haida Nation.

that identified the islands as Haida Gwaii. The globes would be distributed to local schoolchildren in a gesture "symbolizing the restoration of their history to future generations" (British Columbia 2010-11).

The historic day marked a turning point in the Haida's century-long struggle for their culture and nationhood. As Haida Nation president Guujaaw put it: "What we are doing here is unwinding colonialism" (quoted in Working Together for Haida Gwaii 2011, 6).

POWER, PLANNING, AND SOCIAL CHANGE

Since the land use planning process was first agreed to in 2001, enormous progress has occurred. The Haida Gwaii *Strategic Land Use Agreement* has fundamentally changed how the land is managed and by whom. The new approach is rooted in "a different philosophy on the land base" (Bellis, quoted in Simpson 2008), which, for the first time ever, puts the long-term needs and priorities of the Haida Nation and local communities ahead of corporate profits and government coffers. Major shifts in power have occurred, translating into a more balanced government-to-government relationship between the Haida and the Province, and a more locally controlled governance structure for the land.

Toward this end, the collaborative land use planning process provided an important forum for broadening the scope of values, knowledge, and meanings to be considered in planning. It generated extensive and much-needed information and analyses to assess the current state of the environment of Haida Gwaii. Its co-managed institutional and procedural design contained a variety of measures intended to counteract institutional bias and traditional power differentials between the main actors. Nevertheless, despite these significant advances, politics and power relations remained problematic.

To respond to the problems of inequality and dominance inherent in collaborative planning, the realities of power as they operate in actual processes must be exposed and addressed. These forms of power penetrate and are carried through policy discourses, institutional practices, structural forms, cultural systems, and social relations that underlie planning practices. Without addressing the many ways in which power manifests, planning is unlikely to "disrupt the practices of the already powerful" (McGuirk 2001, 213).

Employing both a conflict and a consensus perspective can be useful in moving past dualistic understandings in which collaborative processes are perceived as either an idealized win-win dynamic or the inevitable co-optation of opposition. The expanded understanding provides for a more constructive engagement with power as it operates through collaborative planning processes and allows one to better assess the benefits or risks that are likely to be encountered by participating.

The study used a conflict understanding of power to expose the problematic relations of inequality and dominance both inside and outside the planning process. It revealed how the consensus-seeking planning forum was constrained by the broader institutional and political structures in which it remained embedded. These included conventional framings and institutions of contract and property rights, forestry, economic development, resource management, governance, and many others. These abstracted, technical, and commercial understandings of the land and resource management prescribed the limits of deliberation while shaping interactions, capacities, and, ultimately, relations of dominance and power. The appearance of neutrality and openness to alternative ways of knowing and valuing was thus secured within a largely unchanged structure of resource extraction. Consequently, interests at the planning forum remained situated in a long history of adversarial politics.

At the same time, a consensus understanding of power was useful for seeing how, at another level, collective power and community capacity were generated through the collaborative process. The Community Planning Forum helped to unite and strengthen relations between community members with very diverse backgrounds and interests. It built internal cohesion by furthering a common understanding of their current and past situation, offering a shared vision for the future, and providing a plan for realizing their vision. It strengthened trust among community members, allowing them to take joint ownership of a progressive set of land use recommendations. Their collective will and solidarity was further strengthened by persistent industry opposition at a highly polarized table. Their mutual perception of powerlessness in the face of overwhelming state and corporate forces motivated them to move beyond their internal differences and create a cohesive front.

The study also illustrated that most situations are not a simple matter of pure consensus or pure conflict but rather a mix of the two, operating simultaneously at different levels. In a particular context, one will often override the other, giving the appearance of either consensus or conflict (Haugaard 1997, 140). Thus, consensus may be reached regarding numerous goals of less significance, but conflict regarding one or two central goals will override the otherwise existing consensus. Or, as in the case of collaborative planning between the Haida and the provincial government, there may be conflict at the broader level of meaning or institutional context but consensus to cooperate on a particular process to reach a common goal. Although such consensus may temporarily eclipse an existing conflict, the study showed the difficulty of separating interests and motivations from the broader underlying conflict. Nevertheless, working flexibly between strategies involving collaboration and contestation can have value. At certain times, the Haida and their community allies collaborated with the government to reach specific goals; at other times, they employed confrontation and collective action to achieve change. The challenge in deciding which course to take is to discern the conditions in which one or the other is most likely to contribute toward long-term goals.

Understanding the potential for social change requires not only a thorough knowledge of the institutions, procedures, and strategies that affect agents in a particular process, but also an awareness of the larger cultural, political, economic, and ideological context that shapes constraints and opportunities at various levels. It is also helpful to be well versed in the many ways that dominant representations have been and continue to be contested, individually and collectively, by First Nations, environmentalists, communities, and other grassroots actors.

Combining a micro-analysis of strategies and tactics with a macroanalysis of institutions and structures can be useful to untangle the many layers of power and their interactions with each other. As the Haida case showed, the dominant social structure of norms and values was institutionalized in state policies and legislation governing land and forest use. These produced the conditions of possibility and constraint for agency that operated within the collaborative planning process. However, these structures and constraints were not fixed but were continually produced and maintained by those in a position of power in response to challenges and demands. Ongoing lawsuits, collective actions, the threat of commercial boycotts, and the building of increasingly powerful alliances gradually shifted the field of power away from traditionally dominant actors in favour of previously marginalized groups. As alternative perspectives gained greater public legitimacy, aspects of the broader social structure became increasingly vulnerable to external challenge.

The Community Planning Forum functioned within this complex and evolving context. Drawing on a larger history of movement building and discourse formation, community members were able to formulate, reinforce, and refine their collective goals and vision. They emphasized cultural and local use values related to the land as opposed to commodities and exchange values. They stressed the maintenance of local culture and locally defined meanings in contrast to standard representations of wealth and progress. And they called for political self-management and islands governance to overcome subordination to the priorities of the provincial state. These three goals, uniquely formulated in the context of Haida Gwaii, resonate with those of many other successful social movements (see Castells 1983, 318-24).

When it became clear that the government would not be acting on the community's recommendations, overall collaboration turned to conflict. By the time the blockade was launched, the islands' leadership possessed the intellectual, relational, social, and cultural capital that would enable it to take full advantage of the possibilities and circumstances before it. The community-backed *Haida Land Use Vision,* supplemented with the community's recommendations for ecosystem-based management, provided a clear and persuasive platform for the demands of blockaders. The Haida negotiators, backed by a strong hand from the courts and armed with an assemblage of maps, ecological inventories, analyses, and a collective community vision, were able to reclaim a substantial measure of control. With conditions ripe for change, the effective and well-timed collective actions of the Haida and community actors helped to shift the structures governing land use to reflect new meanings, values, priorities, and interests.

With the Haida and the Province in government-to-government negotiations, and forestry companies entirely excluded, a new set of possibilities became attainable – ecologically, socially, and politically. With the social order changed, a capacity for action was created on issues that were once outside the realm of possibility. The result was a dramatic change in the direction of forestry and politics on Haida Gwaii.

In the end, though the community planning forum was constrained in its ability to influence decision-makers, the collaborative process made an important contribution to the eventual transformation of forestry on Haida Gwaii by providing critical information, formulating a shared community definition of the problems, strengthening relationships and mutual trust, and ultimately creating a collective cultural force with a clear vision to address its challenges. At the same time, the actions leading to this change were made meaningful, and thus successful, only through the background of broader battles, legal precedents, evolving institutions, and societal shifts toward recognition of the rights of indigenous people, the need to protect the environment, and the connection between the two.

A new political landscape is now emerging on Haida Gwaii. Marked by a fundamental shift in power, roles, and responsibilities, a new governance structure is tackling the many challenges and possibilities set in motion by the *Strategic Land Use Agreement*. Although still in their early phases, the political and economic models unfolding on Haida Gwaii may be a preview of what could emerge in rural communities across British Columbia.

Co-Governing the Land

Remarkably, since the signing of the Land Use Agreement, all the land that the Haida had designated for protection is now protected by provincial legislation. In January 2009, eleven new conservancies totalling 255,778 hectares were established on Haida Gwaii.[2] The conservancy designation was introduced in British Columbia in 2006, in response to assertive appeals by the Turning Point Initiative (now Coastal First Nations) and is the first provincial-level protected-area designation in Canada that explicitly incorporates First Nations' interests. It provides for long-term ecological integrity by restricting commercial logging, mining, and hydroelectric development while allowing for continued social, ceremonial, and cultural uses by First Nations. This means that the Haida continue to hunt, fish, and trap in the protected areas, to gather foods and medicines, and to access monumental cedars for cultural uses. The conservancy designation also allows for some low-impact economic development such as shellfish aquaculture and guided touring and fishing. The Haida and the Province jointly issue permits for these and other activities and co-manage the protected areas.

In a subsequent marine planning process, an unprecedented national marine conservation area was established in the waters surrounding Gwaii Haanas. The 3,500-square-kilometre Gwaii Haanas National Marine Conservation Area Reserve and Haida Heritage Site completes the marine portion of the Haida Heritage Site agreed to in 1993 when the Gwaii Haanas Agreement was signed, and follows the protected area boundary previously designated by the Haida Nation. Together, the park and the marine reserve – the first place in the world to be protected from the mountain tops to the sea floor – encompass over 5,000 square kilometres. The new designation, announced in June 2010, permits fishing and shipping to continue in most of the area but forbids undersea mining, ocean dumping, and oil and gas exploration and development. Detailed planning and management of the new marine conservation area will be taken on by the Archipelago Management Board, which also co-manages Gwaii Haanas National Park Reserve and Haida Heritage Site.

Regarding lands outside of the new protected areas, the legal objectives for implementing ecosystem-based management were formally agreed on under the Haida Stewardship Law and the Province's Land Use Objectives Order. Signed on 17 December 2010. The provincial order builds directly on the *Strategic Land Use Agreement* and covers objectives for maintaining cultural values, aquatic habitat, biodiversity, wildlife, and forest reserves. This includes the establishment of significant cedar stewardship areas and protection of Haida traditional heritage, forest features, and all monumental cedar. These three latter objectives add 26.4 percent protection in old-growth forests that are more than 250 years old (Haida Gwaii Management Council 2011, 16).[3]

The Land Use Objectives Order also provides protection for western yew and a minimum retention of 15 percent of the preharvest composition for red and yellow cedar in stands that originally (pre-1900) contained 30 percent or more cedar. It gives substantial protection to riparian forests in high-value fish habitat, increasing riparian buffers from thirty metres to eighty or a hundred metres.[4] It also provides for significant protection of upland stream areas, sensitive watersheds, active fluvial units, and forested swamps. On the basis of how rare or common the ecology of an area is, the order stipulates how much old forest must be retained in each site series and maps out forest reserves to meet objectives for ecological representation and marbled murrelet nesting habitat. In addition, it affords significant protection for red- and blue-listed ecological communities, and for all black bear dens, northern goshawk reserves, great blue heron nesting sites, and northern saw-whet owl reserves. When the deductions resulting from applying the ecosystem-based management regime are combined with protected lands, private lands, and lands unsuitable for harvesting, 19 percent of the land base, or 188,718 hectares, remains available for logging (Haida Gwaii Management Council 2012b, 7).

With the most immediate threats resolved, the Haida have turned their attention to managing the land. And unlike in the past, the Province no longer has unilateral decision-making powers. The details of the new governance model were spelled out in the historic *Kunst'aa Guu – Kunst'aayah Reconciliation Protocol* (British Columbia/Council of the Haida Nation 2009). The protocol, whose title means "the beginning" in the Haida dialects of Old Massett and Skidegate, was signed on 12 December 2009 and put into effect by the provincial Haida Gwaii Reconciliation Act (2009) and the Council of the Haida Nation's Haida Stewardship Law. It makes unprecedented advancements toward reconciling Crown and Haida title. Most notable is its innovative joint decision-making process, which gives the Haida shared authority over a range of high-level decisions in several important strategic areas. It represents enormous progress in provincial policy, which, for the first time, recognizes the Haida as the rightful stewards of the islands.

The key entities in the new governance structure are the Reconciliation Table, the Haida Gwaii Management Council, and the Solutions Table. The Reconciliation Table acts in much the same capacity as a treaty table, with the chief negotiators for the Province and the Haida engaging in bilateral discussions and ultimately aiming for a trilateral reconciliation agreement between Victoria, the Haida Nation, and Ottawa. In an effort to increase its responsiveness to all islanders, the Reconciliation Table recently invited a representative from the islands' municipal governments to observe tripartite talks. Ottawa has been a less than willing partner on the reconciliation front, but the Province and the Haida Nation have continued to refine their joint decision-making processes.

Two new governance bodies have been created to carry out shared decision making. At the strategic level is the Haida Gwaii Management

Council, which consists of two Haida and two provincial representatives plus a jointly appointed chair. The council is responsible for making high-level decisions in four main areas: implementation and amendment of the 2007 *Strategic Land Use Agreement;* establishment, implementation, and amendment of land use objectives for forest practices; approval of management plans for protected areas, development of policies and standards for conservation of heritage sites; and determination and approval of the annual allowable cut for Haida Gwaii.

Previously, co-management bodies have been empowered only to make recommendations to a provincial minister, Cabinet, or other statutory decision-maker who retained the ultimate decision-making authority. In Haida Gwaii, the management council is the statutory decision-maker for these strategic areas. Its decisions are legally binding, and both the Haida Nation and the Province have entrusted their authorities and jurisdiction in certain areas to the council. This means that neither the Province nor the Haida can unilaterally enact decisions regarding these subjects. Much will depend on the dynamics of the people in the room and their ability to make decisions that satisfy everyone. However, as most council members live on Haida Gwaii, locals are optimistic that their chances of being heard are better than when the Province was exclusively in charge.

At the operational level, the Solutions Table provides recommendations regarding natural resource permits and other technical matters to the joint statutory decision-makers – the Haida Natural Resource Committee and the district office of the Ministry of Forests, Lands and Natural Resource Operations (recently renamed Front Counter Haida Gwaii). Composed of two Haida and two provincial representatives, the Solutions Table is supported by a team of experts. Unlike the paper exercise of referrals and consultation of the past; which involved an iterative process of critique and revision that often resulted in lengthy conflicts and sometimes legal action, the Solutions Table deals with permit applications face-to-face and in real time. With the recent amalgamation of the Province's various natural ministries into one, an arrangement piloted in Haida Gwaii, the Solutions Table deals with matters pertaining not only to forestry, but to all natural resource ministries, including mines, aquaculture, fish habitat management, recreational permits, archaeology, and more. The result is an intergovernmental and interagency approach to resource management that is expected to run far more smoothly than the confrontational and fragmented process of the past.

Nevertheless, bringing together two very different governments, cultures, and management styles has its challenges. Leonard Munt, district manager for Natural Resource Operations and a main proponent of the Solutions Table concept, asserts that the key to success is that the members work together on a daily basis. He explains: "If they were to come together once a week ... it would be them and us having to debate every issue all the time, and we'd be one step forward three steps back by Friday. It's when we're in each other's faces every day, that's when relationships form, trust gets built."[5]

Whereas a handful of other First Nations have also signed reconciliation protocols with the Province, the Haida Reconciliation Protocol is unique in providing shared statutory decision making for the First Nation. This arrangement arises largely from the Haida's strong title case and the Crown's obligation to consult and accommodate First Nations to a degree commensurate with the strength of their land or title claim. In addition, two decades of collaboration between the federal government and the Haida Nation in Gwaii Haanas demonstrate the feasibility of cooperation and co-management on Haida Gwaii.

Through reconciliation, the Haida and the Province now embark on a more predictable future. Moreover, the foundation has been created to build on the broad interests of the island community. As Guujaaw comments: "We set the conditions to balance competing interests on the land. From here, we design the future that will carry us."[6]

Toward a Sustainable Local Economy

In addition to spelling out the new governance arrangement, the Reconciliation Protocol provides for funding to support its implementation. The Province and the Haida Nation also agreed to share revenues from carbon offsets, which are expected to be substantial for Gwaii Haanas, the new protected areas, and the implementation of ecosystem-based management.[7] Developed in alliance with the Coastal First Nations, this arrangement is the first in which carbon offsets are being awarded for old-growth forests under the BC Forest Carbon Offset Protocol. An Atmospheric Benefit Agreement, signed in 2012, gives the Haida Nation full ownership of the carbon offsets (referred to as "distributed atmospheric benefits") and allocates the annual benefits in a ratio of 81 percent to the Haida and 19 percent to the Province. The revenues will be used largely for the management of protected areas. With revenues potentially surpassing profits from forestry, these carbon offsets will provide a huge incentive to protect rather than log old-growth forests.

The most significant funding in the agreement was provided to the Haida to purchase a forest tenure. In earlier discussions, Guujaaw had pointed out to the Province that, even if the Haida won all their protected areas, timber would continue to leave the islands with few benefits returning to the communities. To help remedy the problem, the Province agreed to provide the Haida with $10 million for the purpose of tenure acquisition.[8] Although a sizable sum, the Haida noted that it paled in comparison to a century of resource extraction on the islands.

Negotiations between the Haida and Western Forest Products for purchase of the largest forest tenure on the islands proceeded in the context of failing global markets. In October 2011, after two years of talks, the deal was sealed. The new licence, now known as tree farm licence 60, combines with the existing Haida Aboriginal Tenure (confirmed through the *Strategic Land Use Agreement*) to give a long-term annual harvest of over 500,000 cubic metres. This places a significant amount of wood in the hands of locals and represents a huge shift from the reality of the past, where multinational logging companies reaped most of the benefits, distant agencies made the rules, and locals had little say. Today, the Islands are multinational-free. In addition, the Haida are jointly managing 270,000 hectares of forest in the timber supply area with BC Timber Sales.

The new Haida forestry operations are being managed by Taan Forest, a subsidiary of the recently created Haida Enterprise Corporation, or "HaiCo" as it is more commonly known. As the largest forest licensee on the islands, Taan is striving to create a sustainable local economy that serves local needs and values – something that, oddly enough, has never been tried before. Unlike the big tenure owners of the past, Taan is accountable not to distant shareholders but to HaiCo, the Haida Nation, and a different set of social aims. The valuable monumental cedars once targeted by logging companies are now off-limits, and the new Land Use Objectives Order ensures that future logging will respect the ecological, social, and cultural values in the forest. Although an unprecedented amount of land is now under protection, much remains open for logging – good logging, sustainable logging. And increasingly, this will be controlled by the communities.

The core objectives of HaiCo, the new business arm of the Haida Nation, are to bring more jobs and benefits to the islands and to create a better quality of life for the Haida people. Functioning like a Crown corporation, the company directs its revenues to the treasury of the Haida Nation. HaiCo's first newsletter states that "nations don't succeed in their businesses because they have good assets – location, natural resources, education etc. They succeed because they have organized themselves effectively to make use of those assets" (Haida Enterprise Corporation 2012, 4). In line with the recommendations from the well-known Harvard Project on American Indian Economic Development, the Council of the Haida Nation "insulates" its business enterprises from politics by keeping its involvement at the strategic level.[9] At the same time, all HaiCo projects must be run in accordance with the Haida Nation's priorities of stewardship and cultural and social values.

Leading the business end is HaiCo's board of directors, many of whom come from high-powered business, management, and legal backgrounds. Under their supervision, HaiCo has quickly acquired several other businesses, including Haida House, the former bear-hunting lodge, which was purchased in spring 2011 as part of the deal to end commercial bear hunting on the islands. HaiCo also acquired West Coast Fishing Resorts, which includes the Sandspit Inn and five fishing lodges, two of which are on Haida Gwaii. As the new owners, the Haida are committed to operating their fishing lodges with more respect and to ending the controversial practice of catch-and-release. There is also ongoing discussion around the possibility of requiring fish caught on Haida Gwaii to be processed on Haida Gwaii.

Nevertheless, with no major increase in tourism expected for the near future, the local economy will remain closely tied to the forest. And with potential annual sales of more than $50 million, Taan Forest is clearly the major development force of HaiCo and the Haida Nation (ibid., 9). Although being stewards of the land and owning the largest forest tenure on the islands may appear contradictory, the Haida have always maintained that they are not opposed to logging per se, but to the scale and method of logging in the past. Now, with the fate of the forests in their hands, they are determined "to show that it isn't necessary to spoil the land to make a living" ("President's Report" 2011, 5). The legislated protected areas and land use objectives go a long way toward ensuring that logging is done with greater respect. And Taan is committed to increasing the value of the resources that are taken from the forest by putting them into local businesses and value-added products.

One such initiative is Taan's "local first" policy, which makes wood available to local buyers at market price minus its transport cost to Lower Mainland markets. At this point Taan has committed to supply a local sawmill, run in partnership by Abfam Enterprises and the Haida community of Old Massett, with 60,000 cubic metres of wood for each of the next ten years. The mill, previously working only one week a month due to a lack of wood, will now be in full operation and will create up to twenty new jobs. The Skidegate Band Council also recently established a pole-peeling plant. Similar initiatives are under way with other existing and proposed local manufacturers, and the number of new jobs on Haida Gwaii can be expected to rise. In addition, the recent Forest Stewardship Certification of Taan Forest and BC Timber Sales in Haida Gwaii will give island wood products an edge in the niche markets.[10]

Despite many promising features, Taan must also confront some real challenges. Not only does it face the constraints associated with ecosystem-based management and the new protected areas, the commodity market, with its globally organized practices, prices, and authorities, is extremely competitive. In the past, logging companies on Haida Gwaii high-graded the valuable and marketable cedars, but Taan must find strong markets for all the species it harvests in proportion to the forest profile.

The challenges of the commodity markets are reflected in the fact that a two-by-four that is barged in from Vancouver costs less than one produced locally. It is the classic model of resource extraction, in which the transport costs of shipping raw logs from Haida Gwaii to Lower Mainland mills are subsidized. When the barges arrive in Haida Gwaii to collect the logs, they bring cheaper wood products from places such as Russia, Brazil, or Argentina, where standards and wages are lower, or from beetle-killed trees in the BC Interior that can be logged at very little cost. Nevertheless, opting out of the market economy is not realistic when dealing with a $40 or $50 million per year forestry operation. There is little choice but to find a niche somewhere in the commodity chains that link Haida Gwaii to other regions, nations, and marketplaces in the world.

Taan was created in the wake of the 2008-9 financial meltdown that led to the BC forest industry's worst economic downturn. In addition, the past decade saw very little investment in the industry, leaving aging equipment and degraded roads and bridges in need of replacement. The scope of the undertaking before them is immense. But with so much at stake for both the Province and the Haida Nation, District Natural Resource Operations Manager Leonard Munt insists: "It can't fail ... And this office will do everything it can within legal bounds to make sure that it doesn't fail."[11]

The business orientation of Taan became clearer when its new president was announced. Those who had spent years fighting the forest industry were stunned to hear that Bob Brash, a major adversary of the community and environmental interests at the Community Planning Forum, had been chosen as Taan's president.[12] Commenting on Brash's appointment, Guuujaaw remarks: "He is the smartest one we ever fought."[13] Even the pundits admit that, as the former president of Husby Forest Products and former district forest manager of Haida Gwaii, Brash clearly knows the forests, politics, and economics of Haida Gwaii. Moreover, he has marketing connections around the world and such a reputation among the locals that: "If anyone can make money in forestry, it's Bob Brash."[14]

So far, that assumption is proving true, as new opportunities in China have created a demand for Haida Gwaii's abundant second-growth Sitka spruce, previously almost worthless on the log market. A recently built container port in Kitimat, located directly across the Hecate Strait from the islands, provides the perfect point of export. Container ships that arrive with manufactured goods from China are refilled with logs from Haida Gwaii and elsewhere in British Columbia for the return trip to China.[15] This is a much-needed opportunity to get the fledgling company off the ground.

To some extent, however, the resource extraction model of maximizing revenues and "getting the logs out" remains in place. There is still little public discussion regarding the best end use of the wood or the islanders' aspirations for the forests. Moreover, as a start-up company, Taan's main focus has been on establishing a successful logging and log sales business rather than conversion to a final product. However, with little local ability to use the wood, exporting logs is not really an obstacle to local manufacturing at this stage. Mass production on the islands still faces multiple challenges, such as adequate power generation, transportation issues, and human capacity. The islands have weathered some difficult years, with the drop in the market coming after decades of overharvesting. Many people have been forced to find work elsewhere, taking with them valuable skills and resources needed to keep communities alive. Building up the necessary physical and social infrastructure to galvanize local manufacturing requires capital reserves. And that, in turn, requires selling some trees to China. Paradoxically, some of the factors that constrained decision making in the Community Planning Forum now constrain decision making within Taan.

Nevertheless, there are many hopeful signs of progress. Taan recently initiated a custom-cut program for its higher-quality logs, in which it contracts a mill to cut various products that it then markets under its own name. Although much of the cutting is currently done in Vancouver, the ultimate goal is to increase manufacturing and employment locally. This aim, once largely dismissed by external decision-makers, is getting a boost from a research partnership with the National Research Council to examine various alternative energy projects to help solve Haida Gwaii's long-standing problem of inadequate power generation. Aside from mass production, there are also countless opportunities for the creative entrepreneur to undertake small-scale manufacturing of high-end products, using some of the finest wood in the world.

Amid the momentous changes, the dream of a single islands' forest tenure is still very much alive. In recent years, the proposal to use the now $60 million Gwaii Trust Fund to buy out the remaining forest tenures has moved from fantasy to possibility. It would enable the non-Haida municipalities to become more involved with collective tenure ownership on the islands and give them a voice at the directors' table. Some discussion has occurred within the Protocol Community group, a governance body representing the Haida Nation and islands' communities that signed the *Protocol Agreement*, but, so far, the non-Haida leadership has been reluctant to support the move. Not only is the undertaking far beyond a municipal government's traditional jurisdiction, but local elected officials, with few support staff and generally narrow areas of expertise, have little capacity to take on such a big issue.

However, as the Haida continue to strategize ways of amalgamating all the tenures on the islands, the non-Haida municipalities could become irrelevant to the endeavour. Gowgaia Institute co-director Simon Davies commented: "The municipalities need to step up – the Haida Nation is going to keep moving with or without them."[16] Contemplating the problem, Dale Lore remarked: "We know what we need to do. But my generation has stomached a lot of change and I don't know that they can stomach much more."[17] Travis Glasman, a key proponent of using the Gwaii Trust to buy the tenures, puts it a little differently: "Politics and relationships haven't gotten there yet. The idea has to be stronger than the politics."[18] Integrating all the recent changes mentally, culturally, and politically will take time. Nevertheless, there are plenty of reminders on the islands that when communities speak with one voice, islanders end up farther ahead.

Although in some ways relations between the communities are better than ever before, a fair amount of animosity and distrust remains. At this point, all island communities have signed on to the once radical community *Protocol Agreement*. However, the solidarity and cooperative action that once radiated from the early signatories has lost much of its momentum. Along with changes in leadership, there has been a dramatic shift in power dynamics between the Haida and the non-Haida. Not only do the

Haida now control the largest forest tenure on the islands, their decision-making authority is far beyond anything that a non-Haida community could hope for.

For now, the non-Haida leadership has set its sights on a community forest offer by the Province for 80,000 cubic metres of wood per year. The community forest is a semi-successful attempt to provide the non-Haida municipalities with a counterbalance to the Haida Aboriginal Tenure. The business will be held by a community corporation collectively owned by the villages of Masset, Queen Charlotte, and Port Clements, and the two electoral areas, Sandspit and Rural Graham Island. Like Taan, the community forest is intended to create jobs for islanders and opportunities for local manufacturers. Net revenues will help build up the business and fund community programs and projects. The community forest partially fulfills the dream of the Islands Community Stability Initiative, which dates from the 1990s. But because available wood is already fully subscribed, it will be challenging to steer clear of contentious lands and live up to the ideal of collective community decision making on priorities for the forest.[19]

The additional 80,000 cubic metres of timber needed for the new community forest was one of many considerations facing the Haida Gwaii Management Council in its first big decision: determining the new annual allowable cut. Through the *Strategic Land Use Agreement,* the Province and the Haida Nation had informally decided to temporarily limit the cut to 800,000 cubic metres until an official recalculation could be done. The new determination would need to be consistent with the *Strategic Land Use Agreement* and Land Use Objectives Order but would also need to satisfy current and would-be licensees. Although the decision-makers had changed – previously, only the chief forester determined the cut – the Management Council's decision was still to take into account "as much as possible, considerations similar to those of the chief forester" (Haida Gwaii Management Council 2011, 54).

In April 2012, the new annual allowable cut was announced at 929,000 cubic metres, 48 percent lower than the pre-blockade equivalent of 1.7 million (Haida Gwaii Management Council 2012a). Applauded by environmentalists across the province, it was nevertheless significantly higher than the minimum level of 800,000 cubic metres that had been in effect for the past four years. It was also higher than the 895,266 cubic metres recommended in the Management Council's public discussion paper prepared six months earlier and even slightly higher than the projected long-term cut of 923,558 cubic metres (Haida Gwaii Management Council 2011, 1).[20]

When asked whether scrutiny was still required, Gowgaia Institute co-founder John Broadhead replied: "There is always a need for scrutiny."[21] However, politics are no longer as black and white as they were before the time of Taan, the community forest, and shared management. The Gowgaia Institute, the most steadfast environmental watchdog for the past three decades, has now turned its attention to the Haida title case and the mapping of thousands of Haida place names. At this point, the only real scrutinizing is within the Management Council itself.

On the other hand, all the necessary components are in place to undertake sustainable forest management, including extensive protected areas, ecosystem-based management, and co-management of the land. At this point, the new governance structure, in which local people make local decisions, will have to be insurance enough. If their decisions flout public preferences, they will hear about it from people who are hard to ignore: their neighbours, family, and friends. As Haida Nation member Vince Collison commented: "Local people making local decisions is a great ideal, a great statement, but it comes with a lot of responsibility and a lot of complicated decision making ... Islands governance means a lot of work, a lot of people that need to make decisions, and you're not always going to be popular."[22]

Part of the difficulty, as Magnusson and Shaw (2003, 270) note, is that "the actually existing community does not stand outside the social relations that establish gender hierarchies, put particular nations on top, and make the majority of people into the employees of others. Thus the problem of liberation is always a matter of changing relations within the community itself, as much as it is of freeing the community from external strictures." With the new governance process still in its infancy, it will be years if not decades before its degree of success becomes obvious. There are few precedents when it comes to actualizing the *Strategic Land Use Agreement* and the Reconciliation Protocol. Numerous factors are involved, from markets and investment to ingenuity, relationships, and politics. In the meantime, the challenge for the new governance structure will be to maintain legitimate political authority as power dynamics shift, as the old guard steps back and new actors enter, and as reality is measured against expectations. The need to build consensus around meanings and mental frames will be ongoing as social forms adapt to the ascendant set of interests and values. As sociologist Mark Haugaard (2003, 96), states: "It is frequently easy to forget that social structures which are dominant within a given social order had to be fought for at one time and still need vigilant destructuring practices to maintain them."

Ultimately, success will be judged, not by the transformations at higher political and institutional levels, but by their outcomes in the day-to-day realities of people and communities of Haida Gwaii. As the Haida embark on the next leg of their journey to build a just and sustainable society, a new set of lessons on power, planning, and social change awaits.

THE WINDING ROAD TO RECONCILIATION

The sound of drums and singing filled the air of Windy Bay on Lyell Island as hereditary leaders ceremonially met two incoming canoes and granted them permission to come ashore. On the afternoon of 15 August 2013, some four hundred people arrived at the former site of the momentous logging blockades of 1985. Unlike twenty-five years earlier, when people gathered here to stop logging in Gwaii Haanas, on this day people came together to witness the raising of the "Legacy Pole," the first monumental pole to be raised in Gwaii Haanas in 130 years. Designed by Jaalen Edenshaw, the forty-two-foot pole tells the story of Gwaii Haanas, highlighting the interconnections between the land, the sea, and the people who take care of them. Among the eleven different figures represented on the pole are "five people standing together," a tribute to the people who stood on the line at Lyell Island in order to protect Gwaii Haanas.[23]

The pole, which weighs almost three thousand kilograms, was raised in the traditional manner with six ropes, long wooden poles, and the power of two hundred people. Once it was fully raised, the crowd burst into celebratory song and dance. While the Legacy Pole stands as an important piece of art, culture, and history, it is also a tangible symbol of the Haida Nation's continued title and occupation of the land. "It is like a dream come true," remarked Percy Williams, former president of the Haida Nation, who stood behind the efforts to stop logging in Gwaii Haanas (quoted in "Historic Feast" 2013).

Reflecting on the anniversary, Miles Richardson, president of the Haida Nation at the time of the blockade, explained to CBC Radio's *BC Almanac*,

> People need to understand we weren't protesting, we were upholding our own laws. Haida Gwaii are Haida lands, always have been, always will be ... We had to fight to uphold that and we were willing to pay whatever price it took ...

What we are celebrating here today is that Canada first, and then BC, accepted Haida law and brought their laws in line with ours (quoted in Horter 2013).

The groundbreaking Gwaii Haanas Agreement paved the way for the Haida and the federal government to cooperatively manage the land,

25   Legacy pole raising at Windy Bay. *Source:* Haida Laas, Council of the Haida Nation.

despite their continuing disagreement over who owned it. Their collaborative model has since received wide recognition, including *National Geographic Traveler Magazine*'s selection of Gwaii Haanas as the best-managed protected area in North America (Toutellot 2005). It is this same spirit that infuses the recently signed *Kunst'aa Guu–Kunst'aayah Reconciliation Protocol*, which now brings the rest of the land on Haida Gwaii under co-management by the Haida Nation and the provincial government. Like the Gwaii Haanas Agreement, this latest agreement shows the potential and power of reconciliation as a way of moving past the quandary of ownership to take care of the land together.

While on the surface, reconciliation may appear to be primarily a procedural matter, it is not the result of a benevolent government "giving" over its power. Rather, the Haida Nation had to develop a power base and authority that would enable it to negotiate from a position of strength. This capacity was created through four decades of political strategizing, legal manoeuvring, alliance building, information gathering, public campaigning, media relations, radical land planning, and astute negotiating – over and over again. Through strong leadership and determined action, the Council of the Haida Nation evolved from an organization without resources or influence at its inception in 1973 to a powerful force at the forefront of ecological and social governance thirty-five years later. It was not sidelined by decades of skewed negotiations and government processes intended to delay real action. Instead, as Guujaaw commented: "We learned to welcome any move, particularly the dirty rotten tricks, as a gift ... something for us to use in our favour."[24]

To fully appreciate the success of the Haida Nation, recent events have to be understood within their larger historical context. The true heroes of the story stretch back to early Haida leaders like Alfred Adams, Amos Russ, and Peter Kelly, who fought for recognition of Haida title at the turn of the last century. They continue through several generations of leaders and elders who stood for their beliefs and called out for justice until the outside world began to listen. They include those who persisted with legal challenges against the Crown and industry until their rights could no longer be denied, and those who reached across divides to find common cause with former rivals in order to promote the greater good. It was the effect of these collective endeavours that made possible the recent transformative actions on Haida Gwaii. Current achievements are thus best understood as the successful culmination of a long struggle that goes back a century or two.

Indeed, the transformations that have occurred on Haida Gwaii are a testament to the spirit of the Haida, whose resilience and determination have endured despite centuries of oppression and exclusion. Their story provides an important message to others striving for justice and sustainability, namely, that their struggles must be engaged, with patience and endurance, on multiple fronts until victory is secured.

After thirteen years as president of the Council of the Haida Nation, Guujaaw did not seek a seventh term, remarking a little tongue-in-cheek: "We were becoming too 'establishment.'"[25] Kil tlaats 'gaa,[25] Peter Lantin, became the new Haida Nation president in December 2012. Despite the major advances that his predecessor ushered in, the battle for justice and sustainability continues as the worldviews, interests, and priorities of two very different systems continue to collide.

Tensions are again rising with the Enbridge Northern Gateway Project, a proposal to build a pipeline from the Alberta tar sands to the northern coast of British Columbia, lurking on the horizon. If built, the pipeline would traverse some of the greatest salmon rivers and bring hundreds of supertankers a year through the neighbouring waters of Haida Gwaii. While Enbridge talks down the risk of an oil spill, the Haida and other coastal First Nations counter that one spill by a supertanker could devastate marine life and coastlines that they depend on for their food, livelihoods, and culture.[26] With so much at stake on both sides of the divide, the pipeline is becoming one of the defining political battles of our time.

Following the federal government's approval of the Northern Gateway Project in June 2014, Haida Nation president Peter Lantin announced that the Haida "will take [their] fight to the land, sea and courts to uphold and protect Haida territory" (Council of the Haida Nation 2014). BC First Nation leaders, including the Haida, announced nine separate lawsuits against the Northern Gateway Project within a month of its approval. Meanwhile, the Haida's title case has been strengthened by the landmark Tsilhqot'in decision which, for the first time in Canadian law, declared Aboriginal title to an area of land claimed by a First Nation.[27]

Upcoming battles in the courts and on the land could go a long way toward clarifying what the relations between First Nations and the Crown will look like in this new era of reconciliation. As the struggle to move past the ideas of an outmoded imperial era continues, the Haida are well placed and ready to rise.

APPENDIX

Community Planning Forum
Interests/Sectors and Members

Interest/sector	Member	Related background
Council of the Haida Nation (CHN)	Nika Collison	Council of the Haida Nation member
	Gary Russ	Council of the Haida Nation member
Haida cultural values	Allan Wilson (Sgaann 7iw7waans)	Hereditary chief
	Johnny Williams (Git'Kun)	Hereditary chief
Band councils	Eddie Russ	Skidegate Band Council
	Marlene Liddle/ Leo Gagnon[a]	Old Massett Village Council
Non-timber forest products	Margaret Edgars	Haida elder and plant specialist
	Dwight Welwood	Commercial mushroom gatherer
Local government	Dale Lore	Mayor of Port Clements
	Barry Pages	Mayor of Masset
Provincial government	Herb Langin	Ministry of Sustainable Resource Management
	Warren Mitchell[b]	Ministry of Sustainable Resource Management
Small business forestry (logging contractors)	Stan Schiller	President, Edwards and Associates
	Mike Hennigan	Owner, Slarktooth Logging

▶

Interest/sector	Member	Related background
Major forest tenure holders	Bob Brash	Vice-president, Husby Forest Products
	Dale Morgan	Senior forester, Teal-Jones
Forest-based employment	Deborah Mantic/Betsy Cardell[c]	Forest sector employees (unionized and non-unionized workers)
Terrestrial ecosystems	Travis Glasman	Professional forester, Haida Forest Guardians
	Jacques Morin	Biologist
Aquatic ecosystems	Leandre Vigneault	Marine biologist
	Lynn Lee	Marine biologist
Cultural heritage tourism	Vince Collison	Haida Nation member
	Barb Rowsell	Ecotourism operator
Tourism	Urs Thomas	Hotel owner
	Delina Adea Petit-Pas	Coffee/gift shop owner
Public interest	Carolyn Terborg	Resident at large
	Cathy Rigg	Resident at large
Sub-surface resources	Bob Patterson	Taseko Mines
	Tim Boyko	Haida artist, argillite carver

a The seat was filled sequentially by Marlene Liddle and, subsequently, Leo Gagnon.

b Warren Mitchell attended the last two sets of meetings as the provincial government representative in addition to Herb Langin.

c The two members served consecutively, not simultaneously, at the planning table.

Notes

Chapter 1: Navigating Change on Haida Gwaii

1 Although population estimates differ, the nineteenth-century depopulation was between 90 and 96 percent. Boyd (1999) puts the 1882 Haida population at 1,600, and Van den Brink (1974, 77) suggests that it had declined to 588 by 1915.

2 Although historians dismiss the idea, First Nations people have long contended that smallpox was deliberately spread in their communities as a means of subjugating them. See Swanky (2012).

3 If the manufactured end products of the wood are taken into account, this value increases to between $15 and $18 billion. In addition, stumpage fees on the wood contributed an estimated $1.8 billion to the province. Gowgaia Institute (2007, 11); John Broadhead, pers. comm. (11 September 2012) (all values are in 2004 dollars).

4 Interviews were recorded and transcriptions were given to interviewees for their review and comment. They could choose to be identified with their comments or to remain anonymous. Hence, interviewees who are cited as "anonymous" are known individuals.

Chapter 2: The Nature of Power

1 It should be noted that, although the principles of communicative rationality have been adopted by state-initiated communicative planning processes, Habermas contended that this form of public deliberation could not be sponsored by the state. Moreover, as Huxley (2000, 375) points out: "the purpose of it was for opinion-formation, not decision making."

2 Neutralizing this institutional bias is part of the aim of procedural theorists such as Habermas.

3 For example, in some places same-sex marriages are perfectly legitimate, whereas polygamy is not. Elsewhere, the reverse may be true – same-sex marriages are untenable, and polygamy is accepted. In the latter case, polygamy is compatible with the dominant interpretative

scheme of the place, whereas same-sex marriage is not. The opposite applies in the first case. To marry a monkey, on the other hand, will probably be unacceptable everywhere because it violates the broadest interpretative scheme of what marriage is – a union between humans.

4 Here a distinction may be noted between collective action as "the ensemble of conflictual behavior within a social system" and social movements that engage in "conflictual behavior that does not accept the social roles imposed by institutionalized norms, supersedes the rules of the political system and/or attacks the structure of class [power] relationships of a given society" (Alberto Melucci in Castells 1983, 295).

5 The term "organizational outflanking" was coined by Mann (1986).

6 Although the state retains a monopoly on the "legitimate" use of violence, it cannot monopolize the actual use of violent tactics to further goals. However, most social movements operate non-violently for moral and/or strategic reasons. Nevertheless, the actions of extremists can sometimes help the more moderate elements of a social movement pass through radical reforms (Castells 1983, 294-95).

CHAPTER 3: CLASH OF NATURE, CULTURE, AND ECONOMICS

1 In contrast to the word "state," which refers to "the deliberate organization of governance through which citizens are bound by a common rule of law," the word "nation" refers to "a group of people bound by a common cultural or ethnic identity" (Lane and Hibbard 2005, 173).

2 The potlatch was an important part of the governance systems of the Haida and other west coast First Nations. Its ban came into effect on 1 January 1885.

3 In 2008, the Government of Canada publicly apologized to the victims of Native residential schools and offered monetary compensation for the abuse.

4 *Stolen Lands, Broken Promises* (UBCIC 2005) provides a detailed chronology of the many twentieth-century resistance actions and land title pursuits of BC First Nations.

5 In 1912, delegates of the Interior Tribes, Indian Rights Association, and Nisga'a Land Committee united with First Nation leaders of the Indian Rights Association on matters related to the McKenna-McBride Agreement (UBCIC 2005, 25).

6 Royal Commission on Indian Affairs for the Province of British Columbia, "Queen Charlotte Islands Agency Stenographic Report," reprinted in Council of the Haida Nation (2010b).

7 Ibid., 18.

8 Ibid., 19. When the commission was asked whether specific discussions regarding adjustment to: reserve size would interfere with the Haida's legal claim for land title, the chairman replied: "We cannot say whether it will or will not interfere with your other interests" (ibid., 22).

9 At the founding of the Allied Tribes, the Indian Rights Association was dissolved (UBCIC 2005, 26).

10 At the same time, a map at the United Nations building in New York shows the colonized world and the areas that have been decolonized. According to this map, North America has never been colonized.

11 Guujaaw, pers. comm. (12 August 2013).

12 In contrast to the "three worlds" designation, which is based on ideology or levels of economic wealth, the Fourth World designation unites indigenous peoples temporally

through their histories and traditions, and spatially through their powerful links to their lands and waters (Seton 1999, 1).

13 Drawing on some of the same insights, Stephen Bunker (1985, 1989) provided a useful examination of the spatiotemporal dynamics and differences between extractive and productive (manufacturing) economies, particularly as they relate to the Brazilian Amazon.

14 The concept of ecologically unequal exchange is summarized by Martinez-Alier (2002, 214) as "the fact of exporting products from poor regions and countries, at prices which do not take into account the local externalities caused by these exports or the exhaustion of natural resources, in exchange for goods and services from richer regions. The concept focuses on the poverty and the lack of political power of the exporting region, to emphasize the idea of lack of alternative options, in terms of exporting other renewable goods with lower local impacts, or in terms of internalizing the externalities in the prices of exports, or in terms of applying the precautionary principle to new export items produced with untested technologies."

15 "Ecosystem approach" and "ecosystem management" are somewhat synonymous with "ecosystem-based management," although the latter most clearly indicates that the ecosystem concept forms a basis for management. "Ecosystem management" is vaguer and must be distinguished from approaches that simply modify existing management practices within a largely unchanged understanding. Canada and the United States have been the frontrunners of ecosystem-based management, with international environmental NGOs helping to push it onto the international agenda. By 1995, the ecosystem approach had been introduced as a general principle in the United Nations Convention on Biological Diversity and is being pursued at a conceptual level in the World Bank, European Union, and US AID (Hartje, Klaphake, and Schliep 2003, 7-9, 35).

16 The Resilience Alliance homepage (www.resalliance.org) is a good source of information on this subject.

CHAPTER 4: WAR IN THE WOODS: 1974-2001

1 More recently, community forests and Aboriginal forest tenures have also been created. However, they account for only a small fraction of the total harvesting rights.

2 Marchak, Aycock, and Herbert (1999) note that throughout much of the last century, the rental cost or "stumpage" paid by companies on harvesting remained relatively low, even by a global standard.

3 Although the conflict on Haida Gwaii was shaped by unique events and circumstances, it was similar in many ways to the confrontations throughout British Columbia.

4 The name was changed to Islands Protection Society in 1979.

5 Guujaaw, pers. comm. (26 August 2013).

6 Pearse raised concerns about control of the forest industry by a few large companies, and problems with sustained-yield policies. However, his recommendations did not result in a significant redirection of provincial forest policy.

7 In contrast to subsequent legal cases, this one deliberately avoided the Haida land claim issue since it was deemed unlikely that the court would accept a petition based on such an argument (Pinkerton 1983, 81).

8 Guujaaw, pers. comm. (1 September 2013).

9 Captain Gold, pers. comm. (27 January 2014).

10 Ibid.

11 Ibid.

12 Guujaaw, pers. comm. (5 September 2013).

13 Captain Gold, pers. comm. (27 January 2014); Guujaaw, pers. comm. (12 February 2014).

14 Captain Gold, pers. comm. (27 January 2014); Guujaaw, per. comm. (12 February 2014).

15 For video footage of the event and interviews with participants, see Jones (2003).

16 Those who stood on the line and faced arrest were (in addition to the elders): Brad Collinson, Frederick Davis, Mervin Dunn, Andrew Edgars, Lawrence Jones, Colin Richardson, Ronald Russ, Noel White, Martin Williams, John Yeltatzie, Harold Yeltatzie, Willard Wilson, Diane Brown, Rose Russ, Laura Williams, Richard Williams, Reginald Wesley, James McGuire, Merle Adams, Henry Wilson, Barbara Stevens, Jacqueline Yovanovich, Kenneth Davis, John Jones, Christopher Collinson, Barry Bell, Teddy Williams, Valerie Jones, Laverne Collinson, Diana Hans, Patricia Gellerman, Paulette Robinson, Marni York, Colleen Williams, Audra Collinson, David Brock, James Stelkia, Mervin Dunn, Joey Parnell, Vincent Pearson, Jody Russ, Ronald Wilson, Lawrence Drager, Sally Edgars, Kathleen Pearson, Russell Edgars, Harold Wilson, Herman Collinson, Clayton Gladstone, Gordon Russ, Stuart McLean, Michael Allen, Troy Pearson, Frank Baker, Fred Richardson, Marchel Ann Shannon, Shelley Lavoie, Waneeta Richardson, Jennifer Davidson, Ronald Souza, Alfred Setso, James Stanley, Dorothy Russ, James Young, Linda Day, Beatrice Drager, Ronald George, Nigel Pearson, Harold Williams. Those formally charged and convicted were: Miles Richardson Jr., Guujaaw, John Yeltatzie, Arnie Bellis, Diane Brown, Ernie Collison, Frederick Davis, Colin Richardson, Roberta Olsen, Lawrence Jones, Martin Williams, Michael Nicoll Yaghulanaas, Willard Wilson, and Svend Robinson (the only non-Haida invited to take a stand). Those convicted received suspended sentences and none served time in prison (Council of the Haida Nation 2010a; Guujaaw, pers. comm. [6 September 2013]).

17 By the end, however, R.L Smith advocated for cooperation and was even considered a friend of the Haidas (Guujaaw, pers. comm. [6 September 2013]).

18 Nika Collison, pers. comm. (1 February 2013); see also May (1990, 189-90).

19 See May (1990) for an interesting government insider account of the events, particularly the motives, perceptions, and interactions of the provincial and federal governments.

20 The South Moresby Forest Replacement Account was administered by the Ministry of Forests and the Canadian Forest Service until 2007, when it was transferred to the locally controlled Gwaii Trust Society under the new name Gwaii Forest Charitable Trust.

21 Guujaaw, pers. comm. (12 August 2013).

22 Ibid.

23 Ibid.

24 Ibid.

25 In addition to keeping the annual harvest to a supposedly sustainable level, sustained-yield policies required that private lands be included in tree farm licences so that forestry operations there would fall under provincial regulation. Moreover, the appurtenancy clause obligated tenure-holders to direct logs to certain communities to ensure their economic stability.

26 TFL 24 in South Moresby was overcut by at least 30 percent (Pinkerton 1983, 79), and the Council of the Haida Nation alleged that the 1982 *Queen Charlotte Timber Supply Area Analysis Report* revealed that the cutting rate was two and a half times the long-term sustainable yield (Edenshaw 1982).

27 Already in the 1980s, the capacity of operating mills exceeded the annual allowable harvest by about a third (Marchak 1995, 90).

28 Guujaaw, pers. comm. (12 August 2013); Dale Lore, pers. comm. (29 August 2013).

29 Dale Lore, pers. comm. (29 August 2013).

30 Guujaaw, pers. comm. (6 September 2013).

31 Guujaaw, pers. comm. (12 August 2013).

32 This abbreviated description of events focuses mainly on the tactics of environmentalists, though First Nations and committees such as the Clayoquot Sound Scientific Panel played critical roles. For more details, see Dobell and Bunton (2001, 11-26) and Shaw (2003). For a wealth of background information, see Clayoquot Sound Research Group (2002).

33 Environmental groups included Greenpeace, Western Canada Wilderness Committee, Friends of Clayoquot Sound, Sierra Club, and the Natural Resource Defense Council.

34 This followed the 1994 signing of an interim measures agreement between the Nuu-chah-nulth and the Province, which called for joint management of all land and resource use in the sound. The Clayoquot Sound Central Region Board, consisting of an equal number of appointees from the Nuu-chah-nulth and the Province, was formed to administer the shared management process. The board provides recommendations on all proposed development plans to the Ministry of Forests (Dobell and Bunton 2001, 17-18).

35 Guujaaw, pers. comm. (12 August 2013).

36 The sole show of belligerence came from a union representative who asserted: "If it costs one union job we're out" (ibid). This kind of union attitude made it challenging for left-leaning governments to respond to environmental concerns.

37 Government saw ecosystem-based management as going beyond the mandate of the coastal planning process, First Nations saw it as a distraction from their main concerns, some environmentalists were suspicious of its "green wash" potential, and industry wanted assurances that it would encompass corporate well-being (Tjornbo, Westley and Riddel 2010, 14-15).

38 Guujaaw, pers. comm. (26 August 2013).

Chapter 5: Collaborative Planning in the Face of Conflict

1 For example, when participants in the Vancouver Island CORE round table could not reach consensus, CORE staff presented a plan to Cabinet, based on round-table discussions, which increased protected areas from 10.4 percent to 13.0 percent. This led to a demonstration of approximately fifteen thousand loggers and their supporters at the provincial legislature, much to the embarrassment of the government (Hoberg 2000, 45). Likewise, in Clayoquot Sound, an unsuccessful CORE process was followed by the government's announcement of a plan for the region. In this case, environmentalists were prompted to launch the summer of blockades.

2 Guujaaw, pers. comm. (12 August 2013).

3 John Broadhead, author interview (4 March 2005).

4 This would become the basis for similar agreements with the Sierra Club of BC, Greenpeace, ForestEthics, EcoTrust, Rainforest Action Network, and the David Suzuki Foundation.

5 Guujaaw, pers. comm. (6 September 2013).

6 Ibid.

7 Guujaaw, pers. comm. (12 August 2013).

8 The quote is from the updated 2005 version of the *Haida Land Use Vision*. Subsequent references cite the 2004 version, which was in use for this process.

9 The Haida Constitution was adopted in principle by the Haida House of Assembly in 1985. It was formally adopted in 2003. See Bellis (2004).

10 This poem, written by Guujaaw, was originally published in Swanton (1995, vii). A short-ened version also appears in Council of the Haida Nation (2005).

11 There has been no logging in the designated Haida Protected Areas since 1991. The largest area, Duu Guusd, covers almost 145,000 hectares and has been under temporary protection by the BC government since 1999, following heavy public criticism of proposed logging there.

12 For the Coast Information Team, see www.citbc.org/abo.html.

13 The term "natural range" refers to "the range of dynamic change in natural systems over historic time periods" and is used as a benchmark for assessing risk (Coast Information Team 2004a, 7).

14 Assessment refers to the gathering and analysis of the necessary data for plan design as well as the monitoring of outcomes. Design involves merging inventories, knowledge, and technical analysis into proposed plans. Integration refers to subsequent processes of con-sultation and negotiation with regard to the proposed plan. And implementation entails putting the plan into action (Coast Information Team 2004a, 9-10).

15 In the interim, the use of protocols or memorandums of understanding between relevant parties was recommended to clarify the agreed-on understandings and commitments.

16 Marine and coastal planning was not included in this process.

17 The process management team would later be expanded to include two process managers.

18 Betsy Cardell, author interview (1 March 2005).

19 Dale Lore, author interview (27 January 2012).

20 For an example of the national media coverage, see the *Maclean's* article by Mark Reid (2002).

21 Ironically, the Haida would later justify their blockade of Weyerhaeuser operations by citing the company's breach of this agreement.

22 Guujaaw, pers. comm. (12 August 2013).

23 Ibid.

Chapter 6: Actors and Interests

1 The government team consisted of Leah Malkinson as process coordinator, Carol Kulesha as co-chair, and Gary Reay as process manager. The Haida team consisted of Carrie Carty as process coordinator, Tamara Rullin as co-chair, and Amos Setso, Arnie Bellis, Elsie Stewart-Burton, and Irene Mills sharing the process manager position. Only one of the four Haida process managers acted in that capacity at any single meeting.

2 The team consisted of: Alan Cober (Province), John Broadhead (Gowgaia Institute), Kiku Dhanwant (Haida Forest Guardians), Glen Dunsworth (Weyerhaeuser), Tony Hamilton (Province), Dorthe Jakobsen (Province), Peter Katinic (Haida Fisheries Program), Leah Malkinson (Province), Keith Moore (consultant), Stephen Northway (Weyerhaeuser), and John Sunde (Province). Halfway through the process, Weyerhaeuser would pull its two representatives from the technical team.

3 The forum membership started at twenty-seven and increased to twenty-nine by the end of the process, with each interest represented by two members. The only exception to this was "forest-based employment," which maintained just one seat throughout. Note that while thirty-one names are listed in Appendix 1, only twenty-nine representatives sat at any one time. This is because two seats (forest-based employment, and Old Massett Village Band Council) had a change of representatives part way through the process.

4 Warren Mitchell attended the last two sets of meetings as the provincial government representative in addition to Herb Langin.

5 This estimate is based on *Timberline Second Growth Volume Study for the Queen Charlotte TSA*, a study prepared for Husby Forest Products (Timberline Forest Inventory Consultants 2002).

6 One example of forest use zones and their order of establishment is as follows: cultural use; ecologically sensitive areas; fish and wildlife habitat; tourism and botanical forest products; hunting, fishing, and trapping; and lastly timber management. See Hammond (1994) for more details.

7 Captain Gold, a Haida elder, noted that some strong medicinal plants that thrive in old-growth forests cannot survive for long in second growth (British Columbia/Council of the Haida Nation 2003-05, Meeting 5, 7).

8 Due to the rich soil fertility of these areas, they also contain very high timber values.

9 Yew bark is used to produce taxol, a drug for cancer treatment.

10 Wilson and Williams were selected by the Hereditary Chiefs' Council. Wilson spoke for the chiefs of the north/Old Massett area, and Williams represented the chiefs of the south/Skidegate area.

11 At the time, Masset and Port Clements were the only two incorporated towns on Haida Gwaii, and thus the only towns with mayors. Queen Charlotte City was incorporated in 2006, and Carol Kulesha, who co-chaired the forum, was elected as mayor.

12 Masset has two fish-processing plants, a custom fish-packing plant, and several small-scale wood manufacturers. Its tourism opportunities are also increasing (British Columbia/Council of the Haida Nation 2003b, 4).

13 Dale Lore, author interview (7 March 2005).

14 Similar initiatives in Old Massett are the Community Feast House and the Old Massett Heritage Resource Program. The latter encompasses a cultural centre, a monumental carving house, and the Old Massett Museum, which will house repatriated Haida collections from museums and institutions around the world (British Columbia/Council of the Haida Nation 2003b, 19). Marlene Liddle and Leo Gagnon represented the Old Massett Village Council at the forum.

15 In general, band councils are responsible for community development within the reserve boundaries, whereas the Council of the Haida Nation is responsible for broader political and sovereignty issues.

16 At the same time, many of these unemployed people are engaged in subsistence food gathering, the arts, and other activities that contribute to a high quality of life.

17 The seat was first filled by Deborah Mantic and subsequently by Betsy Cardell.

18 Due to the economic importance of tourism and its potential impact, it was assigned four seats at the forum: two addressed the concerns of small-business owners, and two dealt with cultural heritage tourism.

19 Guide-outfitting potentially conflicted with a resolution by the Council of the Haida Nation, which called for a moratorium on recreational bear hunting. Also, some fishing lodges are situated on lands considered sacred by the Haida.

20 Here the term "community representatives" refers to a group of locally based forum participants who supported a common set of land use recommendations, later known as "viewpoint 2." Although it suggests a large degree of solidarity on issues, not all community representatives were vocal or supportive regarding all issues.

21 An additional provincial representative seat was added to the forum in the final months, bringing the total to twenty-nine.

22 The only exception was Betsy Cardell, who, on principle, continued to sit at the table as an unpaid volunteer.

23 In an effort to alleviate the time constraint, the number of monthly meeting days was expanded from two to three, but the end date remained the same. Ultimately, the actual time extended to eighteen months, mainly to allow the recommendation report to be written. No formal extension as such was made.

24 Betsy Cardell, author interview (1 March 2005).

CHAPTER 7: STATE OF THE LAND AND COMMUNITY

1 Indicator species or ecosystems have the ability "to 'indicate' some ecological values larger than their own populations." In addition, good indicators should meet most of the following criteria: "Responsive to changes, relevant to the needs of potential users, based on accurate, available, accessible data that are comparable over time, understandable by potential users, comparable to thresholds or targets, cost effective to collect and use, [and] unambiguous in interpretation" (Holt 2005, 1-3).

2 Old forests can also be defined by their old-growth characteristics, such as large old trees, large coarse woody debris, and multi-layered canopy.

3 An example would be allowing second-growth forests to attain old-growth characteristics. The report also noted the need for strategies to control deer browse, which was hindering tree regeneration.

4 A watershed, an area or region drained by a river or stream, is regarded as a fundamental ecological unit.

5 The methodology for this was developed for the Bulkley Valley Land and Resource Management Plan, based on the work of Wilford and Lalonde (2004).

6 After 2050, the amount of old forest landscape is expected to remain fairly constant, though its location may shift as young forests reach old-growth proportions.

7 The report also noted that invasive species such as rats and racoons, which prey on goshawk eggs and young, must be managed.

8 A population decline, however, would reduce this estimate. For example, a 30 percent drop would produce a 77 to 79 percent probability of survival, whereas a 50 percent decline would diminish the probability to 70 to 71 percent.

9 These include the marbled murrelet, Cassin's auklet, rhinoceros auklet, Leach's and fork-tailed storm petrels, tufted and horned puffins, pigeon guillemot, glaucous-winged gull, pelagic cormorant, ancient murrelet, and common murre.

10 For a full list of recommendations, see Harfenist (2003).

11 Whereas some species had made remarkable recoveries during this period (such as pink salmon), others showed dramatic declines (coho). Data limitations, however, were thought to reduce the reliability of some trend analysis. Further trend analyses were recommended to determine salmon abundance in specific locations.

12 This is based on the methodology chosen to assess biological functioning in watersheds (as noted in the watershed condition section), which uses the percent of riparian areas harvested as the primary indicator of biological functioning. According to the thresholds recommended by the Coast Information Team, a riparian area with greater than 30 percent logging is at high risk, whereas one with less than 10 percent is at low risk.

13 Red cedar is used for longhouses, canoes, and totem poles, whereas yellow cedar is used for textiles (capes and regalia), traditional clothing, and feast hats.

14 John Broadhead, author interview (2 February 2012).

15 Companies seek out the small high-growth sites where the most valuable trees tend to be located. Consider that one prime monumental yellow cedar could be worth $60,000 to $70,000. Dale Lore, author interview (7 March 2005).

16 Acknowledging this limitation, Holman and Nicol (2004, 3) noted that the report could not "fully reflect the unique nature and sense of community of the islands."

17 The 34 percent figure was based on census data from 2001 (ibid., 6).

18 Economic conditions were summarized in a separate document titled *Summary of Current Economic Conditions* (Ministry of Sustainable Resource Management 2004). Although the *Summary* was based on the *Socio-Economic Base Case*, there were small differences in the sector numbers cited.

19 Several base case scenarios were also used for methodological purposes.

20 For a summary of timber supply impacts in each management unit and all of Haida Gwaii, see Cortex Consultants and Gowlland Technologies (2004, 13).

21 Second-growth forests were generally defined as less than sixty years old. An area of Tlell that regenerated after a fire more than a century ago was also included.

22 For example, high infant mortality rates can be related to a lack of health care services on the islands and the fact that Haida Gwaii is five to seven hours from the nearest trauma centre.

23 Anonymous interviewee, author interview (7 March 2005).

24 John Broadhead, author interview (4 March 2005).

25 This was in line with a presentation made at an earlier forum session by forest ecologist and Coast Information Team member Herb Hammond, who asserted that control of land and resources is key to dictating which options are available or not (British Columbia/Council of the Haida Nation 2003-05, Meeting 5, 8).

26 Dale Lore, author interview (7 March 2005).

27 There was an estimated thirty-five to forty years of old-growth timber left if the calculation were based on Weyerhaeuser's previous allowable annual cut of 1.2 million cubic metres. If the calculation were based on Weyerhaeuser's reduced allowable annual cut of 600,000 cubic metres, an estimated fifty years of old-growth timber remained. Dale Morgan, author interview (21 July 2005).

28 From "Coast Forest Strategy – An Example of Ecosystem-Based Management," Bill Beese's PowerPoint presentation to the Community Planning Forum.

29 John Broadhead, author interview (4 March 2005).

Chapter 8: Land Use Recommendations and the Widening Gap

1 The final *Land Use Plan Recommendations Report* (British Columbia/Council of the Haida Nation Process Management Team 2006) was released in January 2006.

2 Viewpoint 1 was generally supported by two to four industry representatives, whereas viewpoint 2 was supported by thirteen to fifteen community representatives. There were abstentions by three to six members, depending on the issue. The two provincial representatives abstained altogether from voting.

3 The final *Land Use Plan Recommendations Report* (British Columbia/Council of the Haida Nation Process Management Team 2006) repeated the same recommendation for viewpoint 1. However, a subsequent report, *Socio-Economic and Environmental Assessment of Haida Gwaii/Queen Charlotte Islands Land Use Viewpoints: Summary* (Pierce Lefebvre Consulting 2006), completed on 31 March 2006, specified that viewpoint 1 called for the preservation of twelve Haida Protected Areas.

4   In the *Land Use Plan Recommendations Report* (British Columbia/Council of the Haida Nation Process Management Team 2006), viewpoint 2 called for riparian reserves of two tree lengths. This relative measurement reflects the reality that sites of higher productivity produce larger trees and thus require greater reserve zones. The subsequent *Socio-Economic and Environmental Assessment of Haida Gwaii/Queen Charlotte Islands Land Use Viewpoints: Summary* (Pierce Lefebvre Consulting 2006) gave a fixed riparian reserve distance of eighty metres for viewpoint 2.

5   The Haida Forest Guardians began implementing Haida Cultural Value Surveys on TFL 39, following the 2002 Supreme Court of British Columbia ruling that obligated Weyerhaeuser and the Province to consult with the Haida Nation. After the 2004 Supreme Court of Canada ruling on the TFL 39 case, the surveys were mainly conducted in areas under the provincial BC Timber Sales Program.

6   Dale Morgan, author interview (21 July 2005).

7   All quotations in this paragraph are taken from the author's transcript of the December 2004 Community Planning Forum meetings.

8   Quotation from author's transcript of February 2005 Community Planning Forum meeting.

9   Supporters typically included the two major forest licensees and one or more of the representatives for small-business forestry, industrial mineral resources, and tourism.

10 The remaining forum members either abstained from voting or were absent from the meeting. For voting lists, see British Columbia/Council of the Haida Nation (2006, 180-82).

11 Anonymous interviewee, author interview (10 March 2005).

12 Anonymous interviewee, author interview (14 March 2005).

13 Anonymous interviewee, author interview (14 March 2005).

14 Betsy Cardell, author interview (22 July 2005).

15 Dale Lore, pers. comm. (29 August 2013).

16 Ibid.

17 Over the next four years, the Community Protocol Agreement was signed between all the remaining non-Haida communities and the Council of the Haida Nation.

18 Guujaaw, author interview (27 July 2005).

19 Guujaaw, pers. comm. (6 September 2013.

20 First Nations Summit press conference, 25 November 2004.

21 Guujaaw, pers. comm. (12 August 2013).

Chapter 9: Uprising

1   John Broadhead, author interview (4 March 2005).

2   Simon Davies, author interview (4 March 2005).

3   In February 2005, following the Supreme Court of Canada decision in the TFL 39 case, the BC premier committed to establishing a "new relationship" with First Nations leadership. Meetings between First Nations and the government resulted in a five-page document titled "The New Relationship" (British Columbia 2008a), which outlined new approaches to consultation and accommodation, and a vision for dealing with pressing First Nations concerns.

4   Dale Lore, author interview (7 March 2005).

5   Guujaaw, author interview (27 July 2005).

6   Incidentally, Adrienne Clarkson had recently become an adopted member of a Haida family.

7 Guujaaw, pers. comm. (12 August 2013).

8 The name chosen for the blockade, Islands Spirit Rising, was not written with an apostrophe.

9 This estimate was given by Simon Davies of Gowgaia Institute, though the media put the value as high as $50 million (see, for example, Vassallo 2005b).

10 Simon Davies, pers. comm. (4 March 2005).

11 Dale Morgan, author interview (21 July 2005).

12 This situation was illustrative of the difficult position in which many non-Haida islanders found themselves. Though they may have felt that the Council of the Haida Nation better represented their interests than the provincial government, they were not formally represented by the council.

13 Dale Lore, author interview (3 June 2005).

14 This would later take the form of the Community Viability Strategy.

15 Some protected areas were under a thirty-day Government Action Regulation. Temporary protection of these areas was extended under the Regulation as negotiations continued past the deadline. Other areas were placed under part 13 of the Forest Act, which protected them until a final land use plan was completed.

16 Many of those who signed the petition later apologized to Lore, explaining that they had been obliged to sign if they wished to keep their jobs. Dale Lore, pers. comm. (29 August 2013).

17 The checkpoints remained in place until the end of June 2005.

18 Betsy Cardell, author interview (22 July 2005). Cardell was in charge of distributing the funds.

19 Dale Lore and his family later became the successful owners of the local store in Port Clements, established a hostel, and began offering eco-tours for tourists. Dale also co-founded Haida Gwaii Hydrogen, a company dedicated to building sustainable energy solutions for the islands.

20 When the Hupacasath First Nation launched a legal challenge over the removal of the private lands, the court agreed that the lands should not have been removed without first consulting affected First Nations. Nevertheless, the court refused to quash the removal, arguing that doing so would prejudice Brascan in its deal with Weyerhaeuser (Hupacasath First Nation and Hutchins Grant and Associates 2005). This logic appeared absurd, considering that the court had previously refused an injunction filed by the Hupacasath to stop the deal for this very reason.

21 Incidentally, not only was Western Forest Products a major financial contributor to the ruling Liberal Party during the year in which the private lands were removed, but the minister of forests who approved their removal, Rich Coleman, had a brother who worked for Western Forest Products as its manager of strategic planning (Horter 2008). When investigated by British Columbia's conflict of interest commissioner, however, Rich Coleman was cleared of allegations (British Columbia 2008b).

22 Dale Lore, author interview (27 January 2012).

23 Guujaaw, author interview (27 July 2005).

24 For example, if the final land use plan called for a 70 percent reduction in logging, instead of one company having a 10 percent reduction in cut, and another company a 60 percent reduction (based on the location of their licences and the lands taken out of operation for protection), the reduction would be proportional, so that both companies would have a 35 percent reduction in cut (ibid.).

25 Guujaaw. author interview (27 July 2005).

26 This is a common problem with standard cost-benefit analysis due to the virtual impossibility of assigning monetary values to such things as culture, survival of a species, thousand-year-old trees, or even Haida sovereignty. Whose values are to count in allocating a dollar figure to such things?

27 An e-mail message from Villa-Arce surfaced that showed that he had coached local opposition on how to oppose the agreement that he himself was negotiating with the Haida. John Broadhead, author interview (2 February 2012); Guujaaw, pers. comm. (12 August 2013).

28 Guujaaw, pers. comm. (12 August 2013). In one example, Plant had offered to complete negotiations with the bear-hunting lodge and licensee to end the bear hunt. On several occasions, he stated that the talks were going well, but the licence-holder maintained that he had never met with Plant.

29 Guujaaw, pers. comm. (6 September 2013).

30 The logging history video is available at http://www.spruceroots.org/LogVideo/LogVid. html.

31 John Broadhead, author interview (2 February 2012). His understanding was inspired by *Leverage Points: Places to Intervene in a System* (Meadows 1999).

32 For example, a major barrier to processing resources on-island is the inadequacy of the power supply, which is due to Haida Gwaii's isolation from the province's main electricity grid.

33 John Broadhead, author interview (2 February 2012).

34 Ibid.

35 Ibid. This statistic was not made public.

36 Only Port Clements was not represented at the meeting. According to its mayor, its council had not had time to review the draft agreement, and no one had been available to attend the meeting due to the short notice.

37 Guujaaw, pers. comm. (26 August 2013).

38 Ibid.

39 The allowable annual cut was temporarily reduced in October 2006 from 1.7 million cubic metres to 1.2 million cubic metres to accommodate the 83,000 hectares that had been placed under temporary protection following the blockade and while the land use negotiations were under way.

CHAPTER 10: NEW POLITICAL LANDSCAPE

1 The name change had taken effect during the previous week, when the provincial legislature passed the Haida Gwaii Reconciliation Act.

2 The conservancy names and sizes (hectares) are as follows: Daawuuxusda 70,293, Damaxyaa 822, Duu Guusd 143,496, Kamdis 1,896, Kunxalas 3,344, K'uuna Gwaay 1,756, Nang Xaldangaas 6,897, SGaay Taaw Siiwaay K'adjuu 597, Tlall 16,214, Yaaguun Gandlaay 2,493, and Yaaguun Suu 7,970. See Haida Gwaii Management Council (2011).

3 This breaks down as 13.7 percent for monumental cedar, 7.7 percent for culturally modified trees, and 5.0 percent for Haida traditional forest features. See Haida Gwaii Management Council (2011, 16). A monumental cedar is defined as greater than 120 centimetres diameter at breast height.

4 An exceptional stand of trees could have buffers as large as 150 to 180 metres. John Broadhead, pers. comm. (11 September 2012).

5 Leonard Munt, author interview (3 February 2012).

6 Guujaaw, pers. comm. (6 September 2013).

7 Guujaaw, pers. comm. (1 February 2012).

8 Guujaaw, pers. comm. (6 September 2013). The significant handover of money received relatively little media attention. Guujaaw recalls that, when the Reconciliation Protocol was about to be signed, Premier Gordon Campbell asked the Haida delegation whether it would prefer to announce the Queen Charlotte Islands name change at the same time or later. The chiefs agreed that it should be announced at the signing of the Reconciliation Protocol. The timing of the announcement in this way ensured that the name-change ceremony rather than the $10 million would be the focus of attention (Guujaaw, pers. comm. [6 September 2013]).

9 The project showed that First Nations that owned businesses that were separated from political councils were four times more likely to succeed than those run by councils and presidents (Cornell and Kalt 1998, 200).

10 The potential for the Haida Gwaii brand to invoke the Haida's renowned relationship with the forests was illustrated by an art installation in Victoria by Emilio Portal that showcased red cedar boards, each displaying the Haida Forest Products stamp. The installation ran in May and June 2012 at Open Space Gallery.

11 Leonard Munt, author interview (3 February 2012).

12 Brash would be appointed as HaiCo's chief operating officer in 2012.

13 Guujaaw, pers. comm. (6 September 2013).

14 John Broadhead, author interview (2 February 2012).

15 In China, the logs are manufactured into value-added products, which are then exported to Japan. See British Columbia 2012, 17.

16 Simon Davies, author interview (1 February 2012).

17 Dale Lore, author interview (27 January 2012).

18 Travis Glasman, author interview (1 February 2012).

19 Most wood on Haida Gwaii is already committed to existing forest licensees. The only wood still available is in the timber supply area. This suggests that the community forest would probably be managed under the rules set by BC Timber Sales, with only token input from the communities on such things as the location of logging.

20 Haida Gwaii Management Council 2012a, 6. According to the official rationale, the reason for the higher than projected cut was the new recognition that a 1999 "taper and loss" study, previously used to calculate timber supply, was now believed to underestimate the supply in the base case by 12 percent (ibid., 8-9). When the 12 percent underestimate was combined with a 9.7 percent overestimate in other areas, the net underestimate was 3.8 percent. Interestingly, the public discussion paper (Haida Gwaii Management Council 2011) of six months earlier also noted the 12 percent higher number for the taper and loss study but rejected it, citing various problems with the calculation.

21 John Broadhead, pers. comm. (6 April 2012).

22 Vince Collison, author interview (14 March 2005).

23 From bottom to top, the figures represented are sculpin, grizzly bear, five people standing together, Raven, Sacred One Standing and Moving, Wasco, dog, marten, visitor, three Watchmen, and Eagle.

24 Guujaaw, pers. comm. (26 August 2013).

25 Ibid. (6 September 2013). The remark alludes to the fact that the Haida Nation under Guujaaw's watch succeeded in protecting all of the lands they set out to protect. Although

no longer serving as president, Guujaaw remains as a representative on the Council of the Haida Nation and will be fully involved in battles to come.

26 Even without a spill, ballast waters from tankers would be discharged into Haida waters making them vulnerable to contaminants and invasive species from across the Pacific. The Haida have united with approximately 150 First Nations in British Columbia and Alberta who have publicly declared their opposition to the pipeline. This includes declarations by the Coastal First Nations alliance and seventy signatories to the "Save the Fraser River Declaration," which bans pipelines and supertankers from crossing their territories and watersheds. For a list of the First Nations opposing the pipeline, see "Did You Know ..." 2012, 7.

27 Full decision of *William v. British Columbia* 2014, SCC 34986 can be accessed at http:// www.scc-csc.gc.ca/factums-memoires/34986/FM010_Appellant_Roger-William.pdf.

References

Arts, Bas, and Jan Van Tatenhove. 2004. "Policy and Power: A Conceptual Framework between the 'Old' and 'New' Policy Idioms." *Policy Sciences* 37: 339-56.

Association of Haida Gwaii/Queen Charlotte Islands Forest Workers. 2002. "Letter to Weyerhaeuser Employees and Contractors," June. http://www.haidanation.ca/ (accessed 30 March 2005; page now discontinued).

Bachrach, P., and M.S. Baratz. 1962. "Two Faces of Power." *American Political Science Review* 56: 947-52.

Barnes, Trevor J., Roger Hayter, and Elizabeth Hay. 2001. "Stormy Weather: Cyclones, Harold Innis, and Port Alberni, BC." *Environment and Planning A* 33: 2127-47.

BC Wild. 1996. "Taking It All Away: Communities on Haida Gwaii Say Enough Is Enough." http://www.spruceroots.org/.

Beldessi, Bill. 2007. "Leadership Is the Point," letter to the editor. *Queen Charlotte Islands Observer*, 6 December.

Bellis, Arnie. 2004. *The Haida Constitution, Business and the Environment*. Gowgaia Institute Speakers' Series, Transcript No. 5, 22 April. http://www.spruceroots.org/.

Berman, Tzeporah. 2006. "Corporate Campaigns and the New Environmentalism." Plenary address at the 2006 Bioneers conference. http://www.sacfoodcoop.com/PDFs/april-june07_17-22.pdf.

Boyd, David R., and Terri-Lynn Williams-Davidson. 2000. "Forest People: First Nations Lead the Way toward a Sustainable Future." In *Sustaining the Forests of the Pacific Coast: Forging Truces in the War in the Woods,* ed. Debra J. Salazar and Donald K. Alper, 123-47. Vancouver: UBC Press.

Boyd, Robert. 1999. *The Coming of the Spirit of Pestilence: Introduced Infectious Diseases and Population Decline among Northwest Coast Indians, 1774-1874.* Seattle: University of Washington Press.

Brealey, Larry. 2005. "Charter Being Violated," letter to the editor. *Queen Charlotte Islands Observer*, 2 June, 7.

British Columbia. 2003. "British Columbia Offers Treaty Land to Haida Nation." *Information Bulletin,* 3 September. Treaty Negotiations Office.

—. 2004a. *Forest and Range Practices Act, Forest Planning and Practices Regulation.* Reg. 14/2004. http://www.bclaws.ca/.

—. 2004b. "Forest Stewardship Plans Produce Enforceable Results." Backgrounder. January 2004.

—. 2004c. "Provincial Interest Statement for Haida Gwaii/Queen Charlotte Islands Land Use Planning Process." Presentation to the Community Planning Forum. http://archive. ilmb.gov.bc.ca/slrp/lrmp/nanaimo/haidagwaii/docs/Prov_Govt_Interest_Statement.pdf.

—. 2005. *Land Use Objectives Regulation.* Reg. 357/2005. http://www.bclaws.ca/.

—. 2006. *A New Direction for SLUP.* Victoria: Government of British Columbia.

—. 2008a. "The New Relationship." http://www.gov.bc.ca/arr/newrelationship/down/ new_relationship.pdf.

—. 2008b. *Opinion of the Conflict of Interest Commissioner Pursuant to Section 18(1) of the Members' Conflict of Interest Act in the Matter of a Request by the Honourable Member for Fort Langley-Aldergrove, Rich Coleman, with Respect to Any Appearance of Conflict of Interest under Section 2(2) of the Members' Conflict of Interest Act (September 18, 2008).* Victoria: Government of British Columbia.

—. 2010. Haida Gwaii Reconciliation Act. S.B.C. 2010.

—. 2010-11. "New Relationships with Aboriginal People and Communities in British Columbia: Annual Report on Progress, 2010-2011." http://www.newrelationship.gov.bc. ca/shared/downloads/new_relationships_aboriginal_people_and_communities_2010-11. pdf.

—. 2012. "Forestry Innovation Investment Service Plan 2012/2013-2014/2015." http://www. bcbudget.gov.bc.ca/2012/sp/pdf/agency/fiil.pdf.

British Columbia Coalition for Sustainable Forest Solutions. 2005. "Coalition Calls on Province to Deal Honourably with the Haida Nation and Communities of Haida Gwaii." News release, 15 April.

British Columbia/Coastal First Nations (Gitga'at, Haida, Haisla, Heiltsuk, Kitasoo/Xaixais, Metlakatla, Old Massett Village Council, and Skidegate Band Council). 2001. "General Protocol on Land Use Planning and Interim Measures." http://www.coastforest conservationinitiative.com/pdf/finalprotocol.pdf.

British Columbia/Council of the Haida Nation. 2001. *Protocol on Interim Measures and Land Use Planning,* 17 April.

—. 2003a. "Haida Gwaii/Queen Charlotte Islands Land Use Plan." *Newsletter,* March.

—. 2003b. *Haida Gwaii/Queen Charlotte Islands Strategic Land Use Plan: Planning Process Framework,* March.

—. 2003-05. *Community Planning Forum Meeting Summaries 1-17.*

—. 2007. *Haida Gwaii Strategic Land Use Agreement.* Victoria: Government of British Columbia. http://archive.ilmb.gov.bc.ca/slrp/docs/Haida_SLUPA_Dec_07.pdf.

—. 2009. *Kunst'aa Guu – Kunst'aayah Reconciliation Protocol.* Signed 12 December 2009.

British Columbia/Council of the Haida Nation Process Management Team. 2005. *Haida Gwaii Queen Charlotte Islands Land Use Plan – Draft Recommendations Package.* Presented to the Haida Gwaii/Queen Charlotte Islands Community Planning Forum, meeting #17.

—. 2006. *Haida Gwaii Queen Charlotte Islands: Land Use Plan Recommendations.* Haida Gwaii/Queen Charlotte Islands Community Planning Forum. *Report. Victoria:*

Government of British Columbia. http://www.llbc.leg.bc.ca/public/PubDocs/bcdocs/ 400881/FinLUPPackageJan26b.pdf.

British Columbia Ministry of Forests. 1996. *Queen Charlotte Timber Supply Area: Rationale for Annual Allowable Cut Determination (Summary of Public Input),* 1 May.

British Columbia Ministry of Sustainable Resource Management. 2004. "Summary of Current Economic Conditions – Haida Gwaii/Queen Charlotte Islands." Prepared for HG/QCI Community Planning Forum.

British Columbia and Yukon Chamber of Mines and Mining Association of British Columbia. N.d. "Haida Gwaii/Queen Charlotte Islands Land Use Planning – Mineral Exploration and Mining." Presentation to the Community Planning Forum. http:// archive.ilmb.gov.bc.ca/slrp/lrmp/nanaimo/haidagwaii/docs/Minerals_presentation_no_ photos.pdf.

Broadhead, John. 1984. "Islands at the Edge." In *Islands at the Edge: Preserving the Queen Charlotte Islands Wilderness,* ed. Islands Protection Society, 121-42. Vancouver: Douglas and McIntyre.

–. 2005. "And So the Story Goes." *SpruceRoots Magazine,* August.

–. 2007. "On the Land Use Plan," letter to the editor. *Queen Charlotte Islands Observer,* 24 September.

Brosius, Peter J. 1999a. "Analyses and Interventions: Anthropological Engagements with Environmentalism." *Current Anthropology* 40, 3: 277-309.

–. 1999b. "Environmentalism, Indigenous Rights and Transnational Cultural Critique." *Identities* 6 (2-3): 180-81.

Bunker, Stephen G. 1985. *Underdeveloping the Amazon: Extraction, Unequal Exchange, and the Failure of the Modern State.* Chicago: University of Chicago Press.

–. 1989. "Staples, Links, and Poles in the Construction of Regional Development Theories." *Sociological Forum* 4, 4: 589-610.

Burrows, Mae. 2000. "Multistakeholder Processes: Activist Containment versus Grass-roots Mobilization." In *Sustaining the Forests of the Pacific Coast,* ed. Debra Salazar and Donald Alper. Vancouver: UBC Press.

Castells, Manuel. 1983. *The City and the Grassroots: A Cross-Cultural Theory of Urban Social Movements.* Berkeley: University of California Press.

Chomsky, Noam, and Michel Foucault. 1974. "Human Nature: Justice versus Power." In *Reflexive Water: The Basic Concerns of Mankind,* ed. F. Elders, 135-97. London: Souvenir Press.

Clayoquot Sound Research Group. 2002. "The Clayoquot Documents." *A Political Space: Reading the Global through Clayoquot Sound.* http://web.uvic.ca/clayoquot/clayoquot Documents.html.

Clegg, Stewart R. 1989. *Frameworks of Power.* London: Sage.

Coast Information Team. 2004a. *Ecosystem-Based Management Framework.* Victoria: Coast Information Team. http://www.citbc.org.

–. 2004b. *Ecosystem-Based Management Planning Handbook.* Victoria: Coast Information Team.

–. 2004c. *Hydroriparian Planning Guide.* Victoria: Coast Information Team.

"Community Sustainability (Draft)." N.d. Presented to the Haida Gwaii/Queen Charlotte Islands Community Planning Forum, meeting #16.

CORE (Commission on Resources and Environment). 1992. *Report on a Land Use Strategy for BC.* Victoria: Queen's Printer.

–. 1993. *Land Use Goals Workbook*. Victoria: Government of British Columbia.

–. 1994. *Provincial Land Use Strategy*. Vol. 3: *Public Participation*. Victoria: Government of British Columbia.

Cornell, Stephen, and Joseph P. Kalt. 1998. "Sovereignty and Nation Building: The Development Challenge in Indian Country Today." *American Indian Culture and Research Journal* 22, 3: 198-214.

Cortex Consultants and Gowlland Technologies. 2004. *Haida Gwaii/Queen Charlotte Islands LUP Timber Supply Analysis – Analysis of Base Cases*. Nanaimo, BC: Ministry of Sustainable Resource Management.

Cortex Consultants and HiMark Forest Consultants. 2004. "Second-Growth Timber Opportunities on Haida Gwaii/QCI." Nanaimo, BC: Ministry of Sustainable Resource Management.

Council of the Haida Nation. 1976. "A Report from the President, Godfrey Kelly." 30 March, 2.

–. 2002. "Statement of Claim." *Haida Nation v. British Columbia*. Vancouver, Action no. L020662, 14 November (BC SC). http://www.haidanation.ca/Pages/legal/pdfs/Statement_of_Claim.pdf.

–. 2003. *Constitution of the Haida Nation*. Council of the Haida Nation. http://www.haidanation.ca/Pages/governance/pdfs/HNConstitutionRevisedOct2010_official unsignedcopy.pdf.

–. 2004. *Haida Gwaii Yah'guudang* [Respect for this place]: *Haida Land Use Vision*. Council of the Haida Nation. http://archive.ilmb.gov.bc.ca/slrp/lrmp/nanaimo/haidagwaii/docs/HLUVpublic.pdf.

–. 2005a. *Haida Land Use Vision: Haida Gwaii Yah'guudang* [Respect for Haida Gwaii]. Council of the Haida Nation. http://www.haidanation.ca/Pages/documents/pdfs/land/HLUV.lo_rez.pdf.

–. 2005b. "Islands Bulletin 1." 19 March. http://archive-ca.com/.

–. 2005c. "Islands Bulletin 3." 23 March. http://archive-ca.com/.

–. 2010a. "Athlii Gwaii: 25 Years Down the Road." *Haida Laas: Newsletter of the Haida Nation*, November.

–. 2010b. "Indian Affairs, 1913." *Haida Laas: Journal of the Haida Nation*, September.

–. 2014. *Haida Nation Challenges Constitutionality of the Northern Gateway Project*. Press release, 14 July.

Council of the Haida Nation and Gowgaia Institute. 2002. "Protocol Agreement." *Haida Laas: Newsletter of the Haida Nation*, June, 12.

Council of the Haida Nation and the Municipalities of Port Clements and Masset. 2004. *Protocol Agreement*. http://www.haidanation.ca/Pages/Agreements/pdfs/Protocol_Communities.pdf.

Curran, Deborah, and Michael M'Gonigle. 1999. "Aboriginal Forestry: Community Management as Opportunity and Imperative." *Osgoode Hall Law Journal* 37, 4: 711-74.

Dahl, R.A. 1961. *Who Governs? Democracy and Power in an American City*. New Haven: Yale University Press.

"Dear Residents of Haida Gwaii." 2005. *Queen Charlotte Islands Observer*, 14 July 2005, 20.

"Declaration of First Nations of the North Pacific Coast: Turning Point Conference, Vancouver June 13, 2000." 2006. *Haida Laas*, June. http://www.haidanation.ca/Pages/Agreements/pdfs/Turning_Point.pdf.

"Did You Know: Approximately 150 First Nations and Band Councils Have Publicly Declared Their Opposition to the Proposed Enbridge Pipeline Project." 2012. *Haida Laas*, February 2012, 7.

Dobell, Rod, and Martin Bunton. 2001. "Sound Governance: The Emergence of Collaborative Networks and New Institutions in the Clayoquot Sound Region." Background paper for Clayoquot Sound Regional Workshop, Tofino, BC, 25 September.

"Draft Islands' Declaration." 2005. Presented to the Haida Gwaii/Queen Charlotte Islands Community Planning Forum.

Duffy, Dorli, Lisa Hallgren, Zane Parker, Robert Penrose, and Mark Roseland. 1998. *Improving the Shared Decision-Making Model: An Evaluation of Public Participation in Land and Resource Management Planning (LRMP) in British Columbia.* Vancouver: Department of Geography and School of Resource and Environmental Management, Simon Fraser University.

EAGLE Law. 2008. "Haida TFL 39 Case," 66. http://nativemaps.org/files/Haida%20Nation%20v.%20BC%20%28Minister%20of%20Forests%29%20and%20Weyerhaeuser.pdf.

"Ecosystem Interest Statement." N.d. Presentation to the Community Planning Forum. http://archive.ilmb.gov.bc.ca/slrp/lrmp/nanaimo/haidagwaii/docs/ecosystem_interest_statement1.pdf.

Edenshaw, Gary (for the Council of the Haida Nation, Forest and Research Committees). 1982. "Letter to Jack Biickert, Regional Manager of BC Forest Service." 24 March.

Edwards, Bob, and John McCarthy. 2004. "Strategy Matters: The Contingent Value of Social Capital on the Survival of Local Social Movement Organizations." *Social Forces* 83: 621-52.

Erasmus, Georges, and Joe Sanders. 2002. "Canadian History: An Aboriginal Perspective." In *Nation to Nation: Aboriginal Sovereignty and the Future of Canada,* ed. John Bird, Lorraine Land, and Murray Macadam, 3-11. Toronto: Irwin.

Fedje, Daryl, Alexander Mackie, Rebecca Wigen, Quentin Mackie, and Cynthia Lake. 2005. "Kilgii Gwaay: An Early Maritime Site in the South of Haida Gwaii." In *Haida Gwaii: Human History and Environment from the Time of Loon to the Time of the Iron People,* ed. Daryl Fedje and Rolf Mathewes, 187-203. Vancouver: UBC Press.

Fisher, Roger, and William Ury. 1983. *Getting to Yes: Negotiating Agreement without Giving In.* New York: Penguin Books.

Flyvbjorg, Bent. 2001. *Making Social Science Matter: Why Social Inquiry Fails and How It Can Succeed Again.* Trans. Steven Sampson. Cambridge: Cambridge University Press.

Forester, John. 1989. *Planning in the Face of Power.* Berkeley: University of California Press.

—. 1999a. *The Deliberative Practitioner: Encouraging Participatory Planning.* Cambridge, MA: MIT Press.

—. 1999b. "Reflections on the Future Understanding of Planning Practice." *International Planning Studies* 4, 2: 175-93.

Foucault, Michel. 1973. *The Birth of the Clinic: An Archaeology of Medical Perception.* New York: Pantheon Books.

—. 1977. *Discipline and Punish: The Birth of the Prison.* London: Penguin Books.

—. 1988. *Politics, Philosophy, Culture: Interviews and Other Writings, 1977-1984.* Ed. Lawrence Kritzman. London: Routledge.

Frame, Tanis, Thomas Gunton, and J.C. Day. 2004. "The Role of Collaboration in Environmental Management: An Evaluation of Land and Resource Planning in British Columbia." *Journal of Environmental Planning and Management* 47, 1: 59-82.

Frank, Andre Gunder. 1969. *Latin America: Underdevelopment or Revolution.* New York: Monthly Review Press.

—. 1975. *On Capitalist Underdevelopment.* New York: Oxford University Press.

Franklin, Jerry F. 1997. "Ecosystem Management: An Overview." In *Ecosystem Management: Applications for Sustainable Forest and Wildlife Resources,* ed. M.S. Boyce and A. Haney, 21-53. New Haven, CT: Yale University Press.

Funtowicz, Silvio, and Jerry Ravetz. 1993. "Science for the Post-Normal Age." *Futures* 25: 735-55.

G.S. Gislason and Associates. 2002. "The QCI Fishing Lodge Industry." Report prepared for the BC Ministry of Agriculture, Food and Fisheries.

Gedicks, Al. 1994. *The New Resource Wars: Native and Environmental Struggles against Multinational Corporations.* Montreal: Black Rose Books.

Giddens, Anthony. 1984. *The Constitution of Society: Outline of the Theory of Structuration.* Berkeley: University of California Press.

Giljum, Stefan, and Klaus Hubacek. 2001. "International Trade, Material Flows and Land Use: Developing a Physical Trade Balance for the European Union." International Institute for Applied Systems Analysis Interim Report IR-01-059, Laxenburg.

Gill, Ian. 2009. *All That We Say Is Ours: Guujaaw and the Reawakening of the Haida Nation.* Vancouver: Douglas and McIntyre.

Gowgaia Institute. 2005. "Forest Economy Trends and Environmental Conditions on Haida Gwaii 1800-2004." Gowgaia Institute brief.

—. 2007. *Forest Economy Trends and Economic Conditions on Haida Gwaii.* http://www.spruceroots.org/Booklets/ForTrends.pdf.

Grumbine, R. Edward. 1994. "What Is Ecosystem Management?" *Conservation Biology* 8, 1: 27-38.

Gunton, Thomas, J.C. Day, and Peter Williams. 2003. "Evaluating Collaborative Planning: The BC Experience." *Environments* 31, 3: 1-11.

Habermas, Jürgen. 1984. *The Theory of Communicative Action.* Vol. 1: *Reason and the Rationalisation of Society.* Boston: Beacon Press.

—. 1987. *The Philosophical Discourse of Modernity.* Cambridge, MA: MIT Press.

Haida Enterprise Corporation. 2012. *HaiCo Quarterly: Newsletter of the Haida Enterprise Corporation,* February.

Haida Gwaii Management Council. 2011. "Haida Gwaii Public Review Period for an Annual Allowable Cut Determination." Public discussion paper, Timber Supply Review, October.

—. 2012a. "Rationale for Annual Allowable Cut (AAC) Determination for Haida Gwaii: Effective April 4, 2012." http://www.haidagwaiimanagementcouncil.ca/Documents/Haida%20Gwaii%20AAC%20Rationale%20April%202012%20Final2.pdf.

—. 2012b. "Timber Supply Review Data Package 2012." Submitted by Joint Technical Working Group, 4 April.

Haida Gwaii/Queen Charlotte Islands Heritage Tourism Strategy Working Group. 2003. *Haida Gwaii/Queen Charlotte Islands Heritage Tourism Strategy.* http://www.mieds.ca/images/uploads/heritage_tourism_strategy%202003(1).pdf.

Haida Nation v. British Columbia (Minister of Forests), 1995 CanLII 1156 (BC SC). http://canlii.ca/t/1drvf.

Haida Nation v. British Columbia (Minister of Forests), 1997 CanLII 2009 (BC CA). http://gsdl.ubcic.bc.ca/collect/firstna1/index/assoc/HASHe7c2/f33cfddo.dir/doc.pdf.

Haida Nation v. British Columbia (Minister of Forests), [2004] 3 S.C.R. 511, 2004 SCC 73. http://scc-csc.lexum.com/.

Hall, Anthony J. 2003. *The American Empire and the Fourth World: The Bowl with One Spoon*. Montreal and Kingston: McGill-Queen's University Press.

Hamilton, Gordon. 2005. "Weyerhaeuser Buyout Completed." *Victoria Times Colonist*, 1 June, B1.

–. 2007a. "Haida Juggle Logging Plan; How Much Timber Is Harvested Main Issue in Queen Charlottes." *Vancouver Sun*, 19 September, D3.

–. 2007b. "Land-Use Pact Halts 'Juggernaut' of Big Logging on the Charlottes: Agreement Resolves Much Conflict with BC Government, Haida Leader Says." *Vancouver Sun*, 13 December. http://www.canada.com/story.html?id=b38a7979-3caa-452d-94e1-954a1b0b7a76.

Hammond, Herb. 1993. "An Ecosystem Based Approach: Wholistic Forest Use." *Silva Forest Foundation*. http://www.silvafor.org/publications/library/docs/Wholistic%20Forest%20Use.pdf (accessed 6 November 2008; page now discontinued).

–. 1994. "Standards for Ecologically Responsible Forest Use." *International Journal of Ecoforestry* 10, 1: 11-15.

Hardy, Cynthia, and Sharon Leiba-O'Sullivan. 1998. "The Power Behind Empowerment: Implications for Research and Practice." *Human Relations* 51, 4 (April): 451-83.

Harfenist, Anne. 2003. *Seabird Colonies: Background Report for the Haida Gwaii/Queen Charlotte Islands Land Use Plan*. http://archive.ilmb.gov.bc.ca/slrp/lrmp/nanaimo/haidagwaii/docs/Seabird-Rpt-Low-Resolution.pdf.

Harris, Cole. 2002. *Making Native Space: Colonialism, Resistance, and Reserves in British Columbia*. Vancouver: UBC Press.

Hartje, Volkmar, Axel Klaphake, and Rainer Schliep. 2003. *The International Debate on the Ecosystem Approach: Critical Review, International Actors, Obstacles and Challenges*. Bonn: Federal Agency for Nature Conservation, Skripten 80.

Haugaard, Mark. 1997. *The Constitution of Power: A Theoretical Analysis of Power, Knowledge and Structure*. Manchester: Manchester University Press.

–. 2003. "Reflections on Seven Ways of Creating Power." *European Journal of Social Theory* 6, 1: 87-113.

Hayter, Roger. 2003. "'The War in the Woods': Post-Fordist Restructuring, Globalization, and the Contested Remapping of British Columbia's Forest Economy." *Annals of the Association of American Geographers* 93, 3: 706-29.

Hayter, Roger, and Trevor J. Barnes. 1997a. "The Restructuring of British Columbia's Coastal Forest Sector: Flexibility Perspectives." In *Troubles in the Rainforest: British Columbia's Forest Economy in Transition*, ed. Trevor J. Barnes and Roger Hayter, 181-203. Victoria: Western Geographical Press.

–. 1997b. "Troubles in the Rainforest: British Columbia's Forest Economy in Transition." In *Troubles in the Rainforest: British Columbia's Forest Economy in Transition*, ed. Trevor J. Barnes and Roger Hayter, 1-14. Victoria: Western Geographical Press.

Healey, Patsy. 1997. *Collaborative Planning: Shaping Places in Fragmented Societies*. London: Macmillan.

Hearne, Margo. 2005. "Islands Spirit Rising." *Council of the Haida Nation*. http://www.haidanation.ca/islands/Margo.1.html (accessed 30 March 2005; page now discontinued).

"Historic Feast Caps Off Special Week." 2013. *Queen Charlotte Islands Observer*, 23 August.

Hoberg, George. 2000. "How the Way We Make Policy Governs the Policy We Make." In *Sustaining the Forests of the Pacific Coast: Forging Truces in the War in the Woods*, ed. Debra J. Salazar and Donald K. Alper, 26-53. Vancouver: UBC Press.

Holman, Gary, and Steve Nicol (Lions Gate Consulting). 2004. *Haida Gwaii/Queen Charlotte Islands Land Use Plan: Socio-Economic Base Case.* Victoria: Ministry of Sustainable Resource Management.

Holt, Rachel. 2001. *An Ecosystem-Based Management Framework for the North Coast LRMP.* Background report, Government of British Columbia. http://www.llbc.leg.bc.ca/public/PubDocs/bcdocs/352574/EBM_framework.pdf.

—. 2005. *Environmental Conditions Report for the Haida Gwaii/Queen Charlotte Islands Land Use Plan.* Victoria: Ministry of Sustainable Resource Management. http://www.llbc.leg.bc.ca/public/pubdocs/bcdocs/373436/full_report.pdf.

Hornborg, Alf. 1998. "Towards an Ecological Theory of Unequal Exchange: Articulating World System Theory and Ecological Economics." *Ecological Economics* 25: 127-36.

Horter, Will. 2008. "Following the Money in Privatization Scandal." *Dogwood Initiative.* http://www.dogwoodinitiative.org.

—. 2013. "The Real Story behind Gwaii Haanas." *Dogwood Initiative,* 4 September. http://www.dogwoodinitiative.org.

Howitt, Richard. 2001. *Rethinking Resource Management: Justice, Sustainability and Indigenous Peoples.* London: Routledge.

Hupacasath First Nation and Hutchins Grant and Associates. 2005. "Hupacasath First Nation Entitled to Consultation regarding Private Timberlands." News release, 7 December.

Hutton, Thomas. 1997. "Vancouver as a Control Centre for British Columbia's Resource Hinterland: Aspects of Linkage and Divergence in a Provincial Staple Economy." In *Troubles in the Rainforest: British Columbia's Forest Economy in Transition,* ed. Trevor J. Barnes and Roger Hayter, 233-61. Victoria: Western Geographical Press.

Huxley, Margo. 2000. "The Limits to Communicative Planning." *Journal of Planning Education and Research* 19: 369-77.

ICSI (Islands Community Stability Initiative). 1996. *The ICSI Consensus.* QCI/Haida Gwaii: ICSI.

Innes, Judith E. 1995. "Planning Theory's Emerging Paradigm: Communicative Action and Interactive Practice." *Journal of Planning Education and Research* 14: 183-89.

Innis, Harold. 1936. "Approaches to Canadian Economic History." *Commerce Journal* 26: 24-30.

—. 1956. *Essays in Canadian Economic History.* Toronto: University of Toronto Press.

—. 1995. "Industrialism and Cultural Values." In *Staples, Markets, and Cultural Change: Selected Essays,* ed. Daniel Drache, 316-24. Montreal and Kingston: McGill-Queen's University Press. (Essay orig. pub. 1950.)

International Network of Forests and Communities. 2002. *Money Doesn't Grow on Trees: The Fallacy of Economic Globalisation and Centralised Development.* Victoria: POLIS Project on Ecological Governance.

Jackson, Tony, and John Curry. 2004a. "Community-Based Sustainability in an Export Dependent Natural Resource Economy: The British Columbian Experiment to Deliver 'Sustainability in One Province.'" http://lib.icimod.org/record/11552/files/3884.pdf.

—. 2004b. "Peace in the Woods: Sustainability and the Democratization of Land Use Planning and Resource Management on Crown Lands in British Columbia." *International Planning Studies* 9, 1: 27-42.

Jones, Marianne, dir. 2003. *Athlii Gwaii: The Line at Lyell.* Video recording. Vancouver: Ravens and Eagles Productions.

Kay, James. 1993. "On the Nature of Ecological Integrity: Some Closing Comments." In *Ecological Integrity and the Management of Ecosystems,* ed. S. Woodley, J. Kay, and G. Francis, 201-12. Delray, FL: St. Lucie Press.

—. 1994. "Some Notes On: The Ecosystem Approach, Ecosystems as Complex Systems and the State of the Environment Reporting." Typescript, University of Waterloo, Waterloo, ON.

Kay, James, Henry Regier, Michelle Boyle, and George Francis. 1999. "An Ecosystem Approach for Sustainability: Addressing the Challenge of Complexity." *Futures* 31, 7: 721-42.

King, Jeff. 2005. "Islands Will Be More Sustainable, More Protected: Guujaaw." *Queen Charlotte Islands Observer,* 22 April.

—. 2007a. "Land Use Agreement Signing Wednesday in Vancouver." *Queen Charlotte Islands Observer,* 10 December.

—. 2007b. "Land Use Agreement within Sight, Says Minister." *Queen Charlotte Islands Observer,* 27 July.

—. 2008a. "Sandspit Signs Protocol Agreement, Called 'an Important Day for Haida Gwaii.'" *Queen Charlotte Islands Observer,* 18 April.

—. 2008b. "Skidegate Hall Filled to Bursting for Thursday's Historic Celebration." *Queen Charlotte Islands Observer,* 2 February.

Koberstein, Paul. 2003. "BC Forests under Siege: George Bush of the North." *Cascadia Times,* summer. http://www.times.org/archives/2003/campbell.htm (accessed November 2003; page now discontinued).

Krajnc, Anita. 2002. "Conservation Biologists, Civic Science and the Preservation of BC Forests." *Journal of Canadian Studies* 37, 3: 219-38.

"Land Use Plan Possible in 2007, Says CHN Vice-President." 2006. *Queen Charlotte Islands Observer,* 11 October.

Lane, Marcus B. 2006. "The Role of Planning in Achieving Indigenous Land Justice and Community Goals." *Land Use Policy* 23, 4: 385-94.

Lane, Marcus B., and Michael Hibbard. 2005. "Doing It for Themselves: Transformative Planning by Indigenous Peoples." *Journal of Planning Education and Research* 25: 172-84.

Lawson Lundell. 2002. "Court of Appeal Reserves Judgment on Further Arguments in Haida Nation Case." June 5. http://www.arcticgaspipeline.com/Reference/Documents &Presentations/Canada/Haida%20June%2020021LAWSON-LUNDELL.pdf.

Lee, Robert G. 2002. *Planning Principles for Integrated Ecosystem-Based Management on the Central and North Coast of British Columbia Including Haida Gwaii.* Seattle: Robert G. Lee.

Lemke, Thomas. 2002. "Foucault, Governmentality, and Critique." *Rethinking Marxism* 14, 3: 49-64.

Lions Gate Consulting, Westcoast CED Consulting and Peak Solutions Consulting. 2007. "Haida Gwaii/Queen Charlotte Islands Community Viability Strategy." Report prepared for the Community Viability Strategy Steering Committee, 17 May.

Little Bear, Leroy. 2005. "Foreword." In Taiaiake Alfred, *Wasáse: Indigenous Pathways of Action and Freedom,* 9-12. Peterborough: Broadview Press.

"Loggers Support CHN." 2002. *Queen Charlotte Islands Observer,* 6 June, 13-14.

Lordon, Ian. 2000. "We Will Draw the Curtain and Show You the Picture." *SpruceRoots Magazine,* March. http://www.spruceroots.org/.

—. 2002. "The Haida Protected Areas." *SpruceRoots Magazine,* April. http://www.spruceroots. org/.

—. 2003. "Serving Notice: Tuning up the Tenure Holders on Haida Gwaii." *SpruceRoots Magazine,* April. http://www.spruceroots.org/.

Lukes, Steven. 1974. *Power: A Radical View.* London: Macmillan.

M'Gonigle, R. Michael. 1999. "Ecological Economics and Political Ecology: Towards a Necessary Synthesis." *Ecological Economics* 28: 11-26.

—. 2003. "Somewhere between Center and Territory: Exploring a Nodal Site in the Struggle Against Vertical Authority and Horizontal Flows." In *A Political Space: Reading the global through Clayoquot Sound,* ed. Warren Magnusson and Karena Shaw, 121-38. Minneapolis: University of Minnesota Press. Mabee, Warren, Evan Fraser, and Olav Slaymaker. 2003. *Evolving Ecosystem Management.* Liu Institute Environment Program Working Paper Series 03-001. Vancouver: University of British Columbia.

MacQueen, Ken. 2003. "West Coast Renaissance." *Macleans,* 20 October, 52.

Magnusson, Warren, and Karena Shaw. 2003a. "Conclusion: Clayoquot and the Politics Beyond." In *A Political Space: Reading the Global through Clayoquot Sound,* ed. Warren Magnusson and Karena Shaw, 263-86. Minneapolis: University of Minnesota Press.

Mann, Thomas. 1986. *The Sources of Social Power.* Vol. 1: *A History of Power from the Beginning to AD 1760.* Cambridge: Cambridge University Press.

Manuel, George, and Michael Posluns. 1974. *The Fourth World: An Indian Reality.* New York: Free Press.

Marchak, Patricia. 1995. *Logging the Globe.* Montreal and Kingston: McGill-Queen's University Press.

Marchak, Patricia, and Denise Allen. 2003. "BC Forests 2003: An Appraisal of Government Policies." Report for the David Suzuki Foundation.

Marchak, Patricia, Scott Aycock, and Deborah Herbert. 1999. *Falldown: Forest Policy in British Columbia.* Vancouver: David Suzuki Foundation.

Martinez-Alier, Joan. 2002. *The Environmentalism of the Poor: A Study of Ecological Conflicts and Valuation.* Cheltenham: Edward Elgar.

—. 1987. *Ecological Economics: Energy, Environment and Society.* Oxford: Basil Blackwell.

Mascarenhas, Michael, and Rik Scarce. 2004. "'The Intention Was Good': Legitimacy, Consensus-Based Decision Making, and the Case of Forest Planning in British Columbia, Canada." *Society and Natural Resources* 17: 17-38.

May, Elizabeth. 1990. *Paradise Won: The Struggle for South Moresby.* Toronto: McClelland and Stewart.

McCarthy, Daniel. 1999. "The Management of Complex Sociobiophysical Systems: Ecosystem-Based Management and the Chesapeake Bay Program." Master's thesis, University of Waterloo.

McCarthy, John, and Mayer Zald. 1977. "Resource Mobilization and Social Movements: A Partial Theory." *American Journal of Sociology* 82: 1212-41.

McCullough, Michael. 2005. "Haida, Supporters Blockade to Demand Sustainable Forestry Sale of Weyerhaeuser's BC Assets, Including Timber Rights in Charlottes, Trigger Protests." *Vancouver Sun,* 4 April.

McGuirk, P.M. 2001. "Situating Communicative Planning Theory: Context, Power and Knowledge." *Environment and Planning A* 33: 195-217.

McKinley, Judy. 2008. "Land Use Agreement Marks Beginning of a New Relationship." *Queen Charlotte Islands Observer,* 18 January.

Meadows, Donella. 1999. *Leverage Points: Places to Intervene in a System.* Hartland, VT: Sustainability Institute.

—. 2000. "The Global Citizen: The Forests of the People Islands." *Alternet.* http://alternet.org.

"Memorandum of Understanding Arising from April 22 2005 Discussions between the Province and the Council of the Haida Nation." 2005. Signed 11 May 2005.

Morigeau, Gerry. 2000. "Today the People of Haida Gwaii Walked Together." *SpruceRoots Magazine,* December. http://spruceroots.org/.

"Name-Change Ceremony Symbolically Cuts Haida Gwaii's Link to Colonial Past." 2010. *Vancouver Sun,* 17 June. http://www.canada.com/vancouversun/news/westcoastnews/story.html?id=5604cded-1d6b-4017-9f2e-c38975bc14ab.

Owen, Stephen. 1998. "Land Use Planning in the Nineties: CORE Lessons." *Environments* 25, 2-3: 14-26.

Pacific Analytics and Don Harrison (EcoTech Consulting). 2004. *Revitalizing British Columbia's Coastal Economy: A New Economic Vision for the North and Central Coast and Haida Gwaii.* http://www.savethegreatbear.org/files/reports/Dec_2004-Revitalizing_coastal_economy.pdf.

Parnell, Gilbert. 2005. Interview by Mark Forsythe. *BC Almanac.* CBC Radio, 23 March.

Paulson, Susan, Lisa Gezon, and Michael Watts. 2003. "Locating the Political in Political Ecology: An Introduction." *Human Organization* 62, 3: 205-17.

Pierce Lefebvre Consulting. 2006. *Socio-Economic and Environmental Assessment of Haida Gwaii/Queen Charlotte Islands Land Use Viewpoints: Summary.* Victoria: Ministry of Agriculture and Lands.

Pinkerton, Evelyn. 1983. "Taking the Minister to Court: Changes in Public Opinion about Forest Management and Their Expression in Haida Land Claims." *BC Studies* 57 (Spring): 68-85.

Premier's Office. 1992. "Harcourt Unveils Comprehensive Land Use Initiative." News release, 21 January.

"President's Report." 2011. *Haida Laas: Newsletter of the Haida Nation,* February, 5.

"Provincial Report Badly Flawed, Says CHN Reps." 2006. *Queen Charlotte Islands Observer,* 2 June.

"Provincial Report Is More Mischief, Says CHN." 2006. *Queen Charlotte Islands Observer,* 2 June, 1, 36.

Prudham, Scott. 2007. "Sustaining Sustained Yield: Class, Politics, and Post-War Forest Regulation in British Columbia." *Environment and Planning D: Society and Space* 25: 258-83.

"Public Interest Statement." 2004. Prepared for the Community Planning Forum.

Rajala, Richard A. 2006. *Up-Coast: Forest and Industry on British Columbia's North Coast, 1870-2005.* Victoria: Royal BC Museum.

Ramsay, Heather. 2006. "Committee Discusses Land Use Viewpoints." *Queen Charlotte Islands Observer,* 22 June, 9.

Ravetz, Jerry, Silvio Funtowicz, and International Society for Ecological Economics. 2007. "Post-Normal Science." In *The Encyclopedia of Earth,* ed. Cutler J. Cleveland. Washington, DC: Environmental Information Coalition, National Council for Science and the Environment. http://www.eoearth.org/article/Post-Normal_Science.

Reid, Mark. 2002. "When *Loggers Turn Green:* A New Dissident Alliance Builds in BC's Forests." *Maclean's,* 17 June, 100.

Rinfret, Alex. 2005a. "Action Group Looking for Forestry Middle Ground." *Queen Charlotte Islands Observer,* 28 July, 1.

—. 2005b. "Delegation Demands Mayor Lore Stop Representing Port." *Queen Charlotte Islands Observer,* 21 April, 4.

—. 2005c. "Loggers Say They Will Miss Their Paycheques – But Many Offer Support to Blockades." *Queen Charlotte Islands Observer,* 24 March, 9.

—. 2006. "Port Sticks with Protocol Agreement." *Queen Charlotte Islands Observer,* 17 May.

—. 2008. "CHN Negotiating to Buy TFL." *Queen Charlotte Islands Observer,* 10 August, 1.

Rinfret, Alex, Jeff King, and Heather Ramsay. 2005. "CHN Seeks Islanders' Ideas." *Queen Charlotte Islands Observer,* 9 June, 9.

Robbins, Paul. 2004. *Political Ecology: A Critical Introduction.* Malden: Blackwell.

Ruebsaat, Norbert. 1988. "Speaking with Diane Brown." Simon Fraser University (unpublished thesis).

Said, Edward. 1979. *Orientalism.* New York: Vintage.

Salazar, Debra J., and Donald K. Alper. 1996. "Perceptions of Power and the Management of Environmental Conflict: Forest Politics in British Columbia." *Social Science Journal* 33, 4: 381-400.

Seton, Kathy. 1999. "Fourth World Nations in the Era of Globalisation: An Introduction to Contemporary Theorizing Posed by Indigenous Nations." *Fourth World Journal* 4, 1. http://cwis.org/FWJ/classic/?issue=118.

Shaw, Karena. 2003. "Encountering Clayoquot, Reading the Political." In *A Political Space: Reading the Global through Clayoquot Sound,* ed. Warren Magnusson and Karena Shaw, 25-66. Minneapolis: University of Minnesota Press.

Shiels, Phil. 2005. "We Question the Deal," letter to the editor. *Queen Charlotte Islands Observer,* 14 October.

Shukovsky, Paul. 2005. "Haida Open Seattle Front in Forest Fight: Weyerhaeuser Riles Tribe with Rich Deal to Sell Logging Rights." *Seattle Post-Intelligencer,* 20 April. http://www.seattlepi.com/local/article/Haida-open-Seattle-front-in-forest-fight-1171323.php.

Simpson, Scott. 2008. "Hands Off Oil, Haida Nation Says: Natural Environment Trumps Drilling in Queen Charlotte Basin, Band Warns." *Vancouver Sun,* 15 July.

"Six Point Agreement [The]." 2002. Published in *Haida Laas – Journal of the Haida Nation,* June 2006, 28.

Sloan, Gordon M. 1945. *The Forest Resources of British Columbia: Report of the Commissioner.* Ottawa: Queen's Printer.

Smith, R.L. 1985. "The Red Neck News." 6 November.

SpruceRoots Magazine. 2003. "An Interview with BC Attorney General Geoff Plant." *SpruceRoots Magazine,* November. http://www.spruceroots.org/.

"Statement of Defence of the Defendant Her Majesty the Queen in Right of the Province of British Columbia" re: *Haida Nation v. British Columbia* (Attorney General) (6 June 2003), Vancouver L020662 (B.C.S.C.).

"Story from the Yakoun No. 4." April. http://archive-ca.com/.

"Supreme Court of Canada Ruling Hailed as Monumental." 2004. *Queen Charlotte Islands Observer,* 25 November, 11.

Swanky, Tom. 2012. *The True Story of Canada's War of Extermination on the Pacific.* Burnaby, BC: Dragon Heart Enterprises.

Swanton, John. 1995. *Skidegate Haida Myths and Histories.* Ed. and trans. John Enrico. Skidegate: Queen Charlotte Islands Museum Press.

Teal-Jones Group. 2007. "Haida Gwaii: Strategic Land Use Agreement – Harvesting and Economic Impacts." News release, 7 September.

Teal-Jones Group, Weyerhaeuser, Husby Forest Products, Western Forest Products Ltd. 2004. "Forest Sector Presentation to HG LUP Community Forum." http://archive.ilmb. gov.bc.ca/slrp/lrmp/nanaimo/haidagwaii/docs/Licensee_LUP_Presentation.pdf.

Tenove, Chris. 2003. "The Spirit of Haida Gwaii." *This Magazine,* January/February 2003, 1.

Timberline Forest Inventory Consultants. 2002. *Queen Charlotte Timber Supply Area Second-growth Volumes Study, Results Update.* Prepared for Husby Forest Products Limited, Sandspit.

Tjornbo, Ola, Frances Westley, and Darcy Riddel. 2010. *The Great Bear Rainforest Story.* Case Study No. 3. Waterloo: Waterloo Institute for Social Innovation and Resilience, University of Waterloo.

Tollefson, Chris. 1998. "Introduction." In *The Wealth of Forests,* ed. Chris Tollefson, 3-15. Vancouver: UBC Press.

Toutellot, Jonathon. 2005. "Destinations Scorecard: National Parks." *National Geographic Traveller,* July-August.

Turner, John C. 2005. "Explaining the Nature of Power: A Three-Process Theory." *European Journal of Social Psychology* 35: 1-22.

Turner, Nancy J. 2004. *Plants of Haida Gwaii.* Winlaw, BC: Sono Nis Press.

–. 2005. *The Earth's Blanket.* Vancouver: Douglas and McIntyre.

Turner, Nancy J., Marianne Boelscher Ignace, and Ronald Ignace. 2000. "Traditional Ecological Knowledge and Wisdom of Aboriginal Peoples in British Columbia." *Ecological Applications* 10, 5: 1275-87.

UBCIC (Union of British Columbia Indian Chiefs). 2005. *Stolen Lands, Broken Promises: Researching the Indian Land Question in British Columbia.* 2nd ed. Vancouver: Union of British Columbia Indian Chiefs.

–. N.d. "Recommendations of the McKenna McBride Royal Commission." *Our Homes Are Bleeding – Digital Collection.* http://www.ubcic.bc.ca/.

UNESCO World Heritage Centre. 1981. "SGang Gwaay." http://whc.unesco.org/en/ list/157.

United Nations General Assembly. 1960. *Granting of Independence to Colonial Countries and Peoples.* Resolution 1514 (XV), in *Official Records, Fifteenth Session,* 14 December. http://daccess-dds-ny.un.org/.

Unity Statement. 2000. *SpruceRoots Magazine,* December. http://www.spruceroots.org/.

Van den Brink, J.H. 1974. *The Haida Indians: Cultural Change Mainly between 1876-1970.* Leiden: Brill.

Vassallo, James. 2005a. "Face-Saving Plan on Table, Says Lore." *Prince Rupert Daily News,* 30 March.

–. 2005b. "Haida Nation Seizes Logs during Protest." *Prince Rupert Daily News,* 30 March.

"Village of Port Clements Intervenor Statement." 2004. *Haida Nation v. British Columbia (Minister of Forests),* http://www.usask.ca/nativelaw/factums/.

Weber, Edward. 2000. "A New Vanguard for the Environment: Grass-Roots Ecosystem Management as a New Environmental Movement." *Society and Natural Resources* 13: 237-59.

Whelan, James, and Kristen Lyons. 2005. "Community Engagement or Community Action: Choosing *Not* to Play the Game." *Environmental Politics* 14, 5: 596-610.

Wilford, D.J., and R. Lalonde. 2004. "A Framework for Effective Watershed Monitoring." *Streamline Watershed Management Bulletin* 8, 1: 5-10.

Williams-Davidson, Terri-Lynn, Guujaaw, and Chief David Walkem. 2005. "Session 7: Consultation and Development, Part 2." University of British Columbia, First Nations Studies Program: Land Claims and Governance Speakers Series, 8 March.

Williams-Davidson, Terri-Lynn, and Louise Mandell. 2002. "Haida Title and Implications." Gowgaia Institute Speakers' Series, Transcript No. 2, 28 November. http://www.spruceroots.org/.

Wilson, Jeremy. 1998. *Talk and Log: Wilderness Politics in British Columbia, 1965-96.* Vancouver: UBC Press.

"Working Together for Haida Gwaii." 2005. *Haida Laas – Newsletter of the Haida Nation.* May 2011.

World Commission on Environment and Development. 1987. *Our Common Future.* Oxford: Oxford University Press.

Yaffee, Steven L. 1999. "Three Faces of Ecosystem Management." *Conservation Biology* 13, 4: 713-25.

Index

Note: "(f)" following a number indicates a figure; "(t)" following a number indicates a table

Aboriginal land claims: and Haida, 55, 56, 70; recognition by federal government, 38

Aboriginal rights and title (BC): and amendments to Forest Act; and Constitution Act, 1982; Crown duty to consult, 94, 157-58; Delgamuukw decision, 71, 95; and ecosystem-based management, 89; fight for (early twentieth century), 34-37; key legal cases post-1970, 70-73; and Royal Proclamation of 1763, 32, 34-35, 38-39. *See also* First Nations; Haida litigation; and *names of specific court cases*

Aboriginal tenure, 171, 176, 184, 197

Adams, Alfred, 35, 206

Adaptive management. *See Ecosystem-Based Management Framework*

alliance building: and Community Planning Forum, 142; Haida and coastal First Nations, 75-76; Haida and local communities, 141, 142, 155-56, 161; Haida and local environmentalists, 52, 64; Haida and local forest workers, 96-98; ICSI, 66-70; and Islands Spirit Rising blockade, 161, 162; and power,
25, 191, 206; and shifting relations on Haida Gwaii, 201-2. *See also* environmental movements; indigenous rights movements

Allied Tribes of British Columbia, 37

annual allowable cut: comparison with actual harvest levels on Haida Gwaii, 130; demands for reduction by ICSI, 67, 68; determination by Haida Gwaii Management Council, 195, 202; and land use recommendations, 146; and strategic land use agreement, 183, 184; and sustained yield policy, 50

Anthony Island Provincial Park. *See* SGang Gwaay

aquatic habitat: legal objectives for, 193. *See also* watersheds

Argillite: interests at Community Planning Forum, 109

Atmospheric Benefit Agreement, 196

BC Supreme Court. *See* Haida litigation and *specific cases*

BC Timber Sales, 197, 199

Bachrach, Peter, 19, 23

Baratz, Morton, 19, 23
Barrett, Dave (Premier): and Gwaii
    Haanas, 52
bear hunt, 143, 144(f), 148(t), 171, 176, 198
bears. *See* black bears
Beban, Frank, 52, 59, 60
Beese, Bill, 138-39
Beldessi, Bill, 66
Bell, Pat, 179, 181, 182, 184
Belsey, Bill, 168
birds: and *Haida Land Use Vision,* 86-87
black bears: analysis of, 118-19; commer-
    cial hunting of, 86, 143, 144(f), 148(t),
    198; draft recommendations for, 143,
    148(t); habitat and residency, 124; and
    Haida Land Use Vision, 86-87; legal
    objective for, 194; and strategic land
    use agreement, 186
blockade, logging. *See* Islands Spirit
    Rising blockade; Lyell Island
Brascan: purchase of TLF, 39, 158, 161, 172-
    73; sale of TFL 39 to Western Forest
    Products, 174-75
Brash, Bob: commenting on land use
    agreement, 183; and Community Plan-
    ning Forum, 103, 150; and ICSI, 67, 68;
    as Taan Forest president, 199-200
British Columbia Coalition for Sustainable
    Forest Solutions, 169
British Columbia Treaty Commission:
    establishment of, 70; limitations of, 71
Broadhead, John: and animated logging
    history, 179; on continuing need for
    scrutiny, 203; founding of Gowgaia
    Institute, 64; and Islands Protection
    Society, 54; mapping capabilities, 82;
    on need for blockade, 160; response to
    socio-economic and environmental
    assessment, 178; on raw log export, 134;
    on riparian forest map and high-value
    fish habitat, 182; on risk thresholds, 139
Brown, Diane, 59-60
Bunker, Stephen, 8

Calder case, 70
Campbell, Gordon, 184, 186, 187, 188(f),
    194

Captain Gold (Richard Wilson): and
    blockade, 167(f); and Haida Watchmen
    Program, 54-55
carbon offsets, 196
Cascadia Forest Products, 173, 174
cedar: in blockade memorandum of
    understanding, 170; cultural significance
    for Haida, 5, 126-28; draft recommen-
    dations for, 145, 148(t); and *Haida Land
    Use Vision,* 86-87; inventories on Haida
    Gwaii, 126-27; legal objectives for, 193;
    and strategic land use agreement, 184;
    thousand year plan, 106, 145. *See also*
    Haida cultural values
Central Coast: Interim Land Use Plan,
    78; Land and Resource Management
    Planning, 75, 76, 113
Chilcotin. *See* Tsihlqot'in
Clayoquot Sound: forest conflict, 73-74;
    recognition as United Nations Biosphere
    Reserve, 74; Scientific Panel for Sustain-
    able Forest Practices, 73
co-management: co-governance model for
    Haida Gwaii, 194-96; and Gwaii Haanas,
    63; and Haida Gwaii land use planning
    process, 151; Haida Gwaii Management
    Council, 194; Solutions Table, 195-96.
    See also Gwaii Haanas National Marine
    Conservation Area Reserve and Haida
    Heritage Site; Haida heritage sites
Coast Information Team: establishment
    of, 88; handbooks by, 88; risk thresholds,
    138-39. *See also Ecosystem-based Manage-
    ment Framework*
Coast Opportunity Funds, 9
Coast Sustainability Trust, 83
Coastal First Nations: and Coast Oppor-
    tunity Funds, 9, 76-77; and Declaration
    of First Nations of the North Pacific
    Coast, 76; formation of, 75; General
    Protocol on Land Use Planning and
    Interim Measures, 77; and Great Bear
    Rainforest, 75, 76; membership of, 76;
    and protocol agreements, 77
collaborative planning: on Haida Gwaii,
    9-10; introduction by BC government,
    12; limitations, 8-9; and power, 8-9;

rationale for, 79, 80. *See also* Commission on Resources and the Environment (CORE); land use planning (Haida Gwaii)

Collison, Dempsey (Chief Skidegate/ Skiidagids), 55, 59, 69(f)

Collison, Vince, 110, 150, 187, 203

colonization: colonial economies, 6; early history of, 30-34; resistance to, 34-38. *See also* imperialism

Commission on Resources and the Environment (CORE): inclusive decision-making approach, 8, 80-81

communicative planning, 16, 17, 151

community forest (Haida Gwaii): and Community Planning Forum, 137; and ICSI, 68; implementation, 202

Community Planning Forum (on Haida Gwaii): community and economic well-being, 145; community sustainability, 133, 136-37; 150-53; Draft Islands' Declaration, 133-34; Draft Recommendations Package, 142-47, 148-49(t); early debates, 111-14; ecosystem integrity, 142-45; environmental conditions report, 116-28; facilitation of, 113-14; general structure of, 9, 12; interest statements, 102-11; and islands governance, 135, 136, 137; and movement building, 190, 191-92; Process Management Team, 101-2, 112; Process Technical Team, 115, 139; socio-economic conditions, 129-31, 133, 134, 136-37; spiritual and cultural values, 145; timber supply analysis, 131-33, 134; time-line, 112-13, 135. *See also Ecosystem-Based Management Framework, Haida Land Use Vision;* land use planning (Haida Gwaii); and *individual sectors/interests*

community protocol agreement. *See Protocol Agreement,* Community

community sustainability: Draft Islands Declaration, 151-52; draft recommendations for, 145-46, 149(t); report to Community Planning Forum, 133, 136-37; and strategic land use plan, 180-81

community viability strategy, 180-81, 182

conservancies, 192-93

consultation. *See* Aboriginal rights and title (BC); Haida litigation

CORE. *See* Commission on Resources and the Environment (CORE)

Council of the Haida Nation. *See* Haida Nation

Cowichan Nation, 34

culturally modified trees: as evidence of Haida history, 5, 8(f); and Haida Forest Guardians, 82; recommendations at Community Planning Forum, 145; and strategic land use agreement, 184

Dahl, Robert, 18

Davidson, Robert, 166, 167(f)

Davies, Simon, 108(f), 201, 160

Delgamuukw case, 71, 95

Delves, Cory, 175

Dixon, George, 5-6

Duu Guusd Tribal Park, 2(f), 58, 185(f)

ecological integrity: and conservancies, 192; and ecosystem approach, 46-47; and *Ecosystem-Based Management Framework,* 88, 90, 91, 116; and risk thresholds, 118, 120, 138-39

ecologically unequal exchange, 7, 8, 42

economic development: community forest, 202; economic conditions, 130-31; Haida Enterprise Corporation, 197-98; recommendations for economic well-being, 145-47; regional economic development strategy, 181; staples development, 40-45. *See also* Community Planning Forum (on Haida Gwaii); forestry industry (Haida Gwaii); forest sector (BC); strategic land use agreement (Haida Gwaii)

ecosystem-based management: adaptive management, 91; co-governance structure, 194-96; comparison of Haida Gwaii and central coast, 181-82; concept, 46-48; draft recommendations for, 147; economic feasibility, 180; *Ecosystem-Based Management Framework,* 88-91; as guiding document for land use planning, 83; guiding principles, 88-89; legal objectives for, 193-94; planning elements for, 89-90; and planning outcomes, 13; reserves, 184; and risk management, 90, 181; risk thresholds, 138-39; and timber resources, 180; and tradeoffs, 91. *See also* Environmental Conditions Report (Haida Gwaii); land use planning (Haida Gwaii)

Ecosystem-Based Management Framework, 83, 88-89, 150, 181

Environmental Conditions Report (Haida Gwaii): additional species of land use concern, 128; methodology, 116; primary indicators, 117-28; risk and social values, 137-38. *See also individual indicators*

environmental conflicts: Clayoquot Sound, 73-74; Great Bear Rainforest, 75-78; Gwaii Haanas, 51-64; Islands Spirit Rising, 159-71; languages of valuation, 11, 12; Meares Island, 73

environmental movements: conservation movement, 45 46; environmentalism, 28, 44-46; preservation movement, 45-46. *See also names of environmental organizations*

First Nations: and Canadian citizenship, 38; and federal franchise, 38; indigenous paradigms, 29-30, 39-40; pre-colonization, 29; resistance to colonization, 34-40; traditional management practices, 29. *See also* Aboriginal rights and title (BC); Indian Act; indigenous rights movements; and *name of specific First Nations*

fish habitat: aquatic ecosystem interests, 104; legal objectives for riparian forests in high-value fish habitat, 193; recommendations for hydroriparian ecosystems, 143, 148(t); salmonids, 125; and watershed condition, 120

fishing industry (Haida Gwaii): employment, 130; and HaiCo, 198; as potential growth sector, 137; sports fishing industry, 110, 198

forest industry (Haida Gwaii): annual allowable cut, 130, 146, 202-3; early history on Haida Gwaii, 6-7; economic diversification, 137; forest-based em-

ployment, 107-8, 130, 177; forestry projects under two viewpoints, 176-78; local manufacturing, 130, 134, 178; mismanagement of, 66; 72; as percentage of income from all sectors, 130; new co-governance model for, 192-96; raw log export, 134; Share groups, 64-65; small business forestry interests, 107; and Taan Forest, 197-200; transformation of, 192; and Weyerhaeuser, 72. *See also* Community Planning Forum (on Haida Gwaii); TFL 39; timber resources (Haida Gwaii)

forest management, regulatory framework: amendments to Forest Act and Forest Practices Code in 2002, 152-54; Forest and Range Practices Act, 152-53, 181; Haida Gwaii Reconciliation Act, 192-96; integrated resource management, 51; removal of private lands from forest tenures, 154; stumpage, 154; sustained yield, 50-51; tenure system, 50

forest reserves: legal objectives for, 194; recommendations for, 143

forest stewardship certification, 146, 199

forest tenure holders, major (Haida Gwaii): and Community Planning Forum, 103, 138, 147, 150; and concerns with land use negotiations, 173; response to blockade, 167-68. *See also* tenure system and *names of individual companies*

Forest Workers Association. *See* Haida Gwaii/Queen Charlotte Islands Forest Workers, Association of

ForestEthics, 75, 179

forestry sector (BC): and economic diversification, 44; environmental conflicts, 51-78; destabilization and declining employment, 65-66; environmental impacts of, 44-45; and fordism, 42-44; integrated resource management, 51; manufacturing, 66; mechanization, 65-66; mismanagement of, 65; regulatory model, 49-51; restructuring, 44, 65; Royal Commission on forestry, 50; staples development, 40-45; tenure system, 50, 68. *See also* forest industry

(Haida Gwaii); forest management, regulatory framework

forests, old growth (Haida Gwaii): analysis of, 118-19; draft recommendations, 143, 148(t); environmental conditions report, 117-20; legal objective for, 194; risk thresholds, 117-18; and strategic land use agreement, 186

Foucault, Michel: communication and power, 17; conflict and resistance, 17-18; disciplinary power, 21-22, 25; genealogical studies, 21; structure and agency, 20; truth and power, 21, 26

fourth world, 38-40. *See also* indigenous rights movements

George, Paul, 54

George Manuel, 38-40

Giddens, Anthony, 20

Gitga'at Nation, 76, 77

Gitxsan: and Delgamuukw case, 71

Gladstone, Percy, 53

Goshawk. *See* Northern Goshawk

government of British Columbia: and Clayoquot Sound, 73-74; colonial land policy, 33; and Commission on Resources and Environment (CORE), 80-81; cut block approvals in contentious areas, 153; duty to consult First Nations, 94, 157-58; and Great Bear Rainforest Agreement, 78; and Gwaii Haanas, 52-64; Haida Gwaii Reconciliation Act, 194-97; interest statement at Haida Gwaii Community Planning Forum, 103; and Islands Spirit Rising blockade, 160, 168, 170; Land Use Objectives Order, 193-94; new relationship agreement, 160, 219(n3); rationale for participatory planning, 79, 80; statement of defence in Haida title case, 99; treaties, 33. *See also* forest management, regulatory framework; forestry sector (BC); Haida litigation; land use planning (Haida Gwaii)

government of Canada: Gwaii Haanas Agreement, 62-63; and Haida land claim, 56; and reconciliation table, 194; and treaty offer, 40

Gowgaia Institute: animated logging history, 179; founding of, 64; relationship with Council of the Haida Nation, 82; on remaining old forest ecosystems, 119; riparian forest map of high-value fish habitat, 125, 182; work on Haida title case by, 203

Great Bear Rainforest: campaign, 75, Coastal First Nations, 75-77; and environmental organizations, 75; Great Bear Rainforest Agreement, 78; Joint Solutions Project, 75

Green, Tom, 66

Greenpeace, 75, 179

Guujaaw: and clam shack negotiation with Province, 77; on co-governance model, 196; in discussion at Islands' Spirit Rising blockade, 166(f); formation of Islands Protection Committee, 52; on implications of Haida title for communities, 156; on Islands' Spirit Rising blockade memorandum of understanding, 171; on launch of Islands' Spirit Rising blockade, 164; and Lyell Island blockade, 59; and negotiations with BC, 179, 184; and purchase of TFL 39, 183, 197; on reconciliation, 187; reflection on Haida success, 188; response to draft land use recommendations, 147-48; response to loggers' concerns during blockade, 166, 174; response to release of socio-economic and environmental assessment, 178; and Share the Rock, 66; steaming a cedar canoe, 105(f), on the strategic land use agreement, 186; on Supreme Court of Canada 2004 decision, 158; on Taan Forest president appointment, 200; and TFL 24 lawsuit, 53-54; on treaty offer by Province, 99

Gwaii Haanas (South Moresby): and Aboriginal rights, 63; Archipelago Management Board, 63, 135, 193; BC-Canada agreement, 62; blockade on Lyell Island, 59-60; Canada-Haida agreement, 63; co-management of, 63; funding for, 62; creation of Gwaii